Shakespeare: The Comedies

ANALYSING TEXTS

General Editor: Nicholas Marsh

Published

Analysing Texts
Series Standing Order ISBN 0–333–73260–X
(outside North America only)

You can receive future titles in this series as they are published by placing a standing order. Please contact your bookseller or, in the case of difficulty, write to us at the address below with your name and address, the title of the series and the ISBN quoted above.

Customer Services Department, Palgrave Ltd
Houndmills, Basingstoke, Hampshire RG21 6XS, England

Shakespeare:
The Comedies

R. P. DRAPER

First published 2000 by
MACMILLAN PRESS LTD
Houndmills, Basingstoke, Hampshire RG21 6XS
and London
Companies and representatives
throughout the world

ISBN 0–333–73967–1 hardcover
ISBN 0–333–73968–X paperback

A catalogue record for this book is available
from the British Library.

This book is printed on paper suitable for recycling and
made from fully managed and sustained forest sources.

10   9   8   7   6   5   4   3   2   1
09   08   07   06   05   04   03   02   01   00

Printed and bound by CPI Antony Rowe,

Published in the United States of America 1998 by
ST. MARTIN'S PRESS, INC.,
Scholarly and Reference Division,
175 Fifth Avenue, New York, N.Y. 10010

ISBN 0–312–22702–7 (cloth)
ISBN 0–312–22703–5 (paper)

To Anne and Sophie, who helped to make me computer-literate

Contents

Contents

General Editor's Preface

This series is dedicated to one clear belief: that we can all enjoy, understand and analyse literature for ourselves, provided we know how to do it. How can we build on close understanding of a short passage, and develop our insight into the whole work? What features do we expect to find in a text? Why do we study style in so much detail? In demystifying the study of literature, these are only some of the questions the *Analysing Texts* series addresses and answers.

The books in this series will not do all the work for you, but will provide you with the tools, and show you how to use them. Here, you will find samples of close, detailed analysis, with an explanation of the analytical techniques utilised. At the end of each chapter there are useful suggestions for further work you can do to practise, develop and hone the skills demonstrated and build confidence in your own analytical ability.

An author's individuality shows in the way they write: every work they produce bears the hallmark of that writer's personal 'style'. In the main part of each book we concentrate therefore on analysing the particular flavour and concerns of one author's work, and explain the features of their writing in connection with major themes. In Part 2 there are chapters about the rest of the author's work, assessing their contribution to developments in literature; and a sample of critics' views are summarised and discussed in comparison with each other. Some suggestions for further reading provide a bridge towards further critical research.

Analysing Texts is designed to stimulate and encourage your critical and analytic faculty, to develop your personal insight into the author's work and individual style, and to provide you with the skills and techniques to enjoy at first hand the excitement of discovering the richness of the text.

NICHOLAS MARSH

A Note on Editions

References to act, scene and line numbers in the four comedies studied in this volume are to *William Shakespeare: The Complete Works*, edited by Peter Alexander, London and Glasgow: Collins, 1951. This is also the volume from which the extracts in the analytical chapters are taken. For editions of individual plays suitably annotated for student use see *Further Reading*.

At the beginning of each prose extract line references are given to the Alexander edition and to the extracts reproduced here; all subsequent text references are to the extracts reproduced in this book.

PART 1

ANALYSING
SHAKESPEARE'S COMEDIES

Introduction: The Nature of Shakespearean Comedy

In his *Glossary of Literary Terms* M. H. Abrams defines a 'comedy' as 'a work in which materials are selected and managed primarily in order to interest, involve, and amuse us: the characters and their discomfitures engage our delighted attention rather than our profound concern. We feel confident that no great disaster will occur, and usually the action turns out happily for the chief characters.' He also adds that it is a term applied to dramatic works only.

This is a loose and broadly inclusive 'definition', as it has to be, since 'comedy', even when confined to drama, is used to cover a wide range of very different kinds of entertainment, ranging from good old farcical standbys such as *Arsenic and Old Lace* and *Charley's Aunt* to Oscar Wilde's wittily sophisticated *The Importance of Being Earnest*, and from popular television programmes such as *Dad's Army* and *The Last of the Summer Wine* to the intellectual debate-pieces of Bernard Shaw and Tom Stoppard. Abrams, of course, fully recognises this diversity, and specifies several different types of comedy 'within the broad spectrum of dramatic comedy', including romantic comedy, satiric comedy, the comedy of manners, farce and 'high' and 'low' comedy.

Much comedy, however – and this is particularly true of English works as opposed to the more genre-conscious productions of classical and French literature – is a mixture of many, if not all, these kinds. Verbal wit is often juxtaposed with the rough-and-tumble, physical action of farce, and characters drawn from the idealised world of romance with more familiar and realistically drawn figures from contemporary city and country life. This is pre-eminently true of Shakespearean comedy. Although plays like *A Midsummer Night's Dream, Much Ado About Nothing, As You Like It* and *Twelfth Night* are usually classified as 'romance comedies' – implying that their themes are love and courtship, their settings remote and exotic, and

3

their plots drawn from tales of adventure and vicissitude which end with the conventional 'they lived happily ever after' typical of romance – they also contain farcical and realistic elements which are equally important in the total effect. Sometimes, indeed, it seems as if these unromantic, or even anti-romantic, elements come near to stealing the show: it is not surprising, for example, that a member of the audience in one of the first performances of *Twelfth Night* found 'A good practice in it to make the steward believe his lady widow [not a widow, actually] was in love with him, by counterfeiting a letter as from his lady', and that Charles I wrote 'Malvolio' in his copy of the play. Many spectators likewise remember Beatrice and Benedick more vividly from *Much Ado About Nothing* than Hero and Claudio; and in *A Midsummer Night's Dream*, for many people, Bottom and the Athenian workmen's rendering of *Pyramus and Thisby* overshadows the mistaken wooings of the lovers. Nevertheless, the proper place of these seemingly discordant elements is as part of a larger whole to which they and the romance constituents jointly contribute, and in doing so help to create a form of comedy which transcends the particular types given in Abrams' list.

The Shakespearean comedy which results from this combining and contrasting of multifarious elements gets the best of many worlds. One of the great pleasures afforded by a good production of a Shakespeare comedy is the sense of harmony in disharmony, of the collision between different worlds, different types of dramatic character and different aesthetic modes, which is felt *as* a collision, and yet simultaneously as an interconnected suppleness and flexibility free from subservience to any one particular genre. If rules are there (and Shakespearean comedy most certainly depends for its functioning on many conventions, both literary and theatrical, which might be called 'rules'), they are also there to be bent, broken, and even flouted, when the comic spirit, with its love of variety rather than uniformity, demands it. And from this delight in juxtaposition also spring effects of comparison and contrast which show an alert critical faculty at work. The kaleidoscopic nature of Shakespearean comedy allows a hundred flowers to flower, but also in the process encourages the making of witty distinctions between the ridiculous and the preposterous, the essentially worthwhile and the pretentiously hollow, which besides being in itself another form of entertainment, also serves to sharpen the wits and heighten that discriminating intelligence on which a truly civilised awareness depends.

In what follows various facets of this complex comic process will be explored by close analysis of passages from the four comedies mentioned above. These plays have been chosen for a number of reasons – first, because they represent what most commentators agree is the very best of Shakespeare's comic achievement (though some might argue that *The Merchant of Venice* deserves a place). Second, taken together they have fascinating interconnections which make them valuable comments on each other: the best aid to understanding any one of them is to read, and, better still, see performances of, the other three (though, as suggested in Chapters 12 and 13, the same argument can, to a lesser degree, be extended to include the whole of Shakespeare's work). At the same time, these plays are not mere repetitions of each other. On the contrary – and this constitutes a third reason for choosing them – they cover different areas of experience which, balanced against each other, illustrate the wide-ranging knowledge of human nature, the breadth of dramaturgical skills and the extraordinary diversity and richness of linguistic energy which make Shakespeare the supreme poet-dramatist in English. The fantasy world of *A Midsummer Night's Dream,* the trenchant counterpoint between romantic and anti-romantic in *Much Ado About Nothing,* the many-sided pastoralism of *As You Like It,* and the skilful blend of farce, satire and refined sentiment in *Twelfth Night* together make up a complementary symphony of the comic imagination. And, fourth, spanning as they do the half dozen or more years in which Shakespeare was especially preoccupied with writing comedies, these four plays appropriately illustrate Shakespeare's comic development – taking him from the exuberantly witty creator of Titania and Bottom in *A Midsummer Night's Dream* to the poet of *Twelfth Night,* whose sense of comedy verges perilously on tragedy in the creation of such contrasting figures as Malvolio, Viola and Feste, and in the melancholy, even bitterness, projected in the language and the songs.

1

Atmospherics

Introduction

Shakespearean comedy is kaleidoscopic. It is anything but homogeneous. Like the architecture of Elizabethan great houses, which can seem a charming jumble of classical and medieval motifs, set in a formal garden, yet opening out on to less tidy English landscapes, it is a happy confusion of characters, genres and contrasting styles. It is usually about young lovers and their mistresses, but also includes statesmen and burghers, old men and the middle-aged. Most come from the aristocratic and 'gentle' levels of society, but maids and servants, clowns, stewards and workmen play important parts as well; and *Twelfth Night* has its sailors, *A Midsummer Night's Dream* its fairies, and *As You Like It* even brings on stage Hymen, the god of marriage. The settings can be both exotic and familiar: the idealised worlds of essentially literary pastoral and romance are juxtaposed with the down-to-earth realism of scenes and characters copied from life. Likewise, satire and rapturous sentiment, irony and passionate feeling are set in contrast with each other to provide varied effects of emotional light and shade; and language, cast in the form of prose or verse, both rhymed and unrhymed, is sometimes allowed to flow easily and freely in the channels of colloquial speech. The weather of a Shakespeare comedy, like 'the uncertain glory of an April day', is constantly on the change, and in that variety lies its complex, evanescent appeal.

The following analyses of passages taken from the four chosen plays illustrate some aspects of these varied atmospherics, and explore their implications for the range and meaning of Shakespearean comedy.

Analyses

A Midsummer Night's Dream, I.ii.1–34 (I.ii.1–33). The Athenian workmen have gathered in the Wood to rehearse their production of *Pyramus and Thisby*, which they intend to present at the wedding of Theseus and Hippolyta.

Quince.	Is all our company here?
Bottom.	You were best to call them generally, man by man, according to the scrip.
Quince.	Here is the scroll of every man's name which is thought fit, through all Athens, to play in our interlude before 5 the Duke and the Duchess on his wedding-day at night.
Bottom.	First, good Peter Quince, say what the play treats on; then read the names of the actors; and so grow to a point.
Quince.	Marry, our play is 'The most Lamentable Comedy and most Cruel Death of Pyramus and Thisby'. 10
Bottom.	A very good piece of work, I assure you, and a merry. Now, good Peter Quince, call forth your actors by the scroll. Masters, spread yourselves.
Quince.	Answer, as I call you. Nick Bottom, the weaver.
Bottom.	Ready. Name what part I am for, and proceed. 15
Quince.	You, Nick Bottom, are set down for Pyramus.
Bottom.	What is Pyramus? A lover, or a tyrant?
Quince.	A lover, that kills himself most gallant for love.
Bottom.	That will ask some tears in the true performing of it. If I do it, let the audience look to their eyes; I will 20 move storms; I will condole in some measure. To the rest – yet my chief humour is for a tyrant. I could play Ercles rarely, or a part to tear a cat in, to make all split.

> 'The raging rocks
> And shivering shocks   25
> Shall break the locks
>   Of prison gates;
> And Phibbus' car
> Shall shine from far,
> And make and mar   30
>   The foolish Fates.'

This was lofty. Now name the rest of the players. This is Ercles' vein, a tyrant's vein: a lover is more condoling.

This is comedy bordering on farce. Its humour is broad and depends to a large extent on incongruities perceived by the audience but lost on the ignorant, though innocent, journeymen actors. The note is hit with the unconscious absurdity of 'wedding-day at night', and continued in the title of the play they are to perform, with its mutually incompatible 'Lamentable Comedy and most Cruel Death'. It is laughable, too, that Bottom speaks wiser than he knows in calling it a good piece 'and a merry'. The organiser, it seems, is Quince, but Bottom rapidly establishes himself as the effective leader by the force of his personality and his sublime belief in himself. He immediately sees himself as the one to take the part of Pyramus, but, in keeping with the incongruity that rules the scene, he oscillates between the tear-jerking vein he thinks appropriate for a lover and the ranting and roaring that he would love to indulge in as a tyrant. In the one he 'will move storms', but the other he speaks of even more enthusiastically as 'a part to tear a cat in, to make all split'; and it is in this style that he proceeds to show what he can do. One can easily imagine the overdone bellowing and ludicrous gesticulations which belong to his interpretation of the part, and these are comical counterparts to the language in which his excerpt is cast. This is in verse, but not the verse found elsewhere as the norm of *A Midsummer Night's Dream*: Bottom's is verse which, by virtue of its short, four-syllable lines, crude rhythms, blatant alliteration and jingling AAABCCCB rhymes, shrieks itself to his untutored sensibility as POETRY. Moreover, its theme is destruction on a supernatural scale, giving Bottom full scope to indulge his fantasy of himself as wielder of irresistible powers. This is the kind of noise he likes: 'This was lofty'. (That it was also a style that audiences of Shakespeare's day would recognise as a gross travesty of earlier sixteenth-century tragic rant would add to the joke, and stamp Bottom's taste as ludicrously old-fashioned.) It is with deliciously comic reluctance that Bottom concedes – even to himself – that the appropriate mode for a lover would have to be 'more condoling'.

*   *   *

A Midsummer Night's Dream, II.i.121–37. Titania refuses to hand over the 'little changeling boy' demanded by Oberon:

> Set your heart at rest;
> The fairy land buys not the child of me.
> His mother was a vot'ress of my order;
> And, in the spiced Indian air, by night,
> Full often hath she gossip'd by my side;   125
> And sat with me on Neptune's yellow sands,
> Marking th'embarked traders on the flood;
> When we have laugh'd to see the sails conceive,
> And grow big-bellied with the wanton wind;
> Which she, with pretty and with swimming gait   130
> Following – her womb then rich with my young squire –
> Would imitate, and sail upon the land,
> To fetch me trifles, and return again,
> As from a voyage, rich with merchandise.
> But she, being mortal, of that boy did die;   135
> And for her sake do I rear up her boy;
> And for her sake I will not part with him.

The speaker in this passage is at the opposite extreme from Bottom. She is Titania, Queen of the Fairies. In accordance with Elizabethan dramatic convention she speaks elegantly refined verse, whereas he speaks down-to-earth, colloquial prose – except, of course, for his 'raging rocks' piece, in which, however, the crudeness of the technique makes an even sharper contrast with the refinement of Titania's language. Her defence of her refusal to hand the boy to Oberon goes far beyond what is required to make her case. A strange, exotic world is evoked, involving the Queen and a votaress of her order whom she treats as an intimate. Remoteness and glamour are suggested by phrases such as 'the spiced Indian air' and 'Neptune's yellow sands'. The human and the natural blend into a heightened poetic diction as the two watch vessels which are not merely commonplace cargo ships, but 'embarked traders on the flood', acting out a version of human pregnancy as they 'grow big-bellied with the wanton wind' (as if the godlike wind – often so depicted in maps of the time – were blowing seed into the ships' holds, or wombs), and are, in their turn, imitated by the Indian mother-to-be as she metaphorically 'sails upon the land' to fetch trifles for Titania, herself thus becoming 'rich with merchandise'. This is a beautifully heightened world, existing solely on the imaginative level, and transcending the everyday human world, but still suffused with what is an essentially human vitality and creativeness.

The imaginative richness of the picture is the main thing, but the context is also worth noting. The cue for the speech is a quarrel between the King and the Queen of the Fairies, and it is this which explains why Titania refuses to give up the boy. Her loyalty to the memory of the dead 'vot'ress' does her credit; but to what extent is she really devoted to the welfare of the boy himself? Is she perhaps simply using him as a tool in her quarrel with her husband? (There are appropriate questions, too, about the motives of Oberon in being so insistent on taking the boy from her.) Such considerations give slightly disturbing, slightly sinister undertones to the speech – as does the mention that the mother proved 'mortal' and died in childbirth. As supernatural creatures neither Titania nor Oberon is subject to the same condition; they are on a different level of existence from the pregnant woman, and, moving as the description of the relationship between the two females is, it is also tinged with a tenderness and melancholy which gives its glowingly imaginative effect another, sadder dimension.

*   *   *

As You Like It, II.i.1–17. Duke Senior speaks to his companions – those who have fled with him to the Forest of Arden after his usurpation by his brother, Duke Frederick – about the consolations of the life they lead in exile.

> Now, my co-mates and brothers in exile,
> Hath not old custom made this life more sweet
> Than that of painted pomp? Are not these woods
> More free from peril than the envious court?
> Here feel we not* the penalty of Adam,   5
> The seasons' difference; as the icy fang
> And churlish chiding of the winter's wind,
> Which when it bites and blows upon my body,
> Even till I shrink with cold, I smile and say
> 'This is no flattery; these are counsellors   10
> That feelingly persuade me what I am'.
> Sweet are the uses of adversity;
> Which, like the toad, ugly and venomous,
> Wears yet a precious jewel in his head;
> And this our life, exempt from public haunt,   15
> Finds tongues in trees, books in the running brooks,
> Sermons in stones, and good in everything.

* Many texts substitute 'but' for 'not'.

On a more normally human level than the previous one, this passage is still, however, idealised and to some extent the work of fantasy. A transforming process involving the human and the natural is going on here, too, as the Duke suggests that he and his followers can find 'tongues in trees, books in the running brooks, / Sermons in stones, and good in everything'. His nature is nature humanised and moralised as if it were an emblematic landscape garden; and the artificiality of the idea is emphasised by the slightly precious, rhetorical quality of the language in which it is expressed (e.g. the balanced alliterative phrasing of 'tongues in trees', 'books in brooks' – where internal rhyme heightens the artificiality still further – and 'Sermons in stones'). The harsher aspects are not ignored, especially if we accept the reading 'Here feel we *but* the penalty of Adam'. Even on the reading 'not' the very mention of original sin (this is the 'penalty' which Adam, having eaten of the fruit of the tree of knowledge, bequeathed to all of subsequent mankind) reminds the audience of the fallen nature of the world they, too, inhabit; and the effects of that penalty are rubbed in by the stinging imagery of the cold wind's 'icy fang', the suggestion of human malevolence in its 'churlish chiding', and the contrast between the physical suffering which it inflicts on those who are exposed to it and the flattery of time-serving courtiers whose underlying wickedness has already been brought home to the Duke by his own banishment. Nevertheless, there is a slightly precious quality in the image of the toad with a jewel in its head which makes ugliness somehow picturesquely attractive, reinforcing the artificiality already noted. The Duke – as Amiens says (somewhat ambiguously) immediately after this speech – shows himself adept at translating 'the stubbornness of fortune' into 'so quiet and so sweet a style' (lines 19–20). The mainly end-stopped, smoothly flowing regularity of the verse lessens its urgency, and gives it an atmosphere of Arcadian relaxation. The world is not forgotten, but the Forest offers compensations for its wickedness.

*   *   *

Much Ado About Nothing, II.iii.8–30 (8–28). Benedick is alone, pondering on the way love has changed his friend Claudio.

> I do much wonder that one man, seeing how much another
> man is a fool when he dedicates his behaviours to love, will,
> after he hath laugh'd at such shallow follies in others, become
> the argument of his own scorn by falling in love; and such a
> man is Claudio. I have known when there was no music with   5
> him but the drum and the fife, and now had he rather hear
> the tabor and the pipe; I have known when he would have
> walk'd ten mile afoot to see a good armour, and now will he lie
> ten nights awake carving the fashion of a new doublet. He was
> wont to speak plain and to the purpose, like an honest man   10
> and a soldier, and now is he turn'd orthography; his words are a

very fantastical banquet, just so many strange dishes. May I be
so converted, and see with these eyes? I cannot tell; I think not.
I will not be sworn but love may transform me to an oyster;
but I'll take my oath on it, till he have made an oyster of me   15
he shall never make me such a fool. One woman is fair, yet I
am well; another is wise, yet I am well; another virtuous, yet
I am well; but till all graces be in one woman, one woman shall
not come in my grace. Rich she shall be, that's certain; wise,
or I'll none; virtuous, or I'll never cheapen her; fair, or I'll   20
never look on her; mild, or come not near me; noble, or not
I for an angel; of good discourse, an excellent musician, and
her hair shall be of what colour it please God.

This is Benedick in his role as the professed enemy of the follies and
sentimental excesses of a man in love (though to have him speaking
in this fashion at this particular point in *Much Ado About Nothing* is
a piece of anticipatory irony on Shakespeare's part, as it is in this
very scene that Benedick is to be tricked into falling in love with
Beatrice). He marvels, as do many young men who have not yet had
the experience of being in love, how anyone who has seen the foolish
behaviour of lovers can join their ranks himself; and the more so,
since he has just seen this happen to his comrade-in-arms, Claudio.
What follows (lines 5–12) is a witty set of variations on the not
uncommon theme in Elizabethan literature of the transformation of
the soldier into the lover: delight in military music (played on a big
drum and the shrill-sounding fife) is exchanged for the civilian pleasure of the tabor (a small drum) and the pipe (a more gentle-
sounding form of woodwind); the hard slog of a soldier whose
enthusiasm for armour would make him think nothing of tramping
ten miles to view a suit of it is exchanged for the self-indulgence of a
man lying in bed for ten nights dreaming up a new style in doublets
(the upper part of a fashionable man's clothing); and the honest,
plain, direct speech of a soldier gives way to the fantastic language of
a lover picking and choosing among all the up-to-the-minute words
and phrases available to an Elizabethan courtier, like a finicky gour-
mand at a banquet of rare dishes. The contrasts are, of course, satirically exaggerated. This is Benedick showing off – not to other

characters on the stage, for this is a soliloquy; but to the theatre audience. And despite its being a soliloquy, and in the more down-to-earth medium of prose rather than verse, it is not by any means a realistic imitation of Benedick's stream of consciousness (the odd, abrupt flotsam and jetsam of thoughts flowing through the mind such as James Joyce was to give to his characters in *Ulysses* three centuries later). On the contrary, what Benedick says is a highly organised performance, owing a great deal to the artificially balanced phrases that became something of a craze in Shakespeare's day as a result of the success of John Lyly's *Euphues* (published in 1588). The two halves of his second sentence both open with 'I have known when ...', and 'the drum and the fife' are antithetically balanced against 'the tabor and the pipe'. Walking 'ten mile afoot' is poised against lying 'ten nights awake', and the adjective/noun combination, 'good armour', against the similarly constructed 'new doublet'. Phrases tend to come in pairs: 'speak plain' and 'to the purpose', for example, with the alliterative 'p' helping the words to come more trippingly off the tongue; and the metaphor of words as 'a very fantastical banquet' is at once explained and balanced by 'so many strange dishes'. (However, the listener has to keep his wits about him: if he falls too easily into the antithetical habit, expecting 'an honest man and a soldier' to be exactly balanced by some such phrase as 'a foolish boy and a lover', he is jolted into renewed attention by the curious expression 'orthography' – an abstract noun rather than an agent, and one of the newly imported words that were giving Elizabethan English a strange, new vitality.)

Having made his rhetorical flourish, Benedick asks himself whether the same transformation could happen to him. He concedes that it might (lines 12–13), in which case he would be shut up like a shellfish, or reduced to what is virtually the most elemental form of existence (two possible meanings of 'made an oyster'). But taking his oath that, till love has had such a reductive effect on him, he will never be as foolish as Claudio, is tantamount to dismissing the possibility as too remote to be taken seriously; and he goes on – via the listing of female qualities followed by the repeated 'yet I am well' (lines 16–18) – to congratulate himself on being immune from such sickness. The possibility has, for all that, been insinuated into the speech, and the more he elaborates the qualities a woman would have to possess to interest him, the more it is kept alive. Though his purpose, of course, is still to mock. Such a woman would be a paragon, and paragons are not to be found in the real world. Benedick's argument runs as follows: he will be satisfied with nothing less than perfection; perfection is not to be found in human beings; all women are human; therefore he will never fall in love with one of them. What this overlooks is the fallibility in all men, including himself, as well as women, and the extent to which such fallibility has crept into his own list. 'Rich' (line 19), for example, is only a 'grace' if one admits a somewhat materialistic sense into the meaning of 'grace' (and, again, though this might not be what Benedick consciously intends, it introduces a decidedly unromantic qualification which Claudio, for one, does seem to have taken into consideration before committing himself as suitor to Hero). A hint of such materialism even qualifies Benedick's fundamental require-ment that the woman must be 'virtuous' (line 20) – 'or I'll never cheapen her', he adds, where the word 'cheapen' carries the sense of 'bargain for'. Marriage (and we hear this again from Rosalind in *As You Like It*) is something that belongs to the market place: suitors make bids for women, and the corollary – perhaps another thing overlooked by Benedick – is that women, and their parents even more so, take into account what title, income and property a suitor has to offer. The subtext is there, once more, in the puns on 'noble' and 'angel' (lines 21–2), which refer to coins as well as social and divine qualities. Even the concept of 'nobility' as such is compro-mised. Benedick, as a gentleman, would expect his mistress to have both a noble, upright mind, i.e. to be a woman of high moral worth, and to meet the more worldly social standards of the time which demand that upper class marries into upper class. Even 'mild, or come not near me' is not without implications of a less than ideal kind. It suggests that Benedick's choice would have to be modest and submissive. Perhaps he is secretly afraid of a self-confident, assertive woman (and this, if true, would have a particular bearing on his relationship with the forthright Beatrice).

The final throwaway remark that 'her hair shall be of what colour it please God' (line 23) reminds us once more that Benedick is the

professed scourge of romantic love. Elizabethan love poems are
obsessed with the beauty of golden-haired women, but in Sonnet
130, where Shakespeare, writing of his 'dark lady', inverts the conventional criteria of beauty, he declares: 'If hairs be wires, black wires
grow on her head.' The Benedick of this speech could well be
aligned with the speaker in this sonnet. He may not be expressing a
preference for black over blonde hair, but in cheerfully dismissing
concern for whatever colour the woman's hair might be, he is
putting the finishing touch to his overall anti-romantic stance. It is
of a piece with his mockery of Claudio's transformation, his deliberately exaggerated list of perfections required in a woman to make
him fall in love with her, and with the overall spriteliness and neat
artificiality of his prose style. Here is a man not to be taken in, as
others are, by the sentimental posturings associated with love. But
the unexamined assumptions implicit in the speech also suggest that
he still has much to learn, and make it a very appropriate beginning
to the comedy that is still to be acted out both in the rest of the
scene and in the play as a whole.

*   *   *

Twelfth Night, V.i.66–86. Antonio has been arrested by Orsino's officers and is accused of being a pirate.

>   Orsino, noble sir,
> Be pleas'd that I shake off these names you give me:
> Antonio never yet was thief or pirate,
> Though I confess, on base and ground enough,
> Orsino's enemy. A witchcraft drew me hither: 70
> That most ingrateful boy there by your side
> From the rude sea's enrag'd and foamy mouth
> Did I redeem; a wreck past hope he was.
> His life I gave him, and did thereto add
> My love without retention or restraint,   75
> All his in dedication; for his sake,
> Did I expose myself, pure for his love,
> Into the danger of this adverse town;

Drew to defend him when he was beset;
Where being apprehended, his false cunning,   80
Not meaning to partake with me in danger,
Taught him to face me out of his acquaintance,
And grew a twenty years removed thing
While one would wink; denied me mine own purse,
Which I had recommended to his use   85
Not half an hour before.

The analysis in this case demands some explanation of Antonio's situation. Antonio has put his life in danger by coming ashore in Illyria, where he has enemies, for the sake of the love he bears Sebastian. He has lent the latter his purse, and subsequently intervened in a duel to protect him – not realising that the person he takes for Sebastian is the disguised Viola. He has just been arrested for this, and is now brought before Orsino, who accuses him of being a thief and pirate. This is Antonio's indignant reply.

It is a more intensely dramatic passage than the previous ones. It shows Antonio defending himself like an animal at bay, but also in a state of angry bewilderment as he believes himself betrayed by one for whom he has risked all – 'pure for his love'. The smooth, end-stopped verse of the *As You Like It* extract gives way to a more abrupt, colloquially stressed verse which breaks through the regularity of the ten-syllable iambic structure (iamb = an unstressed syllable followed by a stressed one) and, as in lines 70, 73 and 76, makes pauses in the middle rather than at the end of the line. Where there is inversion or repetition it is less for the sake of rhetorical balance than passionately felt emotion – as when, extensively in lines 71–3, and again briefly in line 74, the normal order of subject–verb–object is distorted to object–subject–verb; and when, in line 77, Antonio repeats the word 'love' with the emphatic addition of 'pure for' (i.e. 'solely for the sake of '). The language simultaneously highlights the mistaken identity of Viola as the person to whom Antonio is devoted, and intensifies his sense of betrayal, by giving us first the image of the supposedly 'ingrateful boy', standing, it would seem, so coolly by Orsino's side, and afterwards a graphic personification of the storm as an angry sea-god foaming at the mouth, from which – as intensely felt climax –

Antonio redeemed him. 'Redeem' means 'rescue', but its religious overtones are also relevant: in the background is the moving suggestion of Antonio as a Christlike figure sacrificing himself for one who now looks like an ungrateful sinner. The parallelism of 'Did I expose myself' with 'Did I redeem', and the inversion of 'His life I gave him', adds force to this suggestion.

From Antonio's point of view it is something like an evil spell of 'witchcraft' (line 70) that has been cast upon him. The double dealing this seems to imply is reinforced, for him, by the incredible cowardice and 'false cunning' of the supposed Sebastian, who now denies there has ever been any acquaintance between them; and in the linguistically highly original lines 83–4 this translates into a catastrophic telescoping in which the usually slow process of organic change conveyed by 'grew' converts a living human being into a 'thing' (qualified by the highly compressed compound epithet 'twenty years removed', cramming two decades of estrangement into three words) in the time it takes to blink one's eyes. And the speech ends with another suggestion of catastrophic change: Antonio, like the good Samaritan, had also given 'Sebastian' his purse, and that, too, is denied by the now seemingly unworthy object of his love. A generous dispensing of money seems to have been rewarded by a criminal absconding with money, taken from the very person who had acted so altruistically 'Not half an hour before'.

In this speech we sense Antonio's world collapsing about his ears. It opens up a vista of witchcraft, cynicism and betrayal, in a world of radical instability, which leaves the civilised urbanity of the Duke in *As You Like It* far behind, and seems to bring comedy nearer the tragic vision of ingratitude experienced by a King Lear or a Timon of Athens.

Conclusions

The world, or rather worlds, envisaged in the passages analysed above are very different from each other. On the one hand, there is the evocative beauty of the fantasy world which Titania shares with her Indian votaress in *A Midsummer Night's Dream*, and, on the other, the crude burlesque of Bottom's 'Ercles' vein'; both of which contrast with the painful disillusionment of Antonio in *Twelfth*

Night. There is the urbane acceptance of adversity in Duke Senior's speech in *As You Like It*; and there is the elegant mockery of Benedick in *Much Ado About Nothing*, in which the idealised attitudes of conventional lovers are juxtaposed with a more realistic appreciation of how things are in real life. Taken together, these passages (though far from exhaustive) illustrate the wide range of values, emotions and imaginatively created environments which go to make up the complex variety of Shakespearean comedy. Its leading characteristic is openness and responsiveness to different moods and kinds of experience, presented in a way that enhances and expands the imaginative capacities of both audiences and readers.

Each is a world unto itself; but these different worlds are interlinked as well as contrasted, with a sense of interconnection that extends not only to other areas within the same play, but to other Shakespearean comedies as well. The sea-imagery, for example, of the passage from *A Midsummer Night's Dream* cross-connects with the sea-tempest from which Antonio, in the *Twelfth Night* passage, rescues Sebastian, which, in turn, looks back (albeit incongruously) to 'The raging rocks / And shivering shocks' of Bottom's sample of his 'Ercles' vein'. Likewise, the blending of the human and the natural in Titania's speech which metaphorises ships into 'embarked traders on the flood' has a counterpart in the humanising and moralising in Duke Senior's discourse which turns the ice and wind of Arden into 'counsellors' that 'feelingly persuade' him what he is. And, remote as Titania's romantically evocative 'spiced Indian air' may seem from the world of money and commerce, it is precisely this which is called up by her references to 'traders' and 'merchandise', reminding one that seagoing in Elizabethan times had much to do with the more mundane trade in oriental spices. This in its turn connects with the accusation of piracy brought against Antonio, and the enmity between him and Orsino which indirectly suggests a trade war; while – still more indirectly it may be, but not irrelevantly – the 'cheapening' undertone in Benedick's tirade is a reminder of how similar business considerations can affect what purport to be exclusively romantic affairs of the heart.

These are not, of course, necessarily conscious and deliberate attempts on Shakespeare's part at making cross-connections. It would be fairer to regard them as indications of a kind of instinctive reaching out of his imagination from the moods and themes which are the major, and distinct, preoccupations of one passage or play to elements which are present, if only in a subordinate, or even subliminal way, in other passages and plays which seem to have quite different atmospheres and concerns. When passages like those above are put side by side, contrast may well seem more important than points of similarity that can be discovered between them. But, ultimately, the two kinds of effect are complementary. The marked contrasts and differences underline the range and versatility of Shakespearean comedy, its flexibility in dealing with widely disparate areas of experience, and its openness and inclusiveness. The more peripheral-seeming connections, on the other hand, are evidence of the overall synthesising power of an imagination which tends to join experiences together rather than separate and isolate them. Together they illustrate both the diversity and the underlying unity of Shakespeare's comic imagination.

Methods of Analysis

1. *Language.* In both prose and verse look closely at (a) choice of words, including puns, (b) use of rhetorical devices and the structure of sentences, and (c) the use of figurative language. In verse also pay particular attention to (d) metre, rhythm, pauses and the use of end-stopped or run-on lines.

   At the more basic level, as in the dialogue assigned to the Athenian workmen, look for unconsciously comic effects produced by the incongruous juxtaposition of words in such phrases as 'wedding-day at night' and 'Lamentable Comedy and most Cruel Death', and the descent from the would-be sublime to the ridiculous in Bottom's description of a heroic part as one 'to tear a cat in'. On the more romantic level consider the evocative effect of such a combination of epithets as 'spiced Indian' in the phrase 'spiced Indian air' in Titania's speech. What is the effect of her devotee being called 'a vot'ress'? Be on the lookout for puns, which abound in Shakespearean comedy (see the comment on 'noble' and 'angel' in the analysis of Benedick's soliloquy), and for the juxtaposition of familar, monosyllabic words with more complex, polysyllabic words as in Duke Senior's line, 'Sweet are the uses of adversity' or Benedick's 'now is he turn'd orthography'. (Why are these so different in effect?) Use a well-annotated edition which will alert you to words that are still used in present-day English, but have a quite different meaning (e.g. Benedick's 'cheapen').

Get yourself used to hearing the effects of assonance (similarity of vowel sounds), alliteration (similarity of initial sounds) and similar endings, which abound in Shakespeare's language, and consider the different kinds of effect they have. They add, for example, to the smoothness and articulation of Duke Senior's speech, but intensify the farcical effect of Bottom's 'Ercles' vein'. Note the effects of repetition (different again in lines 136–7 of Titania's speech and lines 16–18 of Benedick's), and be aware of balance and antithesis (often emphasised by alliteration, as in the last two lines of Duke Senior's speech). Benedick's prose is rich in balancing effects, which are enhanced by constant parallelism ('I have known when ..., and now had he ...; I have known when ..., and now will he ... He was wont ..., and now is he turn'd ...').

Look for figurative language – a vital part of all Shakespeare's writing. The pregnancy metaphor in Titania's speech and the witchcraft metaphor in Antonio's are examples. Simile is the more self-conscious form (as in Duke Senior's 'like the toad'); metaphor the more immediate (it may be compressed into a single world, as in Titania's use of 'sail' for her votaress's movement like a sailing ship along the land). Personification is a common form, as in Duke Senior's treatment of the winds as 'counsellors' who persuade him by making him feel what he is.

Note the variety in Shakespeare's verse. As suggested in the analysis, Bottom's crude rhyme and rhythm make his 'raging rocks' verse stick out like a sore thumb. The pieces spoken by Titania, Duke Senior and Antonio respectively are subtler. They are all blank verse (examples of rhymed verse will be found in later analyses), but Duke Senior, for example, includes internal rhyme (line 16) and the sequence, 'old', 'woods', 'winter's wind', 'cold', 'toad', 'head', 'haunt', 'Finds', 'books', 'brooks' and 'good', keeps a kind of subliminal half-rhyme going through the whole passage. And, characteristically, none of these speeches is metronomically regular. Notice where they depart from the basic iambic pentameter pattern (te-tum, te-tum, te-tum, te-tum, te-tum), and the effects these departures have. Notice, too, as in the analysis of Antonio's speech, where the rhythm is closer to that of actual speech, and where the sense demands a pause, not at the end of a line, but a run-on into the next line. Hearing both the underlying metric pattern and the surface variations from it, and gauging the extent of the disruptive effect of these variations, should become a natural part of your response to Shakespeare's verse.

2. *Speaker, speech and dramatic context.* Not all speeches are 'in character', but, as far as the text permits, try to hear the words as the expression of a particular character in a particular situation. The dramatic intensity of Antonio's sense of betrayal has been emphasised in the analysis, but bear in mind that the context – all that the audience has seen and heard in the preceding scenes and therefore know of his situation (including knowing more than he does) – contributes powerfully to the effect. So do others on the stage. Be, as it were, mentally aware of them, even if you are not in a theatre actually seeing them there. Clues are often in the text: Duke Senior appeals to his 'co-mates and brothers' who are with him 'in exile', for example, and Antonio points to 'That most ingrateful boy there' on the stage at Orsino's side. Titania's speech is a retort to Oberon ('Set your heart at rest'). How does this qualify her subsequent words? How much does it suggest opposition to her fairy husband rather than concern for her dead votaress's son? Clues as to the quality of a speech, and possible ways in which it might be interpreted, may also be present in the text (e.g. Amiens' comment on Duke Senior's translation of his misfortune into 'so quiet and so sweet a style'). What a character *denies* may also, paradoxically, draw attention to something important, but unrecognised by that character (as in the denials analysed in Benedick's speech).

Suggested Work

In *A Midsummer Night's Dream* analyse the speech in which Hermia swears to meet Lysander in the wood outside Athens ('My good Lysander! I swear to thee ... will I meet with thee', I.i.168–78). What kind of atmosphere is created by the classical references (if you do not understand them, refer to one of the editions mentioned below on p. 258) and by the parallel structures in lines 170–5? Consider the use of rhyme, and the significance of Hermia's references to broken vows.

In *Much Ado About Nothing*, as a contrast to Benedick's speech mocking at love, consider the Friar's speech outlining what he expects to be the effect on Claudio of pretending that Hero is dead ('Marry, this, well carried, shall on her behalf ... Will quench the wonder of her infamy', IV.i.210–39). What is the 'idea' that the Friar hopes to create in Claudio's mind? Consider the contribution to the shaping of this new image made by the metaphors of childbirth, winning and losing a prize, dress, taking aim and quenching (thirst or fire).

In *As You Like It* analyse the exchange between Orlando and Duke Senior in II.vii.102–26 ('What would you have? ... That to your wanting may be minist'red'). Orlando has just burst in upon the Duke and his followers as they are about to eat a meal. To begin with he is peremptory ('Forbear, and eat no more,' line 88), but note how he changes his tune on finding the Duke hospitable. Pay particular attention to the way the syntax and rhetoric of Orlando and the Duke echo each other, and to the qualities that characterise the civilised life for both of them.

In *Twelfth Night* analyse the dialogue between Olivia and Viola at I.v.215–35 ('Good madam, let me see your face ... But, if you were the devil, you are fair'). Viola has been sent, as 'Cesario', to woo Olivia on behalf of Orsino. Olivia's face is covered with a veil, but Viola asks her to remove it. Examine the implications of Olivia's treatment of her veil as if it were a curtain screening a painting, and of her offer to have an inventory taken of her beauty. Note the change from verse to prose and back again to verse. What implications do these changes have for the tone of the exchange?

2

Sympathetic Criticism

Introduction

It is rare for a figure in Shakespearean comedy to be either uncritically admired or mercilessly derided; even a Rosalind has her shortcomings, and even a Malvolio has his 'case'. In the kind of awareness such comedy generates, both judgement and understanding, laughter and compassion are involved. Criticism is balanced by sympathy, and sympathy modified by a cooler quality of intellectual detachment.

To show how these qualities balance each other as a dramatic situation is unfolded the analysis which follows will be applied to the successive developments of one complete scene; but for convenience of discussion this scene will be divided into four sections.

Analysis

As You Like It, II.iv. Rosalind, dressed as a boy and having adopted the name Ganymede, arrives in the Forest of Arden. With her are her cousin, Celia, who has chosen the name Aliena, and the court Fool, Touchstone, who has agreed to join the two young women in their exile. Their journey has been long and wearisome.

Rosalind.   O Jupiter, how weary are my spirits!
Touchstone.   I care not for my spirits, if my legs were not weary.

Rosalind.	I could find in my heart to disgrace my man's apparel, and to cry like a woman; but I must comfort the weaker vessel, as doublet and hose ought to show itself courageous to petticoat; therefore, courage, good Aliena. 5
Celia.	I pray you bear with me; I cannot go no further.
Touchstone.	For my part, I had rather bear with you than bear you; yet I should bear no cross if I did bear you; for I think you have no money in your purse.
Rosalind.	Well, this is the Forest of Arden.
Touchstone.	Ay, now am I in Arden; the more fool I; when I was at home I was in a better place; but travellers must be content. 11
Rosalind.	Ay, be so, good Touchstone.

Both Rosalind and Touchstone are saying, in effect: 'How tired I am!' But Rosalind strikes a loftier tone with her preliminary 'O Jupiter'. Given the prohibition in Elizabethan times against the use of the name of the Christian deity on the stage, 'Jupiter' may simply be a way of avoiding the mention of 'God' (it recurs again as 'Jove' at line 48), but it also has dignified classical associations and is appropriate to Rosalind's adopted name of 'Ganymede'. (We remember that in I.iii she had accompanied her choice of disguise-name with the words, 'I'll have no worse a name than Jove's own page' (line 20), as if wishing, albeit playfully, to ennoble the ruse she is forced to by her banishment.) Likewise, when she speaks of her weariness it is in terms of its effect on her 'spirits', emphasising the psychological rather than the physical.

Not that Rosalind is immune from feeling distress. As lines 3–4 reveal, she is on the brink of tears; but she takes the view that she must suppress them for the sake of Celia/Aliena. It is her duty as a supposed male to 'comfort the weaker vessel', the female; it is what her role as 'Ganymede' demands of her. That role also requires the wearing of different clothes, a feature of gender conventions which is emphasised by the metonymy (substitution of a thing for a person or idea) of Rosalind's reference to 'doublet and hose' versus 'petticoat'. This would seem to suggest that because she wears male dress she must deny her female nature, conforming to a code which is alien to her. However, that she does this so cheerfully also allows for the possibility that the cross-dressing actually enables her to fulfil a need in herself which conventional separation of the sexes denies. Add to this the fact that in Elizabethan productions of *As You Like It* Rosalind would be played by a boy-actor, and one has the more complex situation of a boy playing a girl playing a boy, and, in so doing, fulfilling his nature as a boy. The total effect is thus highly complex, not merely underlining the factitious nature of Rosalind's 'male' chivalry, but also releasing the suppressed maleness within her, and giving the interplay between her and the other two characters on stage a peculiarly comic ambiguity.

To return, however, to line 2: Touchstone's shift from 'spirits' to 'legs' is typical of him. He brings the would-be dignified Rosalind down to earth with deliberate bathos. He may be in the Forest of Arden, but in his more matter-of-fact mind the sheer fatigue of getting there is uppermost. His riposte is typical of his unsentimental approach; and it is reinforced by his calling himself 'the more fool' for being there rather than enjoying the comforts of home. Both remarks are perhaps ironic at the expense of the girls whose boldness has led them to take on more than they can cope with. But if so (and he probably knows this) it rebounds on himself as well. His position is no less ambiguous than Rosalind's. Why has he come at all? Apparently because Celia has been able to rely on his devotion to her. To her confession of weariness (the most plain and straightforward of the three, incidentally) he replies in the same mocking manner, with puns on 'bear' and 'cross' (the latter playing on both its Christian symbolism and its connection with money) which are meant to suggest that only a fool would undertake such a profitless journey – yet, clearly, this is what he has done. Of course, he is a Fool, and can therefore be expected to behave foolishly. But, like other Fools in Shakespeare, wiser, more self-interested behaviour which eschews such folly does not necessarily get his approval. He concludes that he has to be 'content', and Rosalind, who appreciates the nature of his folly, tells him to be so.

At this point Corin and Silvius make their appearance – two denizens of the Forest, as opposed to the three 'travellers' to it whom we have so far heard.

Rosalind.	Look you, who comes here, a young man and an old in solemn talk.	
Corin.	That is the way to make her scorn you still.	15
Silvius.	O Corin, that thou knew'st how I do love her!	
Corin.	I partly guess; for I have lov'd ere now.	
Silvius.	No, Corin, being old, thou canst not guess, Though in thy youth thou wast as true a lover As ever sigh'd upon a midnight pillow. But if thy love were ever like to mine, As sure I think did never man love so, How many actions most ridiculous Hast thou been drawn to by thy fantasy?	20
Corin.	Into a thousand that I have forgotten.	25
Silvius.	O, thou didst then never love so heartily! If thou rememb'rest not the slightest folly That ever love did make thee run into, Thou hast not lov'd; Or if thou hast not sat as I do now, Wearing thy hearer in thy mistress' praise, Thou hast not lov'd; Or if thou hast not broke from company Abruptly, as my passion now makes me, Thou hast not lov'd. O Phebe, Phebe, Phebe!	30 35 *[Exit Silvius.*

The subject of this dialogue is the quintessentially romantic one of love. Silvius is the young, infatuated swain, Corin the older, more experienced man. It rapidly appears, however, that what the courtly exiles have stumbled on are not, after all, realistic country-dwellers (though Corin is nearer to such than Silvius), but personages much more like those of that highly artificial literary form, the pastoral (itself, ironically, more favoured by courtiers than actual country-dwellers). The antithetical positions of the two are those of the standard 'eclogue', or pastoral dialogue, in which the speakers represent Age v. Youth; and the posture of Silvius in particular is recognisably that of the scorned, woebegone lover to be found in countless Elizabethan pastorals and love songs.

It is worth noting, too, that the language has now switched from prose to verse, which also signals something about the tone and genre into which the action has transferred. The normal convention in Elizabethan drama is that noble characters speak in verse and humbler ones in prose. The reversal of that convention here emphasises the artificiality of the situation, and, as Silvius proceeds to make his extravagant claims for the uniqueness of his suffering, its preposterousness as well. This is another form of 'folly' (Silvius admits as much), but divorced from the critical, and self-critical, irony which Touchstone has demonstrated in the preceding exchange with Rosalind. Silvius is wrapped up in the cocoon of his own emotion, which makes 'folly' itself a touchstone of genuine love, and is elevated to the formally serious level of verse.

Silvius's language becomes more patently rhetorical as he weaves himself more deeply into his occluded world of love. Lines 27–35 reveal a pattern of tripled clauses, each of which begins with a conditioned negative aimed at Corin ('If thou rememb'rest not ...', 'Or if thou hast not ...', 'Or if thou hast not ...') and ends with the same, again negatived, main clause: 'Thou hast not lov'd'. This repeated main clause also consists of four syllables only, instead of the normal ten used in the other lines; and the truncation of the line – obvious in print, but also audible on stage, especially to an audience accustomed to verse as the dramatic medium – heightens its emotional impact. 'Love' is what Silvius is experiencing; not to have the same symptoms is not to have loved. And, in effect, as this linguistic foregrounding and isolating suggests, Silvius thinks that no one has ever suffered as he does. Suiting his actions to his final words about breaking from company 'Abruptly', Silvius then sweeps from the stage, histrionically clutching his brow and repeating (again three times) 'O Phebe, Phebe, Phebe!'

This is a delightful comic vignette, executed not simply at the expense of the pastoral as such (for *As You Like It* itself is one of the most fascinating contributions ever made to the pastoral genre), but that stilted and effete variety of it, done to death in the literature of Shakespeare's time, which encouraged an altogether maudlin, self-indulgent pose of self-pity on the part of its standard rejected lover. The theatre audience has watched it, and laughed at it. But the 'eclogue' is also a little play-within-a-play, watched by the on-stage audience of Rosalind, Celia and Touchstone, who are themselves watched as they do so. By means of this device Shakespeare is able to suggest the possibility of there being more than one kind of response to Silvius's passion – as the next part of the scene suggests.

Rosalind.	Alas, poor shepherd! searching of thy wound,
	I have by hard adventure found mine own.
Touchstone.	And I mine. I remember, when I was in love,
	I broke my sword upon a stone, and bid him 40
	take that for coming a-night to Jane Smile;
	and I remember the kissing of her batler, and
	the cow's dugs that her pretty chopt hands had
	milk'd; and I remember the wooing of a peascod
	instead of her; from whom I took two cods, and, 45
	giving her them again, said with weeping tears
	'Wear these for my sake'. We that are true lovers
	run into strange capers; but as all is mortal in
	nature, so is all nature in love mortal in folly.
Rosalind.	Thou speak'st wiser than thou art ware of. 50
Touchstone.	Nay, I shall ne'er be ware of mine own wit till I
	break my shins against it.
Rosalind.	Jove, Jove! this shepherd's passion
	Is much upon my fashion.
Touchstone.	And mine; but it grows something stale with me. 55

Touchstone's response is to find a parallel between the 'folly' of Silvius the demented lover and himself as lover of Jane Smile – though we do not have to believe that he was her lover, or that 'Jane Smile' ever existed; this is simply the jester's spoof. He also reverts to prose, the medium appropriate for his mockingly prosaic anecdote, which knocks love off its romantic pedestal, and brings it down to the banal level of a wooer so deluded that he strikes a stone in mistake for a supposed rival, and woos a pea plant instead of her. More to the point, he makes his story an excuse for alluding to coarse and decidedly unromantic aspects of rural life, such as the 'batler' (laundry stick) used by milkmaids when washing dirty clothes, and the raw, 'chopt' (i.e. 'chapped') hands they get from working the teats of cows. And, with still greater debunking effect, he loads what he says with bawdy double meanings, including verbal play on 'peascod/codpiece' and rather more recondite sexual allusions. Alan Brissenden, for example, suggests that lines 39–41 involve 'punishment of Touchstone's penis for having an embarrassing orgasm in Jane Smile's presence' (Oxford Shakespeare edition of *As You Like It*, p. 135). If this seems preposterous, it is as well to bear in mind that often quite tortuous bawdy is endemic to Shakespearean comedy, and that even characters like Rosalind and Celia indulge in it. Bawdy brings the high-flown sentiments of love down to their origin in sexual appetite, and reminds us that the spiritual and the physical are inseparable in the persons of actual lovers (though it does not have to be cynically reductive to the point of implying that all romantic notions are nothing but a sublimation of lust).

However, Touchstone's Jane Smile piece is only the second response to Silvius. The first comes from Rosalind, and her 'searching of thy wound, / I have by hard adventure found mine own' is much more sympathetic. Silvius's passion for Phebe reminds her of her own love for Orlando; and though it becomes the springboard for Touchstone's exercise in demolition (the partial truth of which she both acknowledges, and detaches herself from, in line 50), at lines 47–8 she reiterates her sympathy for Silvius and the connection she feels with her own love for Orlando. In both instances she also uses the more resonant medium of verse: lines 37–8 continue the earlier blank verse, but lines 53–4 are more emphatic still by being made shorter lines, and having their nominally iambic metre disrupted by heavy stresses on 'Jove' and on the word 'my'.)

Although there is ample evidence later that Rosalind, too, is critical of Silvius, the positiveness of her immediate response is a powerful endorsement of the emotional reality of love. It is a reminder that romance, notwithstanding its liability to extravagance and its capacity to disregard common sense, is founded on something both universal and vital. The juxtaposition of two such diverse responses as hers and Touchstone's illustrates the Shakespearean habit, particularly marked in the comedies, of having his cake and eating it. It is not a question of one being right and the other wrong: both positions, antithetical as they are, belong to the thinking and feeling human being. And the fact that Rosalind's assertion of the primacy of love is also adjusted to a social context of good-humoured mockery – unlike Silvius's, whose passion is anti-social and makes him 'break from company' – allows her to seem that much more properly human. Later in the play she, too, will be allowed to have her cake and eat it by contriving a situation in which she can mock the extravagance of her own lover's love while simultaneously basking in his expression of it.

All this is prompted by Silvius. After his melodramatic exit, however, the presence of Corin, and the reality of the traveller's weariness and hunger, are reasserted:

Celia.	I pray you, one of you question yond man	
	If he for gold will give us any food;	
	I faint almost to death.	
Touchstone.	Holla, you clown!	
Rosalind.	Peace, fool; he's not thy kinsman.	60
Corin.	Who calls?	
Touchstone.	Your betters, sir.	
Corin.	Else are they very wretched.	
Rosalind.	Peace, I say. Good even to you, friend.	
Corin.	And to you, gentle sir, and to you all.	65
Rosalind.	I prithee, shepherd, if that love or gold	
	Can in this desert place buy entertainment,	
	Bring us where we may rest ourselves and feed.	
	Here's a young maid with travel much oppress'd,	
	And faints for succour.	70
Corin.	Fair sir, I pity her,	
	And wish, for her sake more than for mine own,	
	My fortunes were more able to relieve her;	
	But I am shepherd to another man,	

	And do not shear the fleeces that I graze.	75

And do not shear the fleeces that I graze.　　　75
My master is of churlish disposition,
And little recks to find the way to heaven
By doing deeds of hospitality.
Besides, his cote, his flocks, and bounds of feed,
Are now on sale; and at our sheepcote now,　　　80
By reason of his absence, there is nothing
That you will feed on; but what is, come see,
And in my voice most welcome will you be.

Rosalind.　What is he that shall buy his flock and pasture?

Corin.　That young swain that you saw here but erewhile,　85
That little cares for buying any thing.

Rosalind.　I pray thee, if it stand with honesty,
Buy thou the cottage, pasture, and the flock,
And thou shalt have to pay for it of us.

Celia.　And we will mend thy wages. I like this place,　　90
And willingly could waste my time in it.

Corin.　Assuredly the thing is to be sold.
Go with me; if you like upon report
The soil, the profit, and this kind of life,
I will your very faithful feeder be,　　　　　　95
And buy it with your gold right suddenly.

Food and money are issues here that bring us into a very different world from that of Silvius's infatuation with Phebe. As the dialogue progresses between Corin and Rosalind with reference to the purchase of his master' s farm, it emerges that the prospective purchaser is indeed Silvius himself, the 'young swain' who has just made his exit, but 'little cares for buying any thing'. True enough, buying and selling seem irrelevant issues as far as Silvius is concerned. But not for Corin. His speech beginning at line 71 brings in the economic aspects of sheep farming which the kind of literary pastoral to which Silvius belongs usually ignores; or if they are mentioned, it is on the assumption that the shepherd is master of his own flocks, as well as being (in a blurring of the distinction between the classical and Christian asssociations of pastoral) their loving and charitable protector. Corin, however, is a hireling – 'shepherd to another man'; and his master is one who has an unchristianly 'churlish disposition' which makes him care little for finding his way to heaven 'By doing deeds of hospitality'.

The very mention of the master–servant relation brings in social, economic, political, and even religious, matters which literary pastoral tends to gloss over. Corin's master is anti-social in a different way from Silvius; and, it would seem, with less excuse. His denial of 'company' comes from innate churlishness and a selfish refusal to accept those mutual obligations of compassion and charity which make civilised society possible. (These issues are developed more fully in scenes iii, vi and vii of this Act, which respectively anticipate and follow this scene, framing it and giving it further resonance.) The poverty of Corin himself makes it difficult for him, too, to be charitable – at least in the way he would like to be; but he is willing to share what he has, and especially so when Rosalind couples 'gold' with 'love' as a motive to 'buy entertainment' (i.e. food and lodging). However, that Corin reacts as he does to the offer of money does not necessarily imply that his attitude is merely mercenary. His very first response to Rosalind's appeal is one of 'pity' (line 71) for Celia/Aliena, and is only subsequently qualified by the harsher problems of economics. But there is no mistaking the alacrity with which he jumps at Rosalind's suggestion that he might buy the farm which is up for sale, on her and Celia's behalf, especially when Celia adds the inducement of raising his wages. His final couplet – and the one on which the whole scene ends – is one of obvious relish at the prospect of better employment and ready money, the jingling rhyme: 'I will your very faithful feeder be, / And buy it with your gold right suddenly', giving his excitement an almost jaunty note.

The issue of social status also enters into the transaction between Corin on the one hand and Rosalind, Celia and Touchstone on the other. It is Touchstone who addresses the first words to Corin, greeting him condescendingly with 'Holla, you clown!' There is a play here on the word 'clown', meaning both the kind of professional clown that Touchstone himself is, and 'clown' in the sense of a country yokel; but it is one which does Touchstone no credit. Rosalind immediately rebukes him for his rudeness; and when he answers Corin's 'Who calls?' with his rather priggish 'Your betters, sir', he is effectively put down by Corin's rejoinder: 'Else are they very wretched.' It is then Rosalind who takes over the dialogue, and she and Corin exchange courtesies on more amicable terms:

Rosalind.	Good even to you, friend.
Corin.	And to you, gentle sir, and to you all. (lines 67–8)

Corin is not fazed by Touchstone's affectation of superiority; nor does he presume on Rosalind's readiness to address him as a 'friendly' equal. The 'gentle' of his 'gentle sir' is an acknowledgement not only (as it might seem to a twentieth-century audience) of Rosalind's kindliness, but also of the latter's evident status as a gentleman – made apparent, no doubt, despite the disguise, by the quality of the clothes 'he' wears, and particularly the way 'he' speaks. Touchstone's rubbing-in of the social difference is superfluous: Rosalind's status needs no such arrogance to communicate itself. It is absorbed into, and conditions, the subsequent dialogue, and again modifies the pastoral atmosphere by maintaining, albeit un-assertively, the social distinctions which were a real part of the markedly stratified society of Elizabethan England. (It is worth noting, too, that this part of the scene reverts to verse, despite its consciously unromantic matter. This can be attributed to stage con-vention, in that Corin, humble though he is, is talking with gentle-manly characters; but the effect is also to give him a natural dignity.)

That Rosalind and Celia seem to manage these social differences in a more tactful manner than Touchstone does not mean that they ignore them; but it may be that, fundamentally, they are more confi-dent of their position. Touchstone, after all, is himself a court hireling, a hanger-on, even if an indulged one, and to that extent he is anxious to assert distinctions which he cannot take so easily for granted as Rosalind and Celia. Although the 'Peace, fool; he's not thy kinsman' (line 60) which Rosalind directs at him is not a sharp rebuke, it makes a point which the later behaviour of Corin con-firms. The 'clown' is not of kin to the clownishness that Touchstone attributes to him; and, if Touchstone has the smarter wit, Corin may claim to have the better natural manners.

Conclusions

Touchstone remains, of course, one of the most intelligent, adroit and entertaining characters in *As You Like It*, second only to Rosalind in the admiration he arouses in an audience. But the fact that he, who so often worsts others in the play's skirmishes of wit, can himself be occasionally worsted is in tune with the overall spirit of the comedy. In this particular scene he has perhaps, in his Jane Smile anecdote, the speech which scores the most obvious comic success; it is a highly characteristic piece of debunking and an effective antithesis to the amorous mooning of the lovelorn Silvius. On the other hand, Rosalind's tacit criticism of his treatment of Corin temporarily unseats him from his high horse, and her immediate and instinctive recognition of sharing a common experience of love with Silvius goes some way to reinstate a too-easily ridiculed character. Yet again, however, the brittleness and artificiality of the literary tradition to which Silvius's version of pastoral belongs is counterbalanced by a glimpse of the practical economics of sheep farming which comes from the level-headed Corin. And, as a significant undertone to all, the weariness and hunger entailed by the three outsiders' journeying to the Forest of Arden (which, viewed in this perspective, is also in Rosalind's words a 'desert place') both begins the scene and resurfaces towards its end.

The kind of comedy such a scene provides is thus delicately balanced. It excites critical laughter, but it also redeems what is laughed at by a discriminating sympathy. It gives some rein to idealism and romantic sentiment, but also checks and controls them by the keenness of its sense of the absurd. It allows escape into a world which is pure literary fiction, but also confronts that world, both light-heartedly and in more serious style, with the harsher realities on which it would seem to be turning its back. Taken as a whole, therefore, it is a beautifully judged combination of sympathy and criticism; and as such it may be regarded as an expression in miniature of what Shakespearean comedy is all about.

3

Illusion

Introduction

Drama is an art of illusion. Men and women – or, in the Elizabethan theatre, boys – are dressed as characters (*dramatis personae*), and given words to speak and actions to perform which are designed to persuade audiences that they are watching people recognisably akin to themselves (even when these fictional beings are kings and queens) caught up in deeply disturbing or preposterously amusing events. These events are also accepted as taking place in localities which may be either familiar or strange, and in times either contemporary or remote – the appropriate impressions being created either by the use of scenery (which may vary from the elaborately contrived to the merely perfunctory), or linguistic signals in the dramatic script, or both. Modern cinema and television productions, which carry to an extreme the realism of the late-nineteenth-century proscenium-arch theatre, are at one end of this spectrum; and the open-air, apron-stage theatre for which Shakespeare wrote is at the opposite end (though still not as arbitrary and highly stylised as that of the ancient Greeks or Japanese Noh plays). If time and place need to be specified in Shakespeare's theatre, the illusion is more often created by words rather than stage scenery, as in *Much Ado About Nothing*, V.iii.24–7, where the coming of dawn (at the end of the obsequies for the supposedly dead Hero) is announced in an evocative quatrain:

Good morrow, masters; put your torches out;
  The wolves have prey'd; and look, the gentle day,
Before the wheels of Phoebus, round about
  Dapples the drowsy east with spots of grey.

Or, as we have seen in the previous chapter, when the audience
needs to know that Rosalind, Celia and Touchstone have reached the
forest, it is simply informed by Rosalind: 'Well, this is the Forest of
Arden'. Similarly, *Twelfth Night*, I.ii opens with Viola's naive question, 'What country, friends, is this?' and the Captain's answer, 'This
is Illyria' – which is as much for the benefit of the audience as Viola,
and as much as they need to know about the play's place of action.
Again, in II.iii.1–5 when the lateness of the hour is something that
affects the way Sir Toby's and Sir Andrew's carousing is received (and
one should remember this is a scene which, in the Globe Theatre,
would be performed in broad daylight), the necessary information is
conveyed in their verbal banter:

Sir Toby.   Approach, Sir Andrew. Not to be abed after midnight is to
         be up betimes; and 'diluculo surgere' [to rise at dawn] thou
         know'st –
Sir Andrew. Nay, by my troth, I know not; but I know to be up late is to
         be up late.

Yet audiences, whether Elizabethan or modern, are not deceived.
They know all along exactly where they, physically, are, and what
time of day it is. And even though they may become deeply involved
in the most absorbing of dramatic situations, they maintain a dual
awareness that what they see and hear both is, and is not, so – that
they are simultaneously in a theatre on a London afternoon, and in
the imaginative world of Messina, or the Forest of Arden, or by the
sea coast of Illyria. Audiences, that is, of any degree of sophistication, and with enough experience of theatregoing to appreciate the
give-and-take suppositions without which the entertainment they
have paid for cannot proceed. To be an audience is by that very
token to be capable of transcending literal-mindedness, and to be
ready to eke out the limited technical resources available in the

theatre with a more than willing imagination. In the words with which the Chorus in *Henry V* appeals directly to the audience of that play, they must let their 'imaginary forces work' (line 18) and 'piece out' (line 23) the actors' (and the stage's) imperfections with their 'thoughts'.

Playwrights and actors can likewise assume, and build on, such dual awareness in their audiences. Certainly with Shakespeare – and nowhere more so than in his comedies – consciousness of the play *as* a play, and, along with that consciousness, a keen awareness of the nature of illusion as such, is of primary importance. 'All the world's a stage', Jaques is made to say in *As You Like It* II.vii.139, and the metaphorical interrelationship between life and theatre is a recurrent theme. In addition, the deceived–undeceived condition which is fundamental to an audience's participation in the theatrical experience can be used to explore the wider implications of illusoriness as such, manifested in accidental mistakings, deliberate deceptions, disguises and duplicity. The playwright's make-believe, and the audience's condition of willing, yet nonetheless knowing, acceptance of illusion, shade over into comic devices for creating false impressions, and villainous schemes for smirching with false appearances, which are seen for what they are by the audience, but mislead victims, sometimes to their ultimate advantage, sometimes to near-disaster. In an art form peculiarly dependent on illusion, illusion takes on a multiplicity of forms, some of which will be explored in the following passages.

Analyses

A Midsummer Night's Dream, V.i.209–53 (209–55). The Athenian workmen's play of *Pyramus and Thisby* is being performed before Theseus, Hippolyta and the lovers. This extract begins just before Snug enters as the Lion, accompanied by one of his mates carrying a bush of thorns and a lantern to represent Moonshine.

Hippolyta. This is the silliest stuff that ever I heard.
Theseus.   The best in this kind are but shadows; and   210

the worst are no worse, if imagination amend
them.

Hippolyta. It must by your imagination then, and not theirs.

Theseus. If we imagine no worse of them than they of
themselves, they may pass for excellent men.   215
Here come two noble beasts in, a man and a lion.
Enter LION *and* MOONSHINE.

Lion. *You, ladies, you, whose gentle hearts do fear*
The smallest monstrous mouse that creeps on floor,
May now, perchance, both quake and tremble here,
When lion rough in wildest rage doth roar.   220
Then know that I as Snug the joiner am
A lion fell, nor else no lion's dam;
For, if I should as lion come in strife
Into this place, 'twere pity on my life.

Theseus. A very gentle beast, and of a good conscience.   225

Demetrius. The very best at a beast, my lord, that e'er I saw.

Lysander. This lion is a very fox for his valour.

Theseus. True; and a goose for his discretion.

Demetrius. Not so, my lord; for his valour cannot carry his
discretion, and the fox carries the goose.   230

Theseus. His discretion, I am sure, cannot carry his valour;
for the goose carries not the fox. It is well. Leave it
to his discretion, and let us listen to the Moon.

Moon. *This lanthorn doth the horned moon present –*

Demetrius. He should have worn the horns on his head.   235

Theseus. He is no crescent, and his horns are invisible within
the circumference.

Moon. *This lanthorn doth the horned moon present;*
Myself the Man i' th' Moon do seem to be.

Theseus. This is the greatest error of all the rest; the man   240
should be put into the lantern. How is it else the
man i' th' moon?

Demetrius. He dares not come there for the candle; for, you
see, it is already in snuff.

Hippolyta. I am aweary of this moon. Would he would change! 245

Theseus. It appears, by his small light of discretion, that

	he is in the wane; but yet, in courtesy, in all reason, we must stay the time.	
Lysander.	Proceed, Moon.	
Moon.	All that I have to say is to tell you that the lanthorn is the moon; I, the Man i' th' Moon; this thorn-bush, my thorn-bush; and this dog, my dog.	250
Demetrius.	Why, all these should be in the lantern; for all these are in the moon.	255

If we consider the Athenian workmen first, the amateurishness of their performance and the woodenness of their script is obvious enough. We have seen them earlier in rehearsal (e.g. in III.i), and have laughed at their naive anxiety lest their playing of a 'tragedy' in which Thisby is gored by a lion will frighten the ladies in their audience. It is to avoid this that Snug has been given the explanatory piece he recites in this extract. His preoccupation with what is supposed to be standard, 'feminine' timidity is ludicrously overdone, and – thanks to the anonymous author's linguistic incompetence – succeeds in making a monster of a mouse. Given what the audience has already seen and heard previously in *A Midsummer Night's Dream,* this is even more inappropriate, for we know that Hippolyta is a warrior Amazon and that Hermia and Helena have been brave enough to defy the laws of Athens and commit themselves to the perils of the wilderness outside its walls. And yet Snug's eagerness to reassure them is touching in its way. However misplaced, and however misguided as to the nature of theatrical illusion, it shows some humanity and concern.

Not quite the same can be said of the stage audience. Hippolyta makes it plain that she finds the whole business silly and embarrassing. As she had said when the question of the workmen's entertainment originally came up, 'I love not to see wretchedness o'ercharged, / And duty in his service perishing' (V.i.85–6). Theseus's reply (lines 90–105) is more tolerant: he accepts the essentially illusory nature of theatre, and his reference to the role of imagination echoes what he had said earlier and more extensively when he had argued that an inadequate performance, often due to nervousness, needs to be taken 'in might, not merit' (i.e. for the sake of its good intentions rather than the quality of its execution). A botched speech of welcome, uttered 'in the modesty of fearful duty', had often seemed to him preferable to something delivered 'from the rattling tongue / Of saucy and audacious eloquence'; and he had concluded graciously that

> Love, therefore, and tongue-tied simplicity
> In least speak most to my capacity.

Nevertheless, his comments here on the workmen's production, like those of Demetrius and Lysander, tend to be merely scoffing. The men (Hermia and Helena, perhaps significantly, are excluded) get their amusement from poking fun at the ignorance and inadequacies of the workmen's performance. Some of the jokes – for example, Demetrius's pun on 'best' and 'beast' (226), and the overdone play, shared by all three men, on the traditional notion that lion = valour, fox = cunning, and goose = silliness (227–33) – sound facile to modern ears. How they sounded to Shakespeare's original audiences it is difficult to say. Probably much wittier: this kind of wordplay was more in accord with Elizabethan taste; and, from the social point of view, what sounds patronising to us may then have been taken as legitimate puncturing of ridiculous pretension. As implied by Theseus's comment, 'If we imagine no worse of them than they of themselves' (line 214), the workmen are vulnerable to criticism because they seem to have too high an opinion of themselves. In particular, the more self-consciously intellectual members of the audience, including those gallants who sat on the stage and did not refrain from commenting aloud on the action, might well have seen themselves reflected in the aristocratic stage-audience of the workmen's preposterous efforts. But, in that case, what they would have made of such a self-image – and how they, in turn, would be seen by the rest of the theatre audience – is an interesting subject for speculation. For the result of such a combination of play-within-a-play and audience-within-an-audience is to throw into relief, and subject to scrutiny, the whole question of the relationship between an actual audience and the performance it is watching. A simple, uncritical identification of theatre audience with stage-audience is something which it is in the very nature of drama to undercut. Theseus, Demetrius and Lysander are themselves fictitious beings, and the effect of the play-within-a-play device is to heighten awareness of their fictitiousness. If the absurdity of the Athenian workmen's belief in the power of illusion is uproariously comic, and made the more transparent by their performance, there is also the possibility of a boomerang effect on their critics. The latter become similarly exposed to audience response, and in consequence liable to be judged themselves. If the real audience laughs *with* them at the follies of the workmen-actors, it is also liable to laugh *at* them as well. Their bantering and barracking is the kind of audience response that would be capable of ruining any kind of performance in the theatre, and so, in a sense, their wit backfires.

*   *   *

Much Ado About Nothing, III.iii.108–65 (108–67). Borachio, the henchman of Don John, under the influence of drink, confesses to Conrade how he deceived Claudio and Don Pedro into believing Hero unfaithful, and is overheard by the Watch.

Borachio.	Thou knowest that the fashion of a doublet,	
	or a hat, or a cloak, is nothing to a man.	
Conrade.	Yes, it is apparel.	110
Borachio.	I mean the fashion.	
Conrade.	Yes, the fashion is the fashion.	
Borachio.	Tush! I may as well say the fool's the fool.	
	But seest thou not what a deformed thief this	
	fashion is?	115
2 Watch.	[*Aside*] I know that Deformed; 'a has been a vile	
	thief this seven year; 'a goes up and down like a	
	gentleman; I remember his name.	
Borachio.	Didst thou not hear somebody?	
Conrade.	No; 'twas the vane on the house.	120
Borachio.	Seest thou not, I say, what a deformed thief this	

fashion is, how giddily 'a turns about all the hot
bloods between fourteen and five and thirty,
sometimes fashioning them like Pharoah's soldiers
in the reechy painting, sometimes like god Bel's   125
priests in the old church-window, sometime like
the shaven Hercules in the smirch'd worm-eaten
tapestry, where his codpiece seems as massy as
his club?

Conrade. All this I see; and I see that the fashion wears out   130
more apparel than the man. But art not thou thyself
giddy with the fashion too, that thou hast shifted
out of thy tale into telling me of the fashion?

Borachio. Not so neither; but know that I have to-night
wooed Margaret, the Lady Hero's gentlewoman,   135
by the name of Hero; she leans me out at her mistress'
chamber-window, bids me a thousand times good
night – I tell this tale vilely. I should first tell thee
how the Prince, Claudio, and my master, planted
and placed and possessed by my master Don John,   140
saw afar off in the orchard this amiable encounter.

Conrade. And thought they Margaret was Hero?

Borachio. Two of them did, the Prince and Claudio; but the
devil my master knew she was Margaret; and partly
by his oaths, which first possess'd them, partly by   145
the dark night, which did deceive them, but chiefly
by my villainy, which did confirm any slander that
Don John had made, away went Claudio enrag'd;
swore he would meet her, as he was appointed, next
morning at the temple, and there, before the whole 150
congregation, shame her with what he saw o'er night,
and send her home again without a husband.

2 Watch. We charge you in the Prince's name, stand.

1 Watch. Call up the right Master Constable; we have here
recover'd the most dangerous piece of lechery that   155
ever was known in the commonwealth.

2 Watch. And one Deformed is one of them; I know him,
'a wears a lock.

Conrade.	Masters, masters!
2 Watch.	You'll be made bring Deformed forth, I warrant 160
	you.
Conrade.	Masters –
1 Watch.	Never speak, we charge you; let us obey you to go
	with us.
Borachio.	We are like to prove a goodly commodity, being
	taken up of these men's bills. 165
Conrade.	A commodity in question, I warrant you.
	Come, we'll obey you.

Illusion as presented in this passage has most obviously to do with the central episode in the main plot of *Much Ado About Nothing*, the deceiving of Claudio about Hero's virtue. In lines 134–52 Borachio describes how he persuaded Margaret to speak to him from Hero's window and thus give the impression to Claudio and Don Pedro ('the Prince') that Hero was having an affair with him.

The first thing to note is that this crucial episode is reported, not directly presented on the stage. It could be argued that Shakespeare found this dramatically convenient, so as not to diminish the impact of the climactic scene in the church (IV.i); and it also helps to cover some of the difficulties there would be in presenting the deception directly, supposing, as it does, the inability of Claudio and Don Pedro to recognise the difference between Hero and her maid, and the complete ignorance on Margaret's part that she might be injuring Hero's reputation. But these are negative contributions to illusion – things not done, or avoided; whereas the passage itself makes a useful, active contribution to the theme.

Mistaking, misrepresentation, and misleading appearances are woven into the very texture of the scene. To begin with, Borachio is drunk. Just prior to the passage in question he admits to Conrade that he will 'like a true drunkard, utter all to thee' (line 98). This causes him to tell his tale 'vilely', failing to explain first the circumstances which make his nocturnal encounter so treacherous. Before that he also engages in a verbose digression on 'fashion' that has Conrade so impatient with him that he asks testily: 'But art not thou thyself giddy with the fashion too, that thou hast shifted out of thy tale into telling me of the fashion?' Drunkenness muddies the verbal waters so that Conrade, and to some extent the theatre audience as well, receives a somewhat confused picture. And yet, notwithstanding, the digression also has its indirect relevance, for the distinction between 'fashion', the smart clothes a man wears, and the essence of the man himself – a distinction which Conrade, in keeping with the nature of this scene, fails to grasp – is one that emphasises the difference between appearance and reality. As Borachio elaborates the distinction for the benefit of the slower-witted Conrade he also emphasises how 'giddily' this 'fashion' works, especially on young men ('all the hot bloods between fourteen and five and thirty', lines 122–3) who are emotionally immature and unstable. And, seeming to pile digression on digression, he brings home the significance of what he is saying with examples drawn from stories which are familiar to Elizabethans via their representation in pictures, tapestries and church windows, which are respectively 'reechy' (smoky), 'worm-eaten' and 'old'. Again, each of these has to do with deception: Pharoah's soldiers thought the way was clear for them to pursue the Israelites across the parted Red Sea, but the waves closed in and drowned them; the priests of Bel were killed by Cyrus when the prophet Daniel denounced their god as false; and though the reference to Hercules may seem (deliberately, perhaps, given Borachio's drunken condition?) to confuse the story of his being put to spin among the womenfolk by Omphale, with that of Delilah's shearing off the hair of the sleeping Samson, both again suggest fatal distortion and deception. The satirical flavour of the whole digression (increased by the concluding, bawdy reference to Hercules's codpiece seeming as big as his club) both suits Borachio's character here as a blabbing drunkard and gives further emphasis to the overall impression of men blinded by passion and misled by false images.

In the prelude to his story Borachio speaks mockingly of fashion as 'a deformed thief' (line 114). This brings in yet another level of misapprehension, for the second member of the Watch takes this to be a reference to a notorious thief called 'Deformed' who has been at his criminal activities for seven years. That the Watchman is deceived by names and words is in keeping with a play in which both appearances and words so much deceive, and also with the particular character of this Watch as it is writ large in their 'right Master Constable' Dogberry (see Chapter 6, pp. 119–24). Ignorantly aping the linguistic sophistication of their social superiors, they continually say the opposite of what they mean (e.g at line 155 using 'recover'd' for 'discovered' and 'lechery' for 'treachery', and at line 162 saying 'let us obey you' when they mean 'you must obey us').

With the Watchmen's linguistic incompetence also goes incompetence in the discharging of their office (again anticipating Dogberry), as the Second Watchman continues his irrelevant obsession with the mysterious 'Deformed'. 'Deformed' in the sense of lacking form – or of robbing 'form' of its correct meaning as proper order in correspondingly proper shape – sums up what this comically inadequate order-maintaining Watch is about. But, likewise, Borachio's 'fashion', personified as 'a deformed thief', from which this wrongheaded obsession derives, is equally a distortion of what ought to be sensible, appropriate clothing, and thus ultimately a comment on the distortion of inner value by the outward appearance it adopts. The whole scene of drunkenness, bungling and misapprehension is thus on a par with the central distortion which leads to the deception of Claudio and Don Pedro, and to the false accusations levelled at Hero.

However, it is also worth noting that, as in the previous extract from *A Midsummer Night's Dream*, this passage presents the playing – or, in this case, reporting – of a 'tragedy' before both a stage audience (for the Watch is another variation on this device) and the actual audience in the theatre, which the latter find laughably absurd. In *A Midsummer Night's Dream* the potential sting is taken out of 'The most Lamentable Comedy and most Cruel Death of Pyramus and Thisby' by the ludicrous manner in which it is performed by the Athenian workmen. Here – though the most 'tragic' scene is yet to come (in IV.i) – it is through the combination of Borachio's telling his tale so 'vilely' and the misapprehension of the Watch that tragedy, at least for the actual audience in the theatre, is averted in advance. And both scenes are powerfully assisted in accomplishing this effect by the tricks they play with illusion. The perspectives opened up by the play-within-a-play device enable the theatre audience to enjoy others' vulnerability to illusion, while itself being privileged to see through the visual and verbal distortions to the truth beyond. Things are not always so reassuring, even in the world of Shakespeare's comedies, and in this play there is plenty of anguish and suffering to come; but for the time being the way illusion works is in keeping with the spirit of comedy, which is, in Borachio's own words, to make being apprehended (and misapprehended) by the Watch's 'bills' something which is 'like to prove a goodly commodity'. And it is also appropriate that he ends with such a pair of excruciating puns ('bills' = both the Watchmen's weapons and commercial bonds of credit, and 'commodity' = both something useful and goods in a commercial transaction): in their deluded way the Watch are, in fact, contributing to the doing of a deal which will ultimately convert tragedy into comedy and restore lost credit.

*   *   *

Twelfth Night, IV.iii.1–21. The speaker in the following passage is Sebastian, twin brother of Viola. The latter, in her disguise as 'Cesario', has become the object of Olivia's love; but since Viola in her male attire looks exactly like her brother, confusion arises between them. Sebastian (who does not know that his sister is alive and in Illyria, any more than she knows that he is alive) happens to encounter Olivia and, being mistaken for 'Cesario', finds himself both enriched by her and treated as her lover and husband-to-be. The whole situation is for him utterly bewildering, but also delightful and gratifying.

> This is the air; that is the glorious sun;
> This pearl she gave me, I do feel 't and see 't;
> And though, 'tis wonder that enwraps me thus,
> Yet 'tis not madness. Where's Antonio, then?
> I could not find him at the Elephant;   5
> Yet there he was; and there I found this credit,
> That he did range the town to seek me out.
> His counsel now might do me golden service;

For though my soul disputes well with my sense
That this may be some error, but no madness,   10
Yet doth this accident and flood of fortune
So far exceed all instance, all discourse,
That I am ready to distrust mine eyes
And wrangle with my reason, that persuades me
To any other trust but that I am mad,   15
Or else the lady's mad; yet if 'twere so,
She could not sway her house, command her followers,
Take and give back affairs and their dispatch
With such a smooth, discreet, and stable bearing,
As I perceive she does. There's something in't   20
That is deceivable.

The quality of illusion created in this passage is different again from that in the passages from *A Midsummer Night's Dream* and *Much Ado About Nothing*. It results from the plot-complication and confusion over mistaken identities which accelerate towards the end of *Twelfth Night*. Bewilderment is also increased by the fact that Antonio, who had agreed to meet Sebastian at the Elephant, is not to be found, but apparently has been there, and is now wandering about the town in search of Sebastian – the particular way in which this is expressed in lines 4-7, with its juxtaposition of 'I could not find', 'Yet there he was' and 'there I found', seeming to heighten confusion and contradiction. (See also the analysis of Antonio's reaction given above, Chapter 1, pp. 17–18.)

The theatre audience, of course, hold the key which unlocks this confusion; and it is part of the pleasure their superior vantage gives them that they can simultaneously share Sebastian's bewilderment and view it with godlike detachment. But for Sebastian illusion here acquires an air of mystery and wonder, and it makes him question the very nature of the relation between what is normally thought of as 'reason' and 'madness' respectively. Olivia, so little known to him that he still thinks of her simply as 'the lady', at once bewitches and bewilders him. The world in which she moves, and into which he now finds himself inexplicably precipitated, makes him wonder if insanity has suddenly afflicted one or other of them ('I am mad, /

Or else the lady's mad', lines 15–16); while at the same time he recognises, on his part, that he is rational enough to perceive that 'this may be some error', and, on her part, that she could not rule her household, and accept and discharge business, if she were indeed mad (lines 16-20). As he exclaims in his first words – 'This is the air; that is the glorious sun' (line 1) – the external world seems to be there as a normal, objective reality; and he can feel the pressure of the pearl given to him by Olivia in his hand. The senses, that is to say, reassure him that he is living in the real world. (Though it is an additional measure of delight for the theatre audience to know that this 'reality' is dramatic make-believe.) But that which he thinks he sees and feels, and the things that have apparently happened to him, make him ready to distrust both his senses and his reason. The use of nouns like 'wonder', 'accident' and 'flood', and of verbs like 'exceed' and 'wrangle', although balanced against such words as 'instance' (= precedent) and 'discourse' (= discursive reasoning), and the strong affirmation in line 19 of such words as 'smooth', 'discreet' and 'stable', push hard against the rational assumptions on which everyday sense-perceptions are based. Sebastian finds himself in a new world where ordinary criteria no longer seem to apply – a world that apparently contradicts reason and common sense. And yet, as suggested by those repeated assurances of continuity with reason and order, it does not seem to him that the ordinary world is being threatened by any form of irrationality that is destructive. On the contrary, the whole thing, contradictory and bewildering though it is, seems liberating and life-enhancing. There may be something 'deceivable' in it all, but here 'deceivable' does not carry the derogatory meaning of deception practised to trick and subvert. Rather it suggests a breaking-down of ordinary appearances – or, better still, a transcending of them – to create something new and wonderful. This is the incredible and marvellous material of romance defying the common-sense world of day-to-day experience to hint at a richer world of unexpected potentiality which is more appealing, and more satisfying, to the imagination.

Conclusions

From the three passages analysed above it is evident that illusion is a complex theme, and yet absolutely fundamental to drama, especially comedy. To be a member of an audience watching a play is to accept that the illusions being created on the stage are 'real', but only provisionally so. There has to be make-believe – without it there is not entertainment. Nevertheless, the audience retains its consciousness that what it is seeing is 'only a play'. To overestimate the power of illusion, as the workmen do in *A Midsummer Night's Dream*, is to expose oneself to ridicule; and the extract examined above shows how this in itself becomes comic material for the entertainment of both stage-audience and theatre audience. On the other hand, audiences need to show forbearance; when they do not, as exemplified by the aristocratic, on-stage audience, the dramatic situation boomerangs on them, and they in turn become liable to criticism.

Paradoxically, illusion is both vulnerable and necessary. Though often quite capable of being seen through, it can also have powerful effects. In real life, taking the forms of disguise and deception, it may for long periods of time be virtually impenetrable, and this ascendancy of seeming over being can have drastic consequences. When comedy imitates such situations, as happens in the extract from *Much Ado About Nothing*, it may bring the action to the brink of tragedy. The consequences for Hero of the deception practised on Don John's behalf by Borachio, and unwittingly by Margaret, are all but catastrophic. To enable it to remain within the orbit of comedy two conditions have to be fulfilled: (1) the illusion itself needs to be presented not only at second hand, but also within a context of illusion-begetting circumstances (Borachio's drunkenness, the Watch's professional and linguistic incompetence) which are in themselves comic; and (2) the audience need to be kept in such a position of vantage that they can both sympathise with the predicament of the on-stage characters and yet be able to appreciate, as the latter cannot, the fragility of the illusion. The device of the Watch's eavesdropping admirably fulfils both conditions, with the result that even in the harrowing scene of Hero's denunciation the audience are able to remain assured of the comic outcome.

In the third passage, from *Twelfth Night*, another form of mistaken identity leads to an examination of the very nature of illusion, and, by implication, its special role in romantic comedy. The audience again enjoy a double vantage point, which enables them to enter sympathetically into Sebastian's bewildered state of mind while enjoying knowledge of the circumstances which create it (and likewise make it inherently temporary). In addition, through Sebastian's soliloquy, balancing madness against reason and confusion against order, the audience are led towards a more positive view of illusion, which tacitly explains to them their own willingness to accept dramatic fiction as a kind of truth. The very zest with which Sebastian greets the 'air' and the 'glorious sun', and the delight he clearly takes in the madness, which is not madness, of 'the lady', help to project a sense of illusion as something creative and life-enhancing. It becomes the dramatic enactment of that concession to make-believe which raises the merely imaginary to the level of the imaginative. This is illusion as a constructive, poetic force, the activation of which is essential for the kind of romantic entertainment, with its raptures and marvels as well as its follies and absurdities, that *Twelfth Night* and most of Shakespeare's comedies have to offer.

Methods of Analysis (Chapters 2 and 3)

In Chapters 2 and 3 the same attention to linguistic detail has been required as was necessary in Chapter 1, but also even greater awareness of speaker, speech and context. When characters engage in dialogue they act on, and react to, each other. Try to put yourself inside each character's skin in turn – imagine how things look from Corin's perspective, for example, and what his feelings are in his encounter with Touchstone, and likewise imagine yourself as Touchstone sparring verbally with Corin and looking for verbal holds with which to trip him. This is what actors do when they play these parts, and you as a reader need to be several actors at once.

Take into account dramatic circumstances and the effects that one character may be seeking to make on another. Rosalind, for example, instantly sympathises with Silvius's infatuation, but later attacks him for being too uncritical of Phebe; Corin's reaction is that of the older man who has seen it all before; Touchstone debunks it with the deliberately antithetical story of Jane Smile. Look for the meaning behind such dialectical interplay rather than what is to be found in any one particular character's attitude.

Sensitivity to language should include attention to genre. See, for example, how in *As You Like It* the stylised mode of conventional pastoral contrasts with more realistic modes; how the unsophisticated style of *Pyramus and Thisby* brackets it off from the rest of *A Midsummer Night's Dream*, giving it the aural equivalent of inverted commas; how narrative in *Much Ado About Nothing* can be botched by drunkenness or ignorant (if well-meaning) incompetence. Note, too, how even such details as modes of address can take on dramatic significance, as illustrated by the analysis in Chapter 2 of Touchstone's 'Holla, you clown!'

Look out for contrasting effects: comedy frequently gets its laughter through deliberate verbal let-downs – which, for example, is why in the high-falutin' world of romance to which most of Shakespeare's comedies belong there is also so much vulgarity and downright bawdy. 'High' characters versus 'low' characters are used to similar effect (but watch, too, how the 'low' can often score off their supposedly 'high' betters). Similarly, note the effect of one kind of scene or exchange rapidly following on the heels of another: such transitions are often in themselves uproariously comic.

Remember all the time that what you are reading is drama for performance in a theatre. Ask yourself what is the relationship, evidenced within the plays, between actors and audience – more particularly when what is going on on stage is itself witnessed by an on-stage audience (as in the play-within-the-play in *A Midsummer Night's Dream*). How does Shakespeare balance make-believe with the audience's (necessary and healthy) disbelief in the reality of what it sees? What is the effect of having boy-actors, who are known to be boys, playing the women's parts? What is the effect of having these scenes played out in a theatre open to the sky and lit by natural, not artificial, light? How does the audience's knowledge of events compare with that imputed to the characters on the stage?

Try to think of the play not as 'a slice of life', but as what Hardy calls 'a series of seemings' – i.e. as a sequence of invented scenes, having both visual and aural impact, designed to have certain emotional effects on the audience. In other words, a set of illusions.

Suggested Work

Analyse *A Midsummer Night's Dream*, III.i.91–118 (*'Re-enter PUCK, and BOTTOM with an ass's head* ... What angel wakes me from my flow'ry bed?'). The rehearsal of *Pyramus and Thisby* is going on. Bottom has made an exit, and is now due to come back on again; but in the meantime Puck has put the ass's head on him. There are several different characters in this extract, from different levels of being and in different circumstances. What kinds of illusion are they either creating or suffering from? There are also different levels of language. Note all these.

In *Much Ado About Nothing* analyse III.i.81–116 ('Yet tell her of it ... Believe it better than reportingly.'). This is the latter part of the scene in which Hero and Ursula deceive Beatrice into believing Benedick loves her, by speaking where she can overhear them but without, as she thinks, being detected herself. What specific impressions do Hero and Ursula want Beatrice to receive? Note the ironies, given developments in the rest of the play, involved in Hero's references to 'honest slanders' (line 84), 'empoison liking' (line 86) and 'an excellent good name' (line 98). What is implied by the references to Beatrice's 'judgment' and 'wit' (lines 88–9)? Consider the effect of the bird-catching images at lines 104 ('She's lim'd') and 112 ('Taming my wild heart to thy loving hand'). Most of the extract is in blank verse; what is the effect of the rhyming at lines 105–6 and 115–16?

In *As You Like It* analyse the short scene, III.i (Duke Frederick seizes Oliver's goods until he can produce Orlando), and consider how it stands in the sequence of dramatic performance in relation to the conclusion of the preceding scene, II.vii (Orlando re-enters with Adam to share Duke Senior's feast) and the beginning of the next scene, III.ii (Orlando hangs his verses to Rosalind on the forest trees). What variety is there to be found in the use of verse? What elements of love and hatred, altruism and selfishness, romance and realism are here brought into juxtaposition?

In *Twelfth Night* compare the reactions in II.iii.70–110 ('What a caterwauling ... no more cakes and ale?') (bearing in mind both similarities and dissimilarities) of Maria and Malvolio to the late-night carousing of Sir Toby, Sir Andrew and Feste. Consider the variations in prose style between Maria, Malvolio, Sir Toby and Sir Andrew and the effect of the interjected snatches of song. Relate their respective orderliness and disorderliness in the control of language to the theme of 'time' running through the passage. What are the implications of Sir Toby's being a knight and 'consanguineous' (line 75) with Olivia, Maria being waiting woman to 'my lady' (line 71), and Malvolio no more 'than a steward' (line 108)? What kinds of fooling/madness are going on in this scene? What do you make of Feste's [the Clown's] comment with regard to Sir Toby that 'the knight's in admirable fooling' (line 77)?

4

Romantic Sentiment

Introduction

The plots of almost all Shakespeare's comedies are derived from 'romances', i.e. tales which involve marvellous, often quite unrealistic adventures, and characters who are either incredibly virtuous and beautiful, or ugly and wicked. Their most frequently recurring subject is love, and this, too, tends to be of an extravagantly all-embracing kind: the lover worships his mistress as almost a goddess, and she in turn may be impossibly pure, or unapproachably cold and aloof. If they love each other, they have many obstacles to overcome before their love is consummated in marriage. As Lysander says, 'The course of true love never did run smooth' (see the whole exchange between him and Hermia in *A Midsummer Night's Dream*, I.i.132–49).

Above all, love is an overwhelming emotional experience which each lover thinks is unique to him or her – as Silvius characteristically does in the scene from *As You Like It* previously discussed in Chapter 2. It begets the most intense outpouring of feeling, in language which seems to demand the heightened expression peculiar to poetry. No Elizabethan lover, at any rate, would be complete without what Jaques, in the same play, calls 'a woeful ballad / Made to his mistress' eyebrow' (II.vii.148–9); though in practice it was more likely to be a sonnet – much the most favoured verse form, thanks to the widespread influence of the Italian poet, Petrarch (1304–74), whose sonnets to Laura became the most celebrated models of love poetry in the Renaissance.

Frequently, however, love sentiment verges on sentimentality, and so becomes an apt target for mockery and satire. At the very least, the lover is an ambiguous figure, who may excite pity for his painful emotional condition, but also seems ridiculous by virtue of his solipsistic, inward-looking isolation. Romance, especially in romantic comedy, is invariably accompanied by features that are deflatingly anti-romantic. Thus the lover becomes both a figure of awe and a figure of fun. His raptures may be a source of richly flowering, delicate poetry; but, equally, they may lapse into an absurd recital of merely conventional clichés. In his comedies Shakespeare explores the whole gamut of such sentiment, and makes it – as the first of the following passages for analysis suggests –a musical theme adapted to a variety of keys.

Analyses

Twelfth Night, I.i.1–15. These are the opening words of the play, spoken by Orsino, the infatuated lover of Olivia.

> If music be the food of love, play on,
> Give me excess of it, that, surfeiting,
> The appetite may sicken and so die.
> That strain again! It had a dying fall;
> O, it came o'er my ear like the sweet sound   5
> That breathes upon a bank of violets,
> Stealing and giving odour! Enough, no more;
> 'Tis not so sweet now as it was before.
> O spirit of love, how quick and fresh art thou!
> That, notwithstanding thy capacity   10
> Receiveth as the sea, naught enters there,
> Of what validity and pitch soe'er,
> But falls into abatement and low price
> Even in a minute. So full of shapes is fancy,
> That it alone is high fantastical.   15

This speech is preceded and accompanied by music – perhaps some appropriately dreamy and seductive piece, played by one or more players on the lute. As so often in Shakespeare, and more particularly in the comedies, music is an important setter of moods. The love of music is normally a positive quality, indicative of good nature and true civilisation. Thus in *The Merchant of Venice* (at the beginning of Act V) it is not only a mood-setter, but leads on to an important statement which relates harmony, or 'concord', to civilised behaviour in human beings generally:

> The man that hath no music in himself,
> Nor is not mov'd with concord of sweet sounds,
> Is fit for treasons, stratagems, and spoils;
> The motions of his spirit are dull as night,
> And his affections dark as Erebus.
> Let no such man be trusted. (V.i.83–8)

The Elizabethan age was a great one in English music, and its people great music lovers. To that extent, the opening of *Twelfth Night*, with Orsino listening to what was probably a beautifully played piece, might very well have placed him, initially, in a favourable light.

The association of music with love was also as common in Elizabethan times as it is today. The intensification of feeling which belongs to the experience of falling in love leads naturally enough to a greater need for, and appreciation of, the melody, cadence and phonic variety of which music is composed. As it is also most moving when matched to the sadness of unrequited love, it might be expected to have its chief connection with tragedy. But, as already suggested, music, though present in all kinds of Shakespearean drama, is most in evidence in the comedies. The reason for this is already implicit in the above lines from *The Merchant of Venice*: music (of the Elizabethan period, if not necessarily of the twentieth century) is essentially an orderly arrangement of sounds. It may include discord and jarring disruptions of regular rhythm, and it may be conducive to moods of sadness: but the overall structure is one of order, and the end towards which it moves is invariably harmony and resolution. Comedy is similarly varied in texture and capable of verging on tragedy, but likewise leads, overall, to reconciliation and the restoration of order. Its rapprochement with music is therefore peculiarly appropriate.

Nevertheless, comedy also includes an element of mockery and critical irony unknown to music, and one senses this is coming into play – at Orsino's expense – once he begins his speech. He is certainly responsive to the music. Line 4 ('That strain again! It had a dying fall') suggests that he appreciates both the cadence of the composition and the skill of the performer; and the synaesthetic simile which follows (mingling the sound of the music with the scent of violets) succeeds in creating a verbal equivalence which is at once evocative and a tribute to the sensitivity of his ear. But there is also a languishing air about the lines which, coupled with the slightly disturbing connotations of 'dying' and 'stealing', suggests that he is using the music self-indulgently to feed his emotions. This also accords with the curious expression of lines 2–3, where Orsino calls, not for a sufficiency of the music, but, quite deliberately, for 'excess of it', so that in 'surfeiting' (which carries the derogatory sense of having too much to the detriment of good health) the 'appetite' may not merely be reduced, but be made to 'sicken' and ultimately 'die'. The result is not to enhance the charm of the music, but to give it almost a diseased quality – to counter 'the sweet sound / That breathes upon a bank of violets' (lines 5–6) with something sickly and sentimental.

Even the countermanding of his order for 'That strain again' which comes at lines 7–8 has, in this context, a whimsical, slightly capricious air; and the lines which follow, though again they speak of love in positive terms as something 'quick and fresh' (where 'quick' has the meaning of 'alive', contradicting the associations of 'die' and 'dying'), become an elaborate comment on the debasing and diminishing effect of love. If the metaphor of lines 10–11 is meant to exalt the richness and inclusiveness of love, that is negatively qualified by 'notwithstanding', and what follows turns the sea into an appallingly anarchic force which devalues everything – the doubling-up of both the words connoting worth ('validity and pitch') and those connoting worthlessness ('into abatement and low price') adding powerfully to the undermining effect. (And that this happens 'Even in a minute' delivers, one might say, the final, devastating blow.) Finally, the quizzical last line and a half contrive to devalue both love and imagination: 'fancy' here means primarily 'love' (but 'love' in its wayward, unpredictable, Cupid-like character), and 'fantastical' = 'imaginative'; but 'fancy' is also a word for the imaginative faculty, and 'fantastical' carries the derogatory overtone of something capricious and extravagant. Love thus becomes a form of the imagination operating at its maximum level of protean unreliability – a veritable whirlpool of deceptive 'shapes'.

However, an important qualification needs to be made to this analysis. It is not surprising in view of this opening speech that Orsino should later become the object of Feste's oblique mockery: 'Now the melancholy god protect thee; and the tailor make thy doublet of changeable taffeta, for thy mind is a very opal' (II.iv.72–5). Both 'taffeta', a shiny, silk material used in courtly dress, and 'opal', a jewel that changes colour with changing light, have tell-tale connotations of showiness and instability which more than hint at the lack of firmness and good sense in Orsino's attitude to love. What Feste says reinforces the impression implicit in this speech that the Duke is the sentimental victim of overwrought 'fancy'. But the actor playing the part of Orsino has to be wary of presenting him too much in Feste's terms. The elements of excess and affectation, which are there in the speech, and underlined by Feste, constitute a significant part of his character, but they must not be allowed to blot out other aspects which are also there in the initial impression, especially the music-loving sensitivity which marks him out as a cultivated man of the Renaissance. The language itself is beautifully cadenced, and conveys a sense of 'quickness' and 'freshness' even as it undercuts those qualities with its own image of the negative, devaluing sea. To treat the speech simply as satire, on a level, say, with the speeches Ben Jonson gives to his characters in plays like *Volpone* and *The Alchemist*, is to risk oversimplifying it and reducing its evocatively romantic mood to merely self-indulgent twaddle. (And, in the process, to make subsequent developments such as Viola's falling in love with Orsino, and devoted service to him, very difficult to sustain.) The speaker is still the romantic Duke of Illyria who is capable of finding

genuinely nourishing 'food' for love in the charming music that
opens the scene: what the critical undertone does is to identify and
analyse a dangerous 'excess' in his attitude which has the potential to
deny love's 'validity and pitch' (the latter word continuing to remind
us of a musical element necessary to keep the music itself in tune).

*   *   *

Twelfth Night, II.iv.78–123. Orsino sends Viola/Cesario on a second
embassy of love to Olivia.

Orsino.	Once more, Cesario,	
	Get thee to yond same sovereign cruelty.	
	Tell her my love, more noble than the world,	80
	Prizes not quantity of dirty lands;	
	The parts that fortune hath bestow'd upon her,	
	Tell her I hold as giddily as Fortune;	
	But 'tis that miracle and queen of gems	
	That Nature pranks her in attracts my soul.	85
Viola.	But if she cannot love you, sir?	
Orsino.	I cannot so be answer'd.	
Viola.	Sooth, but you must.	
	Say that some lady, as perhaps there is,	
	Hath for your love as great a pang of heart	
	As you have for Olivia. You cannot love her;	90
	You tell her so. Must she not then be answer'd?	
Orsino.	There is no woman's sides	
	Can bide the beating of so strong a passion	
	As love doth give my heart; no woman's heart	
	So big to hold so much; they lack retention.	95
	Alas, their love may be call'd appetite –	
	No motion of the liver, but the palate –	
	That suffer surfeit, cloyment, and revolt;	
	But mine is all as hungry as the sea,	
	And can digest as much. Make no compare	100
	Between that love a woman can bear me	
	And that I owe Olivia.	

Viola.	Ay, but I know –
Orsino.	What dost thou know?
Viola.	Too well what love women to men may owe.

In faith, they are as true of heart as we.   105
My father had a daughter lov'd a man,
As it might be perhaps, were I a woman,
I should your lordship.

Orsino.	And what's her history?
Viola.	A blank, my lord. She never told her love,

But let concealment, like a worm i' th' bud,   110
Feed on her damask cheek. She pin'd in thought;
And with a green and yellow melancholy
She sat like Patience on a monument,
Smiling at grief. Was not this love indeed?
We men may say more, swear more, but indeed   115
Our shows are more than will; for still we prove
Much in our vows, but little in our love.

Orsino.	But died thy sister of her love, my boy?
Viola.	I am all the daughters of my father's house,

And all the brothers too – and yet I know not.   120
Sir, shall I to this lady?

Orsino.	Ay, that's the theme.

To her in haste. Give her this jewel; say
My love can give no place, bide no denay.

This passage is an interesting complement to the previous one. It follows immediately after the comment by Feste quoted above, and with the Fool's irony still ringing in their ears, the audience might well find Orsino's language describing Olivia as 'yond same sovereign cruelty' too much that of a well-worn literary pose. And, given such a context, they might also be inclined to laugh at the grandly elevated tone of his assertion that his love, eschewing all worldly considerations, 'Prizes not quantity of dirty lands' (line 81). As they would know well enough, at the level of the governing classes (and Orsino, after all, is Duke and ruler of Illyria), alliances are rarely made without reference to political and material ends. On the other hand, his very position makes that sweeping disclaimer all the more touchingly romantic. It also has a dimension that makes him sound both generous and passionately wholehearted.

However, that is not the point Viola chooses to take up. She prefers to remind him that love involves two people, that there are Olivia's as well as his own feelings to consider. Orsino's attitude is entirely subjective; he lives within his own private universe of emotion, whereas love is essentially a matter of give and take. The egotism in his attitude is particularly apparent in line 87, where he will not take 'no' for an answer. To his one-sided declaration, 'I cannot so be answered', Viola makes the more objective reply, 'Sooth, but you must.' But Viola herself is not exactly disinterested. The audience is aware how she feels towards Orsino, and what anguish she feels at being used as a messenger of love to a woman whose place she would be only too happy to take. Accordingly, the supposedly hypothetical situation she invents to persuade Orsino that the feelings of the beloved must also come into love's reckoning is less hypothesis and invention than a fictionalised version of her own predicament. In suggesting that some lady might feel as much for him as he professes to feel for Olivia she is, in effect, drawing on her own experience – and almost herself making an admission of love. Furthermore, in supposing that Orsino could not return such love, in which case the 'lady' would have to take 'no' for *her* answer, Viola reveals the potentially tragic situation in which she finds herself, not only because of her disguise, but also because of the gender protocol which condemns the woman to a passive rather than proactive role in love. (Though there is some irony in this, too, given the more active role women enjoy in Shakespearean comedy. See Chapter 8 below.)

It is an aspect of this issue of gender which comes to the fore as Orsino goes on to argue that women are incapable of sustaining the intensity of passion that afflicts him. He makes the extreme assertion that the love of women

> may be called appetite –
> No motion of the liver, but the palate –
> That suffer surfeit, cloyment, and revolt;
> But mine is all as hungry as the sea,
> And can digest as much. (lines 96–100)

Since the liver is the seat of the passions (or was so regarded), Orsino is claiming that women are constitutionally incapable of such depth of feeling as his. If this sounds like mere prejudice, it was perhaps commonplace enough in Elizabethan times; and it might have some excuse here because of the distraught condition to which unrequited love has driven Orsino. But the argument remains an extravagant one, and its extravagance is given further emphasis by the repetition of those images of 'surfeit' and the all-consuming nature of the sea which had figured ironically in his opening speech on music as the 'food of love'.

There is dramatic irony, too; for Orsino's argument for the greater emotional capacity, and therefore suffering, of the male sex is placed, for the theatre audience, in poignant juxtaposition to the stoic endurance which Viola is demonstrating even as she stands and listens to him. The contrast between what he professes and what she silently suffers is then developed far more feelingly and persuasively in the altogether different substance and quality of lines 104–17. Viola's reply is in a form that counterbalances wild, unsubstantiated generalisaton with a more quietly rehearsed story of inward, unspoken grief. Its keynote is 'concealment', tellingly, yet in subdued fashion, crystallised in the mingled metaphor and personification of the canker feeding on the 'cheek' of the damask rose (lines 110–11). This, too, produces 'melancholy', but not of the self-indulgent kind typical of the woebegone male love to whose hackneyed image Orsino himself conforms. It is a much more physiologically convincing 'green and yellow melancholy', the outward sign that the flow of feeling, dammed up, is converting to an internally consuming sickness. And the climax is in another striking personification, that of 'Patience on a monument, / Smiling at grief'. This 'Patience' is not resignation, but suffering (the word derives from the Latin *patio* = 'I suffer'). The outward appearance of happiness ('smiling') belies the pain within – as is the case with Viola/Cesario, who, unlike Orsino, does not make a sentimental display of her suffering. Her condition is comparable with that of the rose in Blake's poem 'The Sick Rose' (which may itself be an echo of this passage from *Twelfth Night*): her frustrated love is 'The invisible worm [serpent or canker] / That flies in the night' (lines 2–3) – the 'dark secret love' that gnaws away at her life.

If there is an element of self-pity in this speech – to balance against the blatant self-pity in Orsino's sense of undeserved slight by 'yond same sovereign cruelty' – it has dramatic endorsement (as Orsino's does not) from what the audience perceive to be the speaker's peculiarly painful situation. Instead of being a merely extravagant assertion, it is the analogue to an actual dilemma being enacted before their eyes. And one consequence of this is that the comparison which Viola goes on to make (in lines 115–17) between men's and women's capacities for love seems to carry much more weight than Orsino's. The impression created is that men do indeed 'say more, swear more' (in a well-worn romantic convention of wordy vows of devotion), but that their actions, unlike those of women, speak less, not more, than their words. Thus the monumental, but quiet stoicism of Viola's 'Patience' more than outweighs the allegedly hungry, all-consuming power of Orsino's sea.

It is also worth noting that, if Viola's anecdote moves the theatre audience, and gives them indirect insight into her necessarily suppressed passion, something akin to that (though fully conscious understanding has not dawned yet) is the effect on Orsino, too. At the end of her tale he is sufficiently intrigued, and moved, to ask, in notably less affected language than before, 'But died thy sister of her love, my boy?' (line 118). And her enigmatic answer (at lines 119–20) leaves him so museful that it is Viola who has to bring his attention back to the matter in hand – the wooing of Olivia. That he needs this reminder suggests the extent to which he has been jolted out of his more sentimental stance; and, paradoxically, it wins him more sympathy from the audience. More genuine emotion is aroused, which does something to neutralise the affected quality of his earlier exclamation. Orsino is now seen to be paying serious attention to someone else's plight; to be moving at least a step or two out of his preoccupation with himself, and consequently gaining in status as a figure of more roundedness and depth than his self-indulgent sentiments too readily make him seem.

Finally, the scene ends with the rhymed couplet (lines 122–3) which, in the Elizabethan theatre, often serves to separate one piece of action from another. Two points may be made about this. The first concerns its nature as a 'scene' ending. Strictly speaking, what we have here is neither a 'scene' nor an ending. In the Elizabethan theatre scenery was virtually non-existent. There was none of that curtain-closing and turning on the lights in the auditorium which, in the modern theatre, tell us a scene has come to its end. (Unless the director has deliberately chosen to ignore this business, and go back to the greater fluidity of the Elizabethan theatre.) One 'scene' rapidly succeeded another. In early productions of *Twelfth Night* it is likely that the '*Exeunt*' indicated in modern editions after line 123 may simply have consisted of Orsino and Viola departing through one exit while Sir Toby, Sir Andrew and Fabian, the characters of scene V, come on at another. This makes for a much more rapid change of mood and tempo. Hardly have Orsino's passionately impatient words died on the air than the audience find themselves listening to fictional beings of a very different kind expressing their relish at the prospect of baiting Malvolio with the spurious love letter from Olivia, and Fabian, in particular, using words ('if I lose a scruple of this sport let me be boil'd to death with melancholy', II.v.2–4) which turn both Orsino's melancholy self-pity and Viola's 'green and yellow melancholy' inside out. Such rapidity of 'scene'-change demands a high degree of flexibility in emotional response. It breaks down any tendency to compartmentalisation of the feelings. Resilience is the keynote. Members of the audience have to adjust to moods and tempi of diametrically opposed kinds, and in so doing are kept very much on their psychological toes.

The second point is related more specifically to the assertion Orsino makes in his parting line: 'My love can give no place, bide no denay.' As far as he is concerned, this is a straightforward reiteration of his own egotistical position – or what is still at least his conscious position. However, the progress of the exchange between him and Viola has given that position a new twist which, though it has not yet altered his mind, has revealed to the audience subtler and more intriguing lines of force between master and supposed page. In spite of himself Orsino has been drawn away from his static and unexamined role as melancholy male romantic, and towards something which is both less fixed and potentially capable of more interesting development. His emphatic 'give no place, bide no denay' contrasts tellingly with Viola's situation. Because of her complicating 'Cesario' role her love is forced to give place and suffer denial. Unlike Orsino, she cannot come out with it openly and passionately, much as she would like to. The most she can do is to invent the frustrating love story of her ambiguous 'sister', which is analogically also one of having to give place and bide denay. On the other hand, the interest which this story arouses in Orsino, as we have seen, is stirring an undercurrent of feeling which is beginning to modify his emotional life quite significantly, and, ironically, to give his seemingly sweeping impatience a subtle check. As an exit line, 'My love can give no place, bide no denay' is thus doubly effective: it marks Orsino's return to the pursuit of Olivia's love, but also sums up the tension which the scene has so dramatically developed.

Taken together, these two points illustrate the remarkable flexibility of Shakespeare's comic skills. Theatrical practice and verbal dexterity cooperate to modify sentiment and liberate it from the static condition in which uncritical convention would seem to fix it. And yet this is done without merely pouring on the mockery to which egotistical sentiment exposes itself. If the audience laugh, for example, with Feste *at* Orsino and enter willingly into the process by which Viola breaks down his simplistic masculine assumptions, they also sympathise *with* him. It is the quality of his romanticism which is questioned rather than his status as romantic hero.

*   *   *

A Midsummer Night's Dream, I.i.226–51. Helena laments that the man she loves, Demetrius, spurns her, and dotes instead on Hermia.

> How happy some o'er other some can be!
> Through Athens I am thought as fair as she.
> But what of that? Demetrius thinks not so;
> He will not know what all but he do know.
> And as he errs, doting on Hermia's eyes,   230
> So I, admiring of his qualities.
> Things base and vile, holding no quantity,
> Love can transpose to form and dignity.
> Love looks not with the eyes, but with the mind;

And therefore is wing'd Cupid painted blind.   235
Nor hath Love's mind of any judgment taste;
Wings and no eyes figure unheedy haste;
And therefore is Love said to be a child,
Because in choice he is so oft beguil'd.
As waggish boys in game themselves forswear,   240
So the boy Love is perjur'd everywhere;
For ere Demetrius look'd on Hermia's eyne,
He hail'd down oaths that he was only mine;
And when this hail some heat from Hermia felt,
So he dissolv'd, and show'rs of oaths did melt.   245
I will go tell him of fair Hermia's flight;
Then to the wood will he to-morrow night
Pursue her; and for this intelligence
If I have thanks, it is a dear expense.
But herein mean I to enrich my pain,   250
To have his sight thither and back again.

This soliloquy of Helena's concludes the scene in which Lysander remarks that 'The course of true love never did run smooth' (line 134). Lysander's own difficulties, and those of Hermia, the woman whom at this point in the play he still loves, derive from the opposition of Hermia's father, Egeus, to their marriage. The lack of smoothness in the progress of Helena's love life derives, as this speech reveals, from the fickleness of the man she admires, Demetrius – now (with Egeus's approval) a suitor to Hermia, though previously Helena's sworn lover. Such obstacles to, and mismatching of, love are standard features of romance, as, again, Lysander's remark suggests, for the unsmooth running of love's course is something which belongs to 'tale or history' (I.i.133). The wrenching of emotion and the plucking of the heartstrings which this involves is a time-honoured part of the appeal of all romantic love stories.

However, Helena's speech does more than reinforce the romantic convention of crossing in love. It subjects love itself to a trenchant examination in brittle, rhymed couplets which wittily expose its essential irrationality. The rhymes underline the perverse contradictoriness of love: that which of itself has 'no quantity' acquires under its influence spurious 'dignity'; the unpredictable subjectivity of 'mind' (here, perhaps with unconscious irony, contrasted with the supposedly more objective evidence of 'eyes') chimes with the representation of Cupid as 'blind'; what should be rational 'taste' clashes with 'unheedy haste' (lines 232–7). The central image on which she dwells is that of the winged Cupid, son of Venus, the goddess of love, and traditionally represented as an archer who shoots the arrows of desire into his victim, but whose eyes are blindfold to signify his complete disregard for the compatibility and reciprocity of those he wounds. Romantic though his business may be, his actions are those of an irresponsible, emotionally unstable and immature 'child'; and his power is used, not to enhance whatever is essentially valuable and admirable, but to put a dubious gloss of attractiveness on persons and things which may be utterly worthless. Indeed, so downright is Helena's denunciation, she asserts categorically that love transforms 'Things base and vile' so that they appear to have 'form and dignity', and utterly misleads lovers as to the true nature of what they extravagantly worship. Likewise, the vows lovers make are equally insubstantial and liable to misdirection. To 'the boy Love' (line 241) perjury is a mere game; and, descending from the general to the particular, Helena cites as examples of this the 'show'rs of oaths' vowed by Demetrius to herself, which melted like hailstones in the hot sun when Hermia took his fancy. The universal characteristics of love thus become irrationality, inconstancy and irresponsibility.

To see all this, however, is not to be above it. For all her sharpness in analysing the folly of love Helena reveals herself to be just as much its victim as those she has hitherto been criticising. (It could, indeed, be argued that her speech is the one-sided tirade of a frustrated woman.) At the end of this passage all consideration for Hermia and Lysander – who had previously confided their plans to her (lines 208–25) – is thrown to the winds as she resolves to betray them to Demetrius. She knows that this is not likely to do her a great deal of good: if her 'intelligence' [news] merely gains her a 'thank you', she will be grateful; and in her final couplet (lines 250–1) she admits that this is little more than an excuse to have further sight of him, which will hurt as much as please her. As she says, ambivalently, it will 'enrich' her 'pain'; and the self-contradiction inherent in that phrase neatly encapsulates the paradox of romantic love. Such love compels lovers to do things which the shrewder ones among them know to be treacherous and fruitless, but it lures them on, nevertheless, with the promise of a delicious satisfaction to be derived from the mere presence of the beloved. Sense and sentiment are competely at odds; insight and action ludicrously compromised.

Conclusions

The last of these passages is the most acerbic in its treatment of the folly of love; the first and second, though critical enough, seem more tolerant of its sentimental extravagances. Yet, strange though it may seem, the latter are from a play written at the point in his career when Shakespeare was making a transition from comedy to tragedy, and the Helena passage when he was just beginning to immerse himself fully in his particular kind of comedy. One conclusion which might be drawn, therefore, is that he did not move through the typical arc from innocence to experience – from delighted acceptance of romantic illusion to dark and bitter disillusionment. From the first, the texture of his comedy is woven both of romantic sentiment and an acute sense of the silliness, and even the dangerously self-deluding treachery, fostered by romantic love. He could never have written, as the Beatles did in the supposedly more knowing twentieth century, 'All you need is love'. The professions of faith, and the failures to live up to those professions, engendered by romantic love, the swearings of devotion and the inevitably subsequent forswearings which it entails, and the way it embroils and exposes to ridicule even those who think they can see it for what it is – all this double-visioned awareness of love and romance seems to have been present to his imagination from the start.

What developed, however, was a more subtle understanding of the simultaneously vitalising and devitalising capacity of love; greater sympathy for the deep, emotional resonance which romantic sentiment could give it, accompanied by a still more penetrating diagnosis of the various states of psychological sickness, Viola's as well as Orsino's, which it could induce. The two passages from *Twelfth Night* reflect this mature awareness of the ambivalent nature of romance. They involve a delicate counterpoint between sympathy and criticism, one which enables audiences of his special music of love to hear both harmonies and discords blended in the same uniquely compelling composition.

5

Wooing

Introduction

Romantic sentiment is bound up with wooing. It is about the elaboration of feelings which lead members of the opposite sex to idealise, and often, indeed, to fantasise each other. This in turn leads on to the approaches which they make to each other to translate feeling into reciprocity of emotion, and ultimately – in the Elizabethan world, and the world of Shakespeare's comedies – to marriage. The late-twentieth-century notion of a non-marital 'relationship', which may, or may not, lead to a couple's living together on a permanent basis which is not sanctified by marriage, is, of course, completely alien to either of these worlds. Wooing is the preliminary to marriage; and marriage is more than a private matter between two individuals: it is the consummation of love between a woman and a man, sealed by a contract which has overwhelmingly important spiritual and social implications. Families are involved, the state is involved, and, above all, God and the Church are involved.

That Shakespeare's comedies have wooing at the centre of their plots is so obvious as scarcely to require statement; and it is almost equally obvious that the dialogue is preoccupied for much of the time with that sounding-out of each other, and testing of emotional responses, which constitute the well-understood ritual of courtship. Wooing scenes are often critical tests of the maturity and humanity of the characters who participate in them. It is, however, perhaps less obvious that wooing scenes are also the points where private and personal values intersect with public ones. The status of the sexes is involved, and the assumptions which society makes about the proper roles of men and women both before and after marriage. These may not be explicitly in the foreground – though it is interesting to note how often Shakespeare's comedy of courtship does, in fact, touch on questions outside the immediate concern of one character's feelings towards another. But there is always tacit recognition of the wider context in which love between individuals is necessarily placed. Shakespearean comedy does not allow its characters to indulge, or at least, not for long, in the illusion that all that matters is what they feel for each other.

Analyses

A Midsummer Night's Dream, I.i.22–82. Egeus complains to Duke Theseus that his daughter, Hermia, refuses to marry Demetrius, the man he has chosen for her, and gives her love instead to Lysander.

Egeus.	Full of vexation come I, with complaint	
	Against my child, my daughter Hermia.	
	Stand forth, Demetrius. My noble lord,	
	This man hath my consent to marry her.	25
	Stand forth, Lysander. And, my gracious Duke,	
	This man hath bewitch'd the bosom of my child.	
	Thou, thou, Lysander, thou hast given her rhymes,	
	And interchang'd love-tokens with my child;	
	Thou hast by moonlight at her window sung,	30
	With feigning voice, verses of feigning love,	
	And stol'n the impression of her fantasy	
	With bracelets of thy hair, rings, gawds, conceits,	
	Knacks, trifles, nosegays, sweetmeats – messengers	
	Of strong prevailment in unhardened youth;	35
	With cunning hast thou filch'd my daughter's heart;	
	Turn'd her obedience, which is due to me,	
	To stubborn harshness. And, my gracious Duke,	
	Be it so she will not here before your Grace	

	Consent to marry with Demetrius,	40
	I beg the ancient privilege of Athens:	
	As she is mine I may dispose of her;	
	Which shall be either to this gentleman	
	Or to her death, according to our law	
	Immediately provided in that case.	45

Theseus.   What say you, Hermia? Be advis'd, fair maid,
To you your father should be as a god;
One that compos'd your beauties; yea, and one
To whom you are but as a form in wax,
By him imprinted, and within his power   50
To leave the figure, or disfigure it.
Demetrius is a worthy gentleman.

Hermia.   So is Lysander.

Theseus.   In himself he is;
But, in this kind, wanting your father's voice,
The other must be held the worthier.   55

Hermia.   I would my father look'd but with my eyes.

Theseus.   Rather your eyes must with his judgment look.

Hermia.   I do entreat your Grace to pardon me.
I know not by what power I am made bold,
Nor how it may concern my modesty   60
In such a presence here to plead my thoughts;
But I beseech your Grace that I may know
The worst that may befall me in this case,
If I refuse to wed Demetrius.

Theseus.   Either to die the death, or to abjure   65
For ever the society of men.
Therefore, fair Hermia, question your desires,
Know of your youth, examine well your blood,
Whether, if you yield not to your father's choice,
You can endure the livery of a nun,   70
For aye to be in shady cloister mew'd,
To live a barren sister all your life,
Chanting faint hymns to the cold fruitless moon.
Thrice-blessed they that master so their blood
To undergo such maiden pilgrimage;   75

> But earthlier happy is the rose distill'd
> Than that which withering on the virgin thorn
> Grows, lives, and dies, in single blessedness.

Hermia.   So will I grow, so live, so die, my lord,
> Ere I will yield my virgin patent up   80
> Unto his lordship, whose unwished yoke
> My soul consents not to give sovereignty.

To begin with the wooing as such: lines 27–36 detail many of the commonplace devices – profoundly traditional, and still to be recognised as having their equivalents today – by which a young man strives to win the heart of a young woman. If serenading is not such a strong feature of the northern tradition, it is certainly well established in the Mediterranean; and in this play, set, at least nominally, in Athens, the singing by moonlight has an additional potency, given the opening lines of this same scene which dwell so romantically on the waxing and waning of the moon, and the recurrence throughout of repeated references to moon and moonlight (including even the actual appearance of Moonshine as a character in the workmen's production of *Pyramus and Thisby*). As the subsequent lines show, these, and the 'trifles' listed by Egeus, have clearly been acceptable to their object, Hermia, who has taken them, not as bribes, but as tokens of Lysander's passionate feeling for her. She returns Lysander's affection, of her own free will; and, more than that, it becomes apparent that she loves him so much she cannot bear the thought of being compelled to marry any other man. So wholehearted is her devotion that she is willing to risk everything for him. Lysander, then, has already wooed and won her in the hallowed fashion of romantic stories of love, and there is complete reciprocity between them.

But this is only one element in the passage; and not the one most intensely brought to the audience's attention. The very account of the wooing is the one given by the outraged father, and it is coloured with his very different view of the procedure. To him it is the result of wicked witchcraft practised by Lysander; the love-gifts are trashy and fraudulent 'gawds, conceits, / Knacks, trifles'; and the serenading is sung with a voice merely 'feigning' devotion, and in verse that is also hypocritically 'feigning'. The biased nature of his version is plain enough – the more so, as Lysander's behaviour and its effect (as indicated above) are commonplace enough. If they are magical, the magic is no more than that of youthful sexuality, heightened by the time-honoured aura of romance. But to Egeus this is witchcraft because it makes Hermia disobedient to his will, and contradicts the marriage choice he has made for her. To him his anger is righteous indignation. As a father he believes himself to have complete owner-ship of his daughter, with the right to dispose both of her body and her feelings; and, in what seems to be the distinctly patriarchal society of Athens, he can appeal to 'ancient privilege' for his determi-nation to have her either married to his choice, Demetrius, or put to death. Wooing, on this basis, is a usurpation of his paternal authority. It is not a private matter between consenting young people, but a criminal encroachment on the absolute power of a father as enshrined in the legal system of the state.

This is where Theseus comes in. The audience has already been introduced to him as a wooer – if a somewhat ambiguous one. The lover of Hippolyta, longing for the coming of their 'nuptial hour' (the very first line of the play), he is also her conqueror, in the literal as well as metaphorical sense: he wooed with his sword, and won her love doing her injuries (lines 16–17). Here he is the Duke, ruler of Athens, and upholder of its laws and customs. As such, he is bound to support Egeus's position, no matter how harsh he might consider it to be. (Though it is worth noting that at line 127 he exits with Egeus and Demetrius as if to confer with them privately, and perhaps with the intention of seeking to mitigate their point of view.) Nevertheless, Theseus's interpretation of the law differs slightly from Egeus's: where Egeus evokes a stark contrast between obedience and death, Theseus introduces another alternative to mar-rying Demetrius, that of the virginal life of a nun. And this is a sig-nificant difference, for, severe as it may still seem to be, it leaves open the possibility of future change – a point vital for comedy. The laws are upheld, but the married life and the virgin life are now seen as each in themselves worthy alternatives. Admittedly, the emphasis in lines 70–5 is on the sterility of the nun's existence ('*barren* sister', '*faint* hymns', '*cold fruitless* moon'), and this, again, suits the needs of comedy, which moves ultimately towards fruition and fulfilment; but it is nonetheless seen as a sanctified condition – 'Thrice-blessed' and a 'maiden pilgrimage'. Marriage is 'earthlier happy', and imaged by the rose which has been distilled into perfume; the virginal life is imaged by the rose withering unplucked on the 'thorn' (with all the derogatory implications that this has), but is, notwithstanding, a condition of 'single blessedness'. Religious issues are here involved, in no matter how subdued a form; and, by introducing these, Theseus mitigates the crudeness of Egeus's stark alternatives. The values of the state (markedly patriarchal as they are, and necessarily upheld by the supreme head of the state, Duke Theseus) are thus softened somewhat by transcendent, religious values, and a more complex sense of the extra-personal issues involved in Hermia's choice is created.

Hermia, however, remains unmoved. With the uncompromising dedication of a truly romantic heroine she reaffirms the supremacy for her of personal choice. She will opt for the life of the rose on the 'virgin thorn' rather than marry where she does not love. And yet, even here, there are hints in the language she uses of issues outside the simplistically romantic ones. For example, in expressing her resistance in terms of a refusal to yield up her 'virgin patent' she employs a metaphor which has legal implications. A patent is an entitlement granting possession of certain rights to an owner, which that owner would not normally surrender without some compensating advantage, often monetary. The suggestion here (albeit only in the background, perhaps) is that Hermia sees herself as a party to a contract, with rights of her own; she is not merely a chattel to be disposed of by her father. And this carries implications for the nature of marriage itself as some kind of legal contract between parties, each of whom has ownership rights. In Hermia's case, the most valuable thing she owns is her virginity, and she will not surrender this without seeing clear advantage to herself. 'Sovereignty' is also involved; and here the implications are to do with the powers of a monarch over the country she/he rules. Marriage will involve surrender of Hermia's sovereignty over herself to another, who will become as a lord, or monarch, to her, but she sees this as something within her right to give or withhold, on the condition of her liking for the person to whom she will surender it. If this is another way of emphasising the importance to her of personal choice, it is also expressed in terms that evoke analogies in the legal and political spheres of life, thus widening the implications of such choice. How Hermia responds to a wooer thus raises issues beyond those of the merely personal; and, especially when taken together with the assumptions made by Egeus and Theseus in the foregoing speeches, her response can be seen as reinforcing the burden of the whole extract – namely, that, important as personal choice is, it functions not in a cut-off world of the romantic imagination, but in a context that has much wider implications.

*   *   *

As You Like It, IV.i.63–178 (63–184). Rosalind, disguised as a boy with the adopted name of Ganymede, invites Orlando, whom she has met in the Forest of Arden, to woo her as if she were indeed his beloved Rosalind.

Rosalind.	What would you say to me now, an I were your very very Rosalind?	
Orlando.	I would kiss before I spoke.	65
Rosalind.	Nay, you were better speak first; and when you were gravell'd for lack of matter, you might take occasion to kiss. Very good orators, when they are out, they will spit; and for lovers lacking – God warn us! – matter, the cleanliest shift is to kiss.	70
Orlando.	How if the kiss be denied?	
Rosalind.	Then she puts you to entreaty, and there begins new matter.	
Orlando.	Who could be out, being before his beloved mistress?	75
Rosalind.	Marry, that should you, if I were your mistress; or I should think my honesty ranker than my wit.	
Orlando.	What, of my suit?	
Rosalind.	Not out of your apparel, and yet out of your suit. Am not I your Rosalind?	80

Orlando.	I take some joy to say you are, because I would be talking of her.
Rosalind.	Well, in her person, I say I will not have you.
Orlando.	Then, in mine own person, I die.
Rosalind.	No, faith, die by attorney. The poor world is almost 85 six thousand years old, and in all this time there was not any man died in his own person, videlicet, in a love-cause. Troilus had his brains dash'd out with a Grecian club; yet he did what he could to die before, and he is one of the patterns of love. Leander, he 90 would have liv'd many a fair year, though Hero had turn'd nun, if it had not been for a hot midsummer-night; for, good youth, he went but forth to wash him in the Hellespont, and, being taken with the cramp, was drown'd; and the foolish chroniclers of 95 that age found it was – Hero of Sestos. But these are all lies: men have died from time to time, and worms have eaten them, but not for love.
Orlando.	I would not have my right Rosalind of this mind; for, I protest, her frown might kill me. 100
Rosalind.	By this hand, it will not kill a fly. But come, now I will be your Rosalind in a more coming-on disposition; and ask me what you will, I will grant it.
Orlando.	Then love me, Rosalind.
Rosalind.	Yes, faith, will I, Fridays and Saturdays, and all. 105
Orlando.	And wilt thou have me?
Rosalind.	Ay, and twenty such.
Orlando.	What sayest thou?
Rosalind.	Are you not good?
Orlando.	I hope so. 110
Rosalind.	Why then, can one desire too much of a good thing? Come, sister, you shall be the priest, and marry us. Give me your hand, Orlando. What do you say, sister?
Orlando.	Pray thee, marry us. 115
Celia.	I cannot say the words.
Rosalind.	You must begin 'Will you, Orlando' –

Celia. Go to. Will you, Orlando, have to wife this Rosalind?

Orlando. I will.

Rosalind. Ay, but when?

Orlando. Why, now; as fast as she can marry us.

Rosalind. Then you must say 'I take thee, Rosalind, for wife'.

Orlando. I take thee, Rosalind, for wife.

Rosalind. I might ask you for your commission ; but – I do take thee, Orlando, for my husband. There's a girl goes before the priest; and, certainly, a woman's thought runs before her actions.

Orlando. So do all thoughts; they are wing'd.

Rosalind. Now tell me how long you would have her, after you have possess'd her.

Orlando. For ever and a day.

Rosalind. Say 'a day' without the 'ever'. No, no, Orlando; men are April when they woo, December when they wed: maids are May when they are maids, but the sky changes when they are wives. I will be more jealous of thee than a Barbary cock-pigeon over his hen, more clamorous than a parrot against rain, more newfangled than an ape, more giddy in my desires than a monkey. I will weep for nothing, like Diana in the fountain, and I will do that when you are dispos'd to be merry; I will laugh like a hyen, and that when thou art inclin'd to sleep.

Orlando. But will my Rosalind do so?

Rosalind. By my life, she will do as I do.

Orlando. O, but she is wise.

Rosalind. Or else she could not have the wit to do this. The wiser, the waywarder. Make the doors upon a woman's wit, and it will out at the casement; shut that, and 'twill out at the key-hole; stop that, 'twill fly with the smoke out at the chimney.

Orlando. A man that had a wife with such a wit, he might say 'Wit, whither wilt?'

Rosalind. Nay, you might keep that check for it, till you met your wife's wit going to your neighbour's bed.

Orlando.	And what wit could wit have to excuse that?	155
Rosalind.	Marry, to say she came to seek you there. You	
	shall never take her without her answer, unless	
	you take her without her tongue. O, that woman	
	that cannot make her fault her husband's occasion,	
	let her never nurse her child herself, for she will	160
	breed it like a fool!	
Orlando.	For these two hours, Rosalind, I will leave thee.	
Rosalind.	Alas, dear love, I cannot lack thee two hours!	
Orlando.	I must attend the Duke at dinner; by two o'clock	
	I will be with thee again.	165
Rosalind.	Ay, go your ways, go your ways. I knew what you	
	would prove; my friends told me as much, and I	
	thought no less. That flattering tongue of yours	
	won me. 'Tis but one cast away, and so, come	
	death! Two o'clock is your hour?	170
Orlando.	Ay, sweet Rosalind.	
Rosalind.	By my troth, and in good earnest, and so God	
	mend me, and by all pretty oaths that are not	
	dangerous, if you break one jot of your promise,	
	or come one minute behind your hour, I will	175
	think you the most pathetical break-promise,	
	and the most hollow lover, and the most unworthy	
	of her you call Rosalind, that may be chosen out	
	of the gross band of the unfaithful. Therefore	
	beware my censure, and keep your promise.	180
Orlando.	With no less religion than if thou wert indeed my	
	Rosalind; so, adieu.	
Rosalind.	Well, Time is the old justice that examines all such	
	offenders, and let Time try. Adieu. [*Exit Orlando.*	

The fascinating thing about this passage is that it is both wooing and not wooing. Orlando is joining in what he takes to be a game in which he pretends that 'Ganymede' is Rosalind, and undertakes to woo her. For Rosalind, however, it is both a game and a serious encounter, giving her the opportunity to tease Orlando and, at the same time, enjoy, and be moved by, his expression of love for her.

Her disguise as a boy also provides her with cover for being far more outspoken and presumptuous than she would ever dare to be as the woman she really is. (And, of course, the further dimension, for the audience, that her 'reality' is male, not female, makes this boyishness both more acceptable and more amusing.) Yet the comic playfulness thus generated also enables her to treat the business of wooing to a satirical scrutiny which educates her somewhat conventionally-minded lover in some of the underlying truths of wooing. She manages to get the best of both worlds – basking in the sun of his warming passion, while pouring a little cold water on its unthinking platitudes.

Orlando's comments tend towards the conventionally proper and romantically pretty: when asked what he would say, he replies that he would kiss before he spoke; and when asked how long he would keep his Rosalind after marrying her, he produces the slightly trite 'For ever and a day.' Rosalind's disconcerting retorts bring these high-flown sentiments down to earth. Kissing is treated as simply a way of filling in the gaps of conversation – mockingly placed on a par with an orator's humming and hawing while he desperately fishes for the next point to make; and Orlando's avowal of eternal love is neatly split into its two verbal components, the 'day' being kept and the 'ever' being thrown away. And what follows the latter piece of humorous deflation is still more effective. It takes wooing into the all-important aftermath of courtship with a satirically exaggerated, but nonetheless telling, glance at the change of emotional weather which comes when maids turn into wives. The madonna-like figure whom the besotted lover places on a pedestal gives way to the unflattering images of cock-pigeon, parrot, ape, monkey and hyena, and the smooth, accommodating mistress of the romantic imagination turns into a woman whose characteristic is perverse opposition to the moods and wishes of her husband.

This, of course, is not cynicism, but intelligent debunkery. It is in line with Rosalind's latter-day revisionism in lines 85–98. There she takes two celebrated examples of ultra-romantic pairs of lovers, Troilus and Cressida and Hero and Leander, and reduces their stories to comically mischievous bathos. It was not his lover's sense of betrayal by Cressida that caused Troilus to fling himself with tragic

abandon into the war against the Trojans, and it was not as a result
of his desperate attempt to keep his tryst with Hero by swimming
the notoriously treacherous Bosphorus that Leander met his death
by drowning – as Rosalind cavalierly puts it, 'he went but forth to
wash him in the Hellespont, and, being taken with the cramp, was
drown'd'. The bathos is there in the language as well as the ludicrously unromantic motivation given to the heroes: that Troilus
should have 'his brains dash'd out with a Grecian club' substitutes
the register of the slaughterhouse for the dignified vocabulary of epic
poetry, and the reduction of Leander's heroic struggle with the elements to the effects of cramp involves a drastic change of tone. Her
conclusion – that 'these are all lies' is, of course, strictly true. There is
no basis in fact for the mythological fictions on which these stories
are based. But the main point of her saying so is not to discredit the
stories as such, but to rid them – at least as far as Orlando is concerned – of their unreal emotional accretions. The cue for her
debunking has been Orlando's 'Then, in mine own person, I die'
(line 84), which is the standard reply of the romantic lover to denial
by his mistress. Rarely, however, does this correspond to feeling in
the real world. Elizabethan love poetry is full of complaints by woebegone lovers that they are dying because the beloved has refused
their suit, to the point where the complaint becomes mere convention and the language in which it is uttered merely trite. In contrast,
Rosalind's language is brisk and refreshingly down-to-earth, and its
form is not that of self-consciously 'poetic' verse (too often bad
verse, like that which Shakespeare deliberately contrives for the love
poetry Orlando writes for Rosalind and pins to the trees in the
Forest of Arden), but rapid-fire, witty, colloquial prose. For all its air
of dismissive contempt, it is lively and energetic, communicating
not only the mocking posture of the boy 'Ganymede', but also the
zest and sexual excitement of the disguised Rosalind, for whom the
encounter with her lover is a kind of delightfully inverted wooing,
conducted – clean contrary to accepted convention – by the woman.

Rosalind perhaps treads on very thin ice when she goes so far (in
lines 153–61) as to suggest that the future might hold cuckoldry for
Orlando. The cuckold joke was funnier to the Elizabethans than it
now seems to us. It runs throughout Shakespeare, and is made much

of in *As You Like It* (as, for example, in IV.ii, and in the present scene
at lines 48–55, both of which harp on the stale tradition that the
cuckold wears horns). Perhaps, therefore, Rosalind's bawdy suggestion that Orlando might find his wife's wit going to his neighbour's
bed is no more than an embroidery on that standard theme. But
coupled as it is with the warning that women have ready tongues,
and can always find an answer to the suspicious questions their hus-
bands might put to them, it goes beyond the merely trite rehearsal of
the joke. Implied in it is the admonition that women cannot be
taken for granted. Not that Rosalind is making a veiled threat of
infidelity; nor is it at all likely that the audience will construe her as
reserving the right to cuckold her future husband if she gets bored
with him. The important thing is not what her remark reveals about
her own intentions, but the way it brings the decidedly *un*romantic
subject of adultery into the same field of semantic play as the conventionally romantic subject of wooing. Orlando's mind is too literary: it it is prone to compartmentalise courtship and marriage, love
and life. Rosalind's underlying purpose is to make him bring the two
together. Separated, they breathe too rarefied an atmosphere, and
become too vulnerable to the colder, cruder airs of the real world,
where devotion is not necessarily undying, vows may be too readily
broken, and gross deception may be practised. To be aware of these
things is a better defence against them than idealistic ignorance, and
to be able to live with that awareness is one of the marks of the
maturity that Rosalind would like to see in her brave, enthusiastic
and much cherished, but nevertheless slightly immature, lover.

And yet when Orlando declares, 'For these two hours, Rosalind, I
will leave thee', Rosalind herself seems to become a temperamentally
petulant girl. She cannot spare his company for two hours; she knew
what he would prove to be like; she was only won over by his false
tongue; she's only a poor girl who has been deceived, but she herself
is now ready to die! (lines 166–70) All this is not, presumably, to be
taken seriously. It is further play-acting on Rosalind's part – or at
least the kind of play-acting she judges appropriate to her adopted
role of boyish Ganymede. On that basis Orlando is still being tested
on his ability to cope with the temperamental variousness of female
moods. Is he man enough to understand, adjust, make allowances?

But, if this is the way her words should be interpreted, perhaps they also provide her with a convenient cover for her own emotional disturbance. Is she, for all her seemingly sophisticated assurance, not quite so self-assured, not quite so much the mature woman herself who can diagnose the immaturity of Orlando? Is playing at wooing, and enjoying a kind of vicarious opportunity to be the wooer, as much a learning scenario for her as well as Orlando? At the very least, the 'Ganymede' pretence of being the petulant girl is a safety valve for the real Rosalind's tension and anxiety, engaged, as she is, in the rather risky stratagem of guying a wooing that she wants, fundamentally, to be the real thing.

At this point it is as well to remember that the dialogue is not solely between Rosalind/Ganymede and Orlando. Celia is also present throughout the exchange, and at line 112 is made, somewhat against her will, an active participant. She seems not to approve the breach of decorum this play-wooing involves, and is clearly reluctant to play the part of officiating minister at the mock wedding ceremony. Rosalind does not discuss the religious implications, but this may well be one of those instances where an absence speaks as loudly as a presence. The dialogue does, however, carry one or two details which perhaps point to the significance of what is not developed in the text. At line 112 Celia is invited to 'be the priest' and marry the lovers. This she cannot be, since priests in Elizabethan England are exclusively male. The fact that it is a game excuses her, of course; but the very mention of 'priest' hints at another supremely important dimension to which wooing normally leads. Likewise, Rosalind's seemingly light-hearted comment after the 'ceremony', 'There's a girl goes before the priest' (lines 125–6), hints at a serious impropriety. Here is a girl who is *not* going before a proper priest; or, on another construction, a girl who is answering the all-important question before he has asked it. Nor is she being led before the priest by her father, who, if he were there, would answer the question, 'Who gives the bride?' Again, an absence signifies as much as, if not more than, a presence. Taken together with Celia's mainly silent presence throughout the passage (a point to be remedied later when, after Orlando's exit, Celia tells Rosalind, 'You have simply misus'd our sex in your love-prate', Alexander text, lines 179–80) and her, at best, laconic performance of the mock-priest's role, these absences may imply yet another level to Rosalind's uneasiness. This is not enough to impair the comedy of wooing. But it is enough perhaps to remind the audience of what is as yet an essential incompleteness in that wooing, and so point forward to elements such as the presence of a father to give away the bride, and the divine sanction, to be embodied in Hymen, the god of marriage, which will ultimately be necessary to complete both the wooing and the comedy.

*   *   *

Much Ado About Nothing, I.i.252–90. Claudio broaches with Don Pedro the question of his wooing Hero.

Claudio.	My liege, your Highness now may do me good.
Don Pedro.	My love is thine to teach; teach it but how,
	And thou shalt see how apt it is to learn
	Any hard lesson that may do thee good. 255
Claudio.	Hath Leonato any son, my lord?
Don Pedro.	No child but Hero; she's his only heir.
	Dost thou affect her, Claudio?
Claudio.	O, my lord,
	When you went onward on this ended action,
	I look'd upon her with a soldier's eye, 260
	That lik'd, but had a rougher task in hand
	Than to drive liking to the name of love;
	But now I am return'd, and that war-thoughts
	Have left their places vacant, in their rooms
	Come thronging soft and delicate desires, 265
	All prompting me how fair young Hero is,
	Saying I lik'd her ere I went to wars.
Don Pedro.	Thou wilt be like a lover presently,
	And tire the hearer with a book of words.
	If thou dost love fair Hero, cherish it; 270
	And I will break with her, and with her father,
	And thou shalt have her. Was't not to this end
	That thou begans't to twist so fine a story?

Claudio.	How sweetly you do minister to love,
	That know love's grief by his complexion! 275
	But lest my liking might too sudden seem,
	I would have salv'd it with a longer treatise.
Don Pedro.	What need the bridge much broader than the flood?
	The fairest grant is the necessity.
	Look what will serve is fit. 'Tis once, thou lovest; 280
	And I will fit thee with the remedy.
	I know we shall have revelling to-night;
	I will assume thy part in some disguise,
	And tell fair Hero I am Claudio;
	And in her bosom I'll unclasp my heart, 285
	And take her hearing prisoner with the force
	And strong encounter of my amorous tale.
	Then, after, to her father will I break;
	And the conclusion is she shall be thine.
	In practice let us put it presently. 290

Here is another kind of proposed wooing, by proxy this time, and a different problem of absences. To take the latter first. The omission of the father's consent is more than remedied here, though it is taken very much for granted by Don Pedro. What seems lacking is any real concern for Hero's consent. Don Pedro, it is true, undertakes to speak to her, but the phrase he uses is 'break with her' (line 271); and though he says 'I'll unclasp my heart' (line 285), as if to pour forth a passionate speech, since he will be in disguise, it will not be *his* heart, but Claudio's, that is unclasped, and in semblance only. With Hero, in particular, the process being suggested sounds more like coercion than wooing. The image Don Pedro uses at lines 286–7 is, in fact, a military one, and this, though appropriate enough perhaps to a soldier just returning from war, has the effect of seeming to reduce Hero to some sort of enemy who is to be taken prisoner by the superior force, not of strength and weapons, it is true, but words. Her will in the matter is all but ignored. And this, one may think, is an ominously significant start to a courtship which the rest of the play will show as running even less smoothly than that referred to by Lysander at *A Midsummer Night's Dream*, I.i.134.

The question that modern audiences of *Much Ado About Nothing* are almost bound to ask is why Don Pedro is brought in to play the role of proxy wooer at all. The answer in part is 'Other countries (or times), other customs.' It would probably not have seemed so odd to the Elizabethans. Proxy wooing occurs elswhere in Shakespeare – notably in *Twelfth Night*, where Viola/Cesario woos Olivia on behalf of Orsino. There is, however, a particular reason in the latter play, for Olivia has shut herself up from all access, and Orsino's only hope of getting his suit heard rests on the insinuating charm of his boylike messenger. In Claudio's case this does not apply. The defence for him might well be that he hopes the prestige and influence of Don Pedro will work in his favour. (And, by subsequent evidence, it is clear that this does work in his favour as far as influencing the beloved's father is concerned!) But that he should require defence is itself slightly disturbing. There seems to be some curious diffidence in him, and some curious uncertainty about his feelings. The first question he puts to Don Pedro is: 'Hath Leonato any son, my lord?', which sounds very much as if he is making sure of Hero's position as an heiress before committing himself further. Only when assured on this point (and having learnt, indeed, that she is Leonato's *only* child) does he embark on a rather florid, circumlocutory account of the state of his heart, full of rather painstaking rhetorical devices – including play, in line 259, on the similar sounds of 'When' and 'went' and 'onward' and 'ended'; the somewhat affected sequence, in lines 260–3, of 'look'd', 'lik'd', 'liking' and 'love'; and the laborious metaphor of lines 263–5 which expresses his change of heart in terms of a room being left vacant by personified 'war-thoughts', thus leaving the opportunity for it to be filled up instead with personified 'desires'. The second half of that metaphor also has to do duty for Claudio's new-found feelings for Hero. But 'soft and delicate' does not suggest much strength of feeling, and 'prompting' – the action attributed to his personified desires in line 266 – calls up the slightly ludicrous image of an inexperienced actor who needs to be reminded of his lines by a prompter. The artificiality and wordiness of it all strikes even the bluff Don Pedro, who characterises Claudio as the kind of lover who will 'tire the hearer with a book of words' (269). His own language is more forthright; and though it suffers from the one-sided presumptuous-ness which has already been analysed above, the directness of the syntax and the plainness of the vocabulary make a telling contrast with Claudio's indirectness. He ends with a simple, short statement, which is the signal for action: 'In practice let us put it presently', i.e. let's do it immediately. With him words go hand in hand with action; Claudio's words are but the prelude to someone else's action.

*   *   *

Twelfth Night, I.v.236–82. This is an example of the proxy wooing in *Twelfth Night* referred to in the previous commentary. Viola/Cesario speaks to Olivia on Orsino's behalf.

Viola.	My lord and master loves you – O, such love
	Could be but recompens'd though you were crown'd
	The nonpareil of beauty!
Olivia.	How does he love me?
Viola.	With adorations, fertile tears,
	With groans that thunder love, with sighs of fire. 240
Olivia.	Your lord does know my mind; I cannot love him.
	Yet I suppose him virtuous, know him noble,
	Of great estate, of fresh and stainless youth;
	In voices well divulg'd, free, learn'd, and valiant,
	And in dimension and the shape of nature 245
	A gracious person; but yet I cannot love him.
	He might have took his answer long ago.
Viola.	If I did love you in my master's flame,
	With such a suff'ring, such a deadly life,
	In your denial would I find no sense; 250
	I would not understand it.
Olivia.	Why, what would you?
Viola.	Make me a willow cabin at your gate,
	And call upon my soul within the house;
	Write loyal cantons of contemned love
	And sing them loud even in the dead of night; 255
	Halloo your name to the reverberate hills,
	And make the babbling gossip of the air

Cry out 'Olivia!' O, you should not rest
Between the elements of air and earth
But you should pity me!

Olivia.   You might do much.   260
What is your parentage?

Viola.   Above my fortunes, yet my state is well:
I am a gentleman.

Olivia.   Get you to your lord.
I cannot love him; let him send no more –
Unless perchance you come to me again   265
To tell me how he takes it. Fare you well.
I thank you for your pains; spend this for me.

Viola.   I am no fee'd post, lady; keep your purse;
My master, not myself, lacks recompense.
Love make his heart of flint that you shall love;   270
And let your fervour, like my master's, be
Plac'd in contempt! Farewell, fair cruelty. [*Exit.*

Olivia.   'What is your parentage?'
'Above my fortunes, yet my state is well:
I am a gentleman.' I'll be sworn thou art;   275
Thy tongue, thy face, thy limbs, actions, and spirit,
Do give thee five-fold blazon. Not too fast! Soft, soft!
Unless the master were the man. How now!
Even so quickly may one catch the plague?
Methinks I feel this youth's perfections   280
With an invisible and subtle stealth
To creep in at mine eyes. Well, let it be.

There is a double process going on here: Viola/Cesario is carrying out the wooing that she is commissioned to do on behalf of Orsino, but in her young man's disguise, and with her readiness of tongue, she, in effect – and quite unintentionally – woos Olivia herself. We hear Olivia rejecting Orsino yet again, and observe her beginning to be susceptible to the proxy wooer. In her brief soliloquy at the end, which enables us to overhear, as it were, what she is saying to herself, the hints given in the foregoing dialogue that this is happening are made explicit.

The expression of this double process also makes the passage illustrative of two kinds of wooing. The first – that which Viola/ Cesario is supposed to be doing – follows the conventions of Elizabethan love poetry. The adoring lover, Orsino, is represented as consumed with passion and grief: loving 'With adorations, fertile tears, / With groans that thunder love, with sighs of fire' (lines 239–40) – a posture entirely familar in the sonnets of the day, and one which, as we have already seen, tends to be made fun of in *Twelfth Night*. (Compare the first passage discussed in Chapter 4 above, and, in the present scene, the satirical response Olivia makes to Viola, at lines 225–33, when she employs very much the argument which Shakespeare uses in his Sonnets to persuade their addressee that he ought to beget an heir so as not to leave his virtues unknown to posterity.) And yet this time it produces a slightly different response from Olivia. Although she repeats her inability to love Orsino, she softens the negative effect of this by conceding that he has pretty well all the qualities that normally make a wooer eligible (but more, one suspects, to mollify Viola than because she is being persuaded to change her mind). At the very least, Viola shows herself to be expert in the use of the conventional devices, and this sets Olivia wondering. However, when Viola asserts that, were she her master, she would refuse to 'understand' denial, and Olivia asks what she would do, there follows something (lines 252–60) which is much more than a set speech, and, though still pursuing the expected plea for 'pity', is far from being merely conventional. The conventional theme is remade by exceptional eloquence and the highly novel conceit which takes the emblem of the weeping willow – in standard poetic usage so conventional that it virtually passes unnoticed – and turns it into an original construction of the imagination, a cabin made of willow branches. Again, the conventional notion that a lover's soul migrates from him to his mistress becomes something quite different when the lover takes up residence in this 'cabin', built by the gate to the mistress's dwelling, and spends his time calling upon his soul within the mistress's house. It creates a highly graphic and arresting picture. The sad poetry bewailing despised love, and the standard lover's serenade, are likewise transformed (and given a quite unexpected touch of humour, too) as this un-ignorable lover sings his verses at full volume 'even in the dead of night', making the name of 'Olivia' echo around the hills so that the very air turns into a 'babbling gossip' (a daring touch of bathos which the intensity of the speech nevertheless enables Viola to get away with).

It is not surprising that, having heard all this, Olivia murmurs, 'You might do much.' The sentence is double-edged – a concession to the effectiveness of such eloquence, but also a hint of the way it is arousing Olivia's feelings for the proxy wooer herself/himself. The otherwise odd-seeming jump Olivia then makes in demanding, 'What is your parentage?' is a result of this arousal. And the answer she gets, cryptic as it is ('I am better than I seem to be in this menial position: I am a gentleman') arouses Olivia still further. Now, in effect, there begins another, covert process of wooing, in a totally different style. Instead of poetic flourishes we have something more psychologically telling as Olivia, almost against her own will, starts to angle for Viola's erotic attention. She is so disconcerted that she does this at first rather unskilfully, making the slightly inept error of offering Viola a tip for her pains. And yet the very pertness of Viola's reply, at lines 268–9, seems to add to Olivia's fascination. As Viola sweeps out with her fine flourish in the conventional style, 'Farewell, fair cruelty', Olivia, virtually unaware of the insult this conveys, is left alone on the stage, brooding in an altogether more realistic manner on the significance of that teasing answer to 'What is your parentage?', and catching herself in the very act of growing too warm in admiration of Viola's tongue, face, limbs, actions and spirit. As with the sudden jump involved in putting this question at line 261, there is another, unexplained jump from 'Soft, soft!', at line 277, to the elliptic 'Unless the master were the man', at line 278.

This represents an interestingly different use of language from the fully laid-out rhetoric and syntactical completeness of the wooing style employed by Viola in her role as Orsino's advocate. 'Unless the master were the man' is a subordinate clause attached to no main clause. The audience has to supply what is missing – which they do readily enough, recognising that Olivia has skipped over a more elaborate process of reasoning. In this hidden subtext Olivia leaps to the idea of loving Viola/Cesario and making 'him' her husband, rejects this on the ground that she cannot marry a servant, but again counters that by suggesting to herself that she might be able to do so if the servant ('the man') were to become the equivalent of the person 'he' serves (Orsino, 'the master'); behind which lies the unspoken implication that she could also bring about that social transformation simply by marrying Viola/Cesario. To spell it out like this makes the thought-process sound somewhat tediously laboured. Reduced, however, as it is in the text, to a sudden jump to the seemingly unattached 'Unless the master were the man', it conveys the impression that Olivia's feverish thoughts are running far ahead of her words. No wonder, then, that she tries to slow herself down, while wondering at the rapidity with which one may 'catch the plague' (279). This is a rapid, insidious, at the most semi-conscious process; it moves, as Olivia suggests at line 281, 'With an invisible and subtle stealth' (like the unseen infection of the plague, all too feelingly known to Shakespeare's original audiences), and the language has to become more abrupt, succinct, and even fragmentary, to express it.

By the end of this passage, then, Olivia has swung round from being the reluctant object of Orsino's wooing, conducted by the proxy wooer, Viola/Cesario, to an emotionally excited and disconcerted woman, on the verge of herself conducting a wooing of that very wooer. But hers is an instinctual, almost unconscious process, quite different from the deliberate wooing conducted (albeit with painful reluctance) by Viola/Cesario. The result is high comedy combined with high, dramatic intensity, and swirling cross-currents of emotion and meaning expressed in vividly appropriate contrasts of language.

Conclusions

The four passages discussed in this chapter by no means exhaust the range of wooing scenes in Shakespearean comedy, but they do illustrate something of the variety of attitudes and styles which they encompass. The passage from *A Midsummer Night's Dream* empha-

sises the broader social context in which wooing necessarily functions, and the complexities which that generates for personal
choice. Rosalind's game of wooing played with Orlando in *As You
Like It* shows sport being used for the more serious purpose of emotional education (though in no didactic spirit); wooing there
becomes a process of maturation, and, in addition, affords fascinating glimpses of life beyond wooing – glimpses that take one
outside the immediate realm of that wooing, winning and happy
achievement of marriage which provides the formal territory of
romantic comedy. The proxy wooings of *Much Ado About Nothing*
and *Twelfth Night* include a variant form of the wooing process
more familiar to the Elizabethans than to modern audiences, and
are ones which throw into stronger relief such issues as those of
dowry, social status, strategy and control over one's own feelings
and actions. They also illustrate how effectively Shakespeare's language and dramatic methods can cope with the significance of
things unspoken and omitted, or breaking to the surface only partially and fragmentarily. But, above all, what these four passages
reinforce is the sense one gets from Shakespearean comedy that,
'romantic' as its wooing stories are, they have to come to terms with
the real world, where the simplifications of romance have to be
modified to meet more difficult and complicating circumstances.
As Rosalind reminds Orlando, 'men are April when they woo,
December when they wed: maids are May when they are maids, but
the sky changes when they are wives'. Wooing is critically important
in the lives of the young people involved in it, but there is also life
after wooing.

Methods of Analysis (Chapters 4 and 5)

Analysis in these chapters involves careful listening to words and
their overtones, awareness of the significance of image clusters, and
consciousness of variations in syntax. Thus in the speech which
opens *Twelfth Night* the images associated with sea, music and food
all require close attention not only for their value as recurring features of the language, but also for the precise way in which they are

deployed and qualified. The full complexity of their meaning must be allowed to come through.

There is also a need to be alert to the implications and reverberations of images which widen the context of meaning, as, for example, occurs with the legal and religious elements in the extract from *A Midsummer Night's Dream*, I.i.22–82.

Syntax makes a difference to the way words register on the minds of the audience. For example, Viola/Cesario's formal style when wooing on Orsino's behalf contributes to the dramatic contrast with Olivia's more elliptical style when catching herself falling in love with the 'boy'.

The way the dramatic situation can modify the effect of what is said also needs attention. Thus in the extract from *Twelfth Night*, II.iv.78–123, Viola's situation as a woman disguised as a boy and in love with Orsino signficantly alters the impression created by Orsino's claims for the depth of male versus female feeling. There is both a surface meaning and an underlying meaning, hidden from Orsino but available to the consciousness of the audience, and both need to be taken into account.

Similarly, absences as well presences call for comment. As the analysis of *As You Like It*, IV.i.63–178 shows, the absence of a proper priest in the mock-wedding is a felt part of its incompleteness; and in the extract from *Much Ado About Nothing*, I.i.252–90 the virtual ignoring of Hero's share in the proposed wooing has ominous implications for what is to follow.

Some awareness of what is commonplace and stereotyped in Elizabethan love literature is helpful in taking the full impact of Shakespeare's mockery of conventionality. This can be gained by a reading of some typical love sonnets of the period (to be found, for example, in *The Oxford Book of Sixteenth Century Verse*); but careful reading will pick up most of the necessary cues from within the texts of the plays. (See, for example, in *As You Like It*, Rosalind's jumping on Orlando's stock responses and her debunking treatment of the stories of Troilus and Cressida and Hero and Leander; and, in *Twelfth Night*, Feste's mockery of Orsino's sentimentality.)

Suggested Work

In *A Midsummer Night's Dream* analyse III.ii.122–61 ('Why should you think that I should woo in scorn? ... all to make you sport'). Lysander has abandoned Hermia and, under the influence of Puck's love-juice, fallen in love with Helena; and now Demetrius does the same. Note the linguistic features which heighten the absurdly mechanical quality of the lovers' reactions, including, for example, rhyme, imagery, extravagant hyperbole and stock rhetorical devices. Note, too, the way similar features intensify Helena's perplexity and indignation. Tell-tale words to look for include 'vow', 'faith' and 'oath'.

As a contrast to the above, in *Much Ado About Nothing* analyse I.i.98–124 ('I wonder that you will still be talking, Signior Benedick ... I know you of old'). This is the first encounter between Beatrice and Benedick. What does it reveal about the relationship between the two? Pay particular attention to the way they each pick up the other's words and play them back and forth like a shuttlecock. Note, too, the use of verbal devices, even though this is in prose. What kind of tone is created by the use of images such as those of food, a turncoat, a dog barking at a crow, a parrot-teacher, etc.? How is the conclusion of this set in the match between the two signalled in the text?

In *As You Like It* analyse III.ii.165–209 ('Trow you who hath done this ? ... Answer me in one word'). Rosalind, in dialogue with Celia, reveals her impatience to know the identity of the person who has been writing verses about her. Note how the eagerness and embarrassment in Rosalind and Celia's good-humoured teasing of her are reflected in such features as the headlong movement of the prose (aided by alliteration), the use of repetition, the piling-on of questions (reaching a climax in lines 204–9) and the use of imagery (especially the 'narrow-mouth'd bottle' and the bawdy pun it prompts at line 190).

In *Twelfth Night* analyse III.i.135–61 ('I prithee tell me what thou think'st of me ... That heart which now abhors to like his love'). Olivia has granted 'Cesario' private access to her, but because she wants to make love to 'him' rather than hear 'his' pleading on

Orsino's behalf. This is the climax of the interview in which the two are at cross purposes, and the perplexing difficulties they respectively experience are exacerbated by Viola's disguise. Show how these complications are reflected in the repetitions, paradoxes and antitheses of the verse, and how they are foregrounded by the use of rhyme in lines 144–61.

6

Fools (1): Dupes

Introduction

A central theme in both comedy and tragedy is the deceiving of one character by another, or others. This being so, there is naturally some degree of overlap in the treatment of deception in the two genres. Both comic and tragic figures may be dupes. In *A Midsummer Night's Dream*, for example, Puck's application of the love-juice tricks both Lysander and Demetrius into falling in love with Helena, and makes Titania besotted with the transformed Bottom. In *Twelfth Night* Malvolio is deceived by the forged letter into thinking that Olivia loves him and is prepared to marry him. With some degree of similarity, the protagonist of *Macbeth* is deceived by the Weird Sisters into thinking that he is destined to become King of Scotland; and in *Othello* Iago tricks Othello into believing that Desdemona is unfaithful to him. The consequences, however, are very different. The love-juice in *A Midsummer Night's Dream* is also used by Puck (on Oberon's instruction) to undo the work of deception where Lysander and Titania are concerned, restoring Lysander to his original love of Hermia, while leaving Demetrius still in love with the reciprocating Helena, and causing Titania to wonder how she could ever have come to dote on the ass-headed Bottom. And though the audience laugh at the folly of the dupes (and in the process learn something about the waywardness of love and lovers), the harmful effects of deception are thus neutralised. With Macbeth and Othello, on the other hand, although there may be gross absurdities in their behaviour – particularly in Othello's – the saving, corrective action either does not come at all, or comes too late to prevent disaster. They are fooled, and may see themselves as 'fools', but the sense of folly adds to the pain of the tragedy, rather than mitigating it, and helping in the end to transform it into happiness.

What, then, constitutes the difference between duping in comedy and tragedy? This is not an easy question to answer. There might at first seem to be an obvious difference in the degree of seriousness involved in the respective acts of deception. Being deceived, as Othello is, into believing one's wife unfaithful, it could be argued, is not at all on the same plane as waking from sleep to think, as Demetrius does, that the woman he once detested is now a 'goddess, nymph, perfect, divine' (*Midsummer Night's Dream*, III.ii.137). And being lured, as Macbeth is, into the belief that one's future is that of a king is more serious than being deceived, as Malvolio is, into thinking that one's employer loves one. But a closer look at the contexts of Demetrius's and Malvolio's deceptions reveals elements which are at least potentially painful. In *A Midsummer Night's Dream*, for example, Demetrius's seeming change of heart does not, as one might have expected, immediately fill Helena with joy. On the contrary, she feels herself as the victim (another kind of dupe) of a cruel hoax, which she resents deeply; and when, in her turn, Hermia finds that she has lost her lover, Lysander, to Helena, she, too, is hurt. The two women find themselves at cross purposes, and turn to quarrelling with each other in a way, again, that has painful overtones. In *Twelfth Night* Malvolio's predicament is something which his overweening vanity and egotism seem to bring on himself, and to that extent the audience laugh at his delusions with no misgivings. But when deception is later carried to the point where he is imprisoned in a dark house and taunted as a madman, that reaction is qualified. His final, unreconciled exit ('I'll be reveng'd on the whole pack of you', *Twelfth Night*, V.i.364), and Olivia's sense that he has 'been most notoriously abus'd' (V.i.365), leave him, if not a tragic figure, then, at least, the victim of a practical joke which stretches comedy to its doubtful limits.

The truth is that Shakespearean comedy is not pure comedy, but a mixture of the comic and tragic, in which the comic elements predominate. (And the corollary is also true – namely, that Shakespearean tragedy is not pure tragedy, like that which Racine, the great French tragedian of the seventeenth century, aimed at, but an alloy composed of both tragic and comic metals.) The controls which enable it to register overall as 'comic' are not hard and fast rules, but the more subtly interacting effects of plot-circumstance, social assumptions and linguistic devices. It is by such means that the elusively 'comic' tone is maintained, and the frequent incursions of the tragic are kept (though sometimes only just) at bay.

In the following passages both the light and the dark in Shakespearean comedy will be explored, with the emphasis on situations in which certain characters are the victims of deception.

Analyses

A Midsummer Night's Dream, II.ii.88–156. Helena, weary from pursuing Demetrius, who at this point in the play still detests her, stumbles upon Lysander asleep. The latter, having been anointed with Puck's love-juice, which causes its 'dupe' to fall in love with the first person his eyes open upon, awakes and immediately dotes on Helena. His former love, Hermia, is also asleep nearby, but does not awake until near the end of the scene.

Helena.	O, I am out of breath in this fond chase!	
	The more my prayer, the lesser is my grace.	
	Happy is Hermia, whereso'er she lies,	90
	For she hath blessed and attractive eyes.	
	How came her eyes so bright? Not with salt tears;	
	If so, my eyes are oft'ner wash'd than hers.	
	No, no, I am as ugly as a bear,	
	For beasts that meet me run away for fear;	95
	Therefore no marvel though Demetrius	
	Do, as a monster, fly my presence thus.	
	What wicked and dissembling glass of mine	
	Made me compare with Hermia's sphery eyne?	

	But who is here? Lysander! on the ground!	100
	Dead, or asleep? I see no blood, no wound.	
	Lysander, if you live, good sir, awake.	
Lysander.	[*Waking*] And run through fire I will for thy sweet sake.	
	Transparent Helena! Nature shows art,	
	That through thy bosom makes me see thy heart.	105
	Where is Demetrius? O, how fit a word	
	Is that vile name to perish on my sword!	
Helena.	Do not say so, Lysander; say not so.	
	What though he love your Hermia? Lord, what though?	
	Yet Hermia still loves you; then be content.	110
Lysander.	Content with Hermia! No; I do repent	
	The tedious minutes I with her have spent.	
	Not Hermia but Helena I love:	
	Who will not change a raven for a dove?	
	The will of man is by his reason sway'd,	115
	And reason says you are the worthier maid.	
	Things growing are ripe not until their season;	
	So I, being young, till now not ripe to reason;	
	And touching now the point of human skill,	
	Reason becomes the marshal to my will,	120
	And leads me to your eyes, where I o'erlook	
	Love's stories, written in Love's richest book.	
Helena.	Wherefore was I to this keen mockery born?	
	When at your hands did I deserve this scorn?	
	Is't not enough, is't not enough, young man,	125
	That I did never, no, nor never can,	
	Deserve a sweet look from Demetrius' eye,	
	But you must flout my insufficiency?	
	Good troth, you do me wrong, good sooth, you do,	
	In such disdainful manner me to woo.	130
	But fare you well; perforce I must confess	
	I thought you lord of more true gentleness.	
	O, that a lady of one man refus'd	
	Should of another therefore be abus'd! [*Exit*	
Lysander.	She sees not Hermia. Hermia, sleep thou there;	135
	And never mayst thou come Lysander near!	

> For, as a surfeit of the sweetest things
> The deepest loathing to the stomach brings,
> Or as the heresies that men do leave
> Are hated most of those they did deceive,   140
> So thou, my sufeit and my heresy,
> Of all be hated, but the most of me!
> And, all my powers, address your love and might
> To honour Helen, and to be her knight! [*Exit.*

Hermia.   [*Starting*] Help me, Lysander, help me; do thy best   145
> To pluck this crawling serpent from my breast.
> Ay me, for pity! What a dream was here!
> Lysander, look how I do quake with fear.
> Methought a serpent eat my heart away,
> And you sat smiling at his cruel prey.   150
> Lysander! What, remov'd? Lysander! lord!
> What, out of hearing gone? No sound, no word?
> Alack, where are you? Speak, an if you hear;
> Speak, of all loves! I swoon almost with fear.
> No? Then I well perceive you are not nigh.   155
> Either death or you I'll find immediately. [*Exit.*

The most obvious dupe in this passage is Lysander, who, thanks to the influence of the love-juice administered by Puck, is now deceived into thinking that the person he really loves is not Hermia, but Helena, and that she loves him. It is a moment of high comedy when he wakes from his sleep to declare passionate love for Helena – a moment increased in its effect by the way he seems to take up Helena's invitation at line 102 to 'awake', and convert it into an expression of love – as if to say, 'Yes, indeed, since you command it, I will awake, and run through fire for your sake.' The preposterousness of this is heightened by the brittle chiming of the rhyme 'awake/sake', which makes Lysander's response sound like the reaction of a programmed automaton. And it is still more comic when he goes on to vary the conventional opposition between Art and Nature by claiming that in this instance Nature itself has demonstrated a capacity for art by making Helena 'transparent' so that he can pierce her bosom and see directly into her heart. The deceived dupe ridiculously asserts that what often deceives, because it is hidden, is made transparently clear to him!

That he subsequently argues (lines 115–22) his change of heart to be the combined result of reason and developing maturity only intensifies the duped irrationality of his behaviour. His claim to have moved on to a superior state of understanding fully justifies the gleeful comment that Puck will make in the later scene (III.ii.115): 'Lord, what fools these mortals be!' Unknowingly, but with delicious appropriateness, Lysander climaxes his argument by asserting that he has now, in fact, reached the pinnacle of human rationality, which leads him to Helena's eyes, where he reads 'Love's stories, written in Love's richest book'. Such stories are indeed fictions, and that they are to be read in the mistress's eyes, conventionally the apex of a lover's appreciation of her beauty, humorously underlines how much such supposed knowledge is only the projection of a deluded lover's passionately distorted seeing. And, one might add, since 'Love's richest book' is equivalent to the romance tradition in which most glamorously idealised love stories are written, Lysander's claim also, unwittingly, becomes a comic exposure of the romantic treatment of love.

But the women in this scene are also deceived. Although they have not been drugged into misapprehension by the love-juice, desire and jealousy have made them dupes, too. Helena, as shown by the opening of this passage, dotes pathetically on Demetrius, and seems to be as much deluded about the 'blessed and attractive' power of Hermia's eyes as Lysander is to become with regard to her own. What she says may, of course, be ironic, and lines 98–9, in particular, may well be merely sarcastic; but her envy of Hermia's ability to command devotion, and despair of her own ability to do the same, is real enough.

Hermia's vision of things is also distorted by her own anxieties. When she wakes from her sleep (at line 145), she no more sees things as they are than Lysander does when he awakes. Properly speaking, she is only half awake, still caught in a nightmare of being attacked by a serpent, and – what is yet more nightmarish for her – of seeing Lysander smile at it indifferently. When she becomes fully awake, she recognises this illusion for what it is – 'a dream' (147);

but she is not comforted, because she finds no comfort from Lysander, and, indeed, goes on to experience the greater disturbance of realising that Lysander has deserted her. A still subtler level of duping is at work here, for the audience knows, as she does not, that she has become the indirect dupe of Puck's misapplied love-juice, losing her love to the unexpected rival, Helena, who is now the one to have acquired 'blessed and attractive eyes'. Moreover, her 'dream' proves to be a form of truth-telling rather than deception; it is a virtual allegory of the betrayal that has taken place while she has been sleeping. Although Hermia does not yet have the capacity to interpret it as such, emotion tells her that something is radically amiss. Feeling, that is, proves a better guide to reality than the 'reason' Lysander prates of in the action that takes place while Hermia is asleep. In a play called *A Midsummer Night's Dream* this cannot be without significance. At the very least, it makes the notion of being duped more than a simple one of illusion v. reality.

What the women's illusions in this passage also do is to emphasise the complex interrelation of comedy with things which are at least potentially tragic. For example, at lines 90–3, where Helena compares herself unfavourably with Hermia, there is an overflow from the half-serious question, 'How came her eyes so bright?' and its answer, 'Not with salt tears', to the more bitterly tinged qualification, 'If so, my eyes are oft'ner wash'd than hers.' There is a hint here that takes one beyond the comic theme of female rivalry to a more painful sense of the grief that unrequited love causes Helena. This is increased when Lysander declares his love for her, as she takes his words as a form of tormenting, which activates her sense of inferiority ('my insufficiency', line 128). Repetitive structures ('Is't not enough, is't not enough' and 'I did never, no, nor never can', 125–6) raise the emotional temperature, and the words with which she makes her exit (lines 133–4) join together her pained sense of being simultaneously 'refus'd' by Demetrius and 'abus'd' by Lysander. More emphatically still, Hermia's frightened exclamations as she wakes from her nightmare and her increasingly desperate questions as she calls on the absent Lysander (lines 147–55) disrupt what has hitherto been the comparatively smooth flow of the verse, and produce a more abrupt, staccato syntax. Reinforced by the dream, with its

twice-repeated image of the serpent (lines 146 and 149) and the suggestion of almost sadistic pleasure in 'smiling at his cruel prey' (150),
these elements of the language seem to convey real disturbance and
anxiety.

However, there are also controlling features which contain this
disturbance and keep it within the bounds of comedy. Chief among
these is the audience's godlike overview of the situation. They know
that all this has come about as a result of mishaps in the application
of the love-juice, intended by Oberon to resolve, not complicate, the
lovers' cross-wooing: it can only be a matter of time before his
authority is reasserted. Meanwhile, the mischief-loving character of
Puck, the agent responsible for these temporary mishaps, also helps
to condition their effect; through him the audience are helped to
take them in the spirit of a practical joke. What we have seen to be
the automaton-like nature of some of the characters' reactions likewise helps to shape the audience's response. In addition, the exaggerated quality that creeps into the language from time to time – its
sense of being ridiculously 'over the top' (for example, in Helena's
self-denigration at lines 94–5, and Lysander's wildly overdone praise
of her at lines 103–5 and 114–22) – contributes to an impression of
disproportion which subtly reminds us that comedy's implicit criteria are good sense and reasonableness. And, finally, the formality of
the verse, continually signalled to us via the neatly chiming rhymed
couplets (even though disruptive elements, as we have seen, also
make themselves felt at various points) puts a kind of bracket, or
frame, round the scene, reminding us that this is art, not nature – a
contrivance for our entertainment, an invented 'reality' rather than
the thing itself, the actors' and the playwright's dream-world, to be
subtly differentiated from the everyday world.

* * *

Twelfth Night, II.v.21–158 (21–71). Malvolio is subjected to the
letter-trick intended to make him think his employer, the Countess
Olivia, is in love with him, and covertly watched by Maria (its
author), Sir Toby Belch, Sir Andrew Aguecheek and Fabian.

Malvolio.	'Tis but fortune; all is fortune. Maria once told me she did affect me; and I have heard herself come thus near, that, should she fancy, it should be one of my complexion. Besides, she uses me with a more exalted respect than any one else that follows 25 her. What should I think on't?
Sir Toby.	Here's an overweening rogue!
Fabian.	O, peace! Contemplation makes a rare turkey-cock of him; how he jets under his advanc'd plumes!
Sir Andrew.	'Slight, I could so beat the rogue – 30
Sir Toby.	Peace, I say.
Malvolio.	To be Count Malvolio!
Sir Toby.	Ah, rogue!
Sir Andrew.	Pistol him, pistol him.
Sir Toby.	Peace, peace. 35
Malvolio.	There is example for't: the Lady of the Strachy married the yeoman of the wardrobe.
Sir Andrew.	Fie on him, Jezebel!
Fabian.	O, peace! Now he's deeply in; look how imagination blows him. 40
Malvolio.	Having been three months married to her, sitting in my state –
Sir Toby.	O, for a stone-bow to hit him in the eye!
Malvolio.	Calling my officers about me, in my branch'd velvet gown, having come from a day-bed – where 45 I have left Olivia sleeping –
Sir Toby.	Fire and brimstone!
Fabian.	O, peace, peace!
Malvolio.	And then to have the humour of state; and after a demure travel of regard, telling them I know 50 my place as I would they should do theirs, to ask for my kinsman Toby –
Sir Toby.	Bolts and shackles!
Fabian.	O, peace, peace, peace! Now, now.
Malvolio.	Seven of my people, with an obedient start, make 55 out for him. I frown the while, and perchance wind up my watch, or play with my – some rich jewel.

	Toby approaches; curtsies there to me –	
Sir Toby.	Shall this fellow live?	
Fabian.	Though our silence be drawn from us with cars,	60
	yet peace.	
Malvolio.	I extend my hand to him thus, quenching my	
	familar smile with an austere regard of control –	
Sir Toby.	And does not Toby take you a blow o' the lips then?	
Malvolio.	Saying 'Cousin Toby, my fortunes having cast	65
	me on your niece give me this prerogative of	
	speech' –	
Sir Toby.	What, what?	
Malvolio.	'You must amend your drunkenness' –	
Sir Toby.	Out, scab!	70
Fabian.	Nay, patience, or we break the sinews of our plot.	
Malvolio.	'Besides, you waste the treasure of your time with	
	a foolish knight' –	
Sir Andrew.	That's me, I warrant you.	
Malvolio.	'One Sir Andrew.'	75
Sir Andrew.	I knew 'twas I; for many do call me fool.	
Malvolio.	What employment have we here?	
	[*Taking up the letter*].	
Fabian.	Now is the woodcock near the gin.	
Sir Toby.	O, peace! And the spirit of humours intimate	
	reading aloud to him!	80
Malvolio.	By my life, this is my lady's hand: these be her	
	very C's, her U's, and her T's; and thus makes	
	she her great P's. It is, in contempt of question,	
	her hand.	
Sir Andrew.	Her C's, her U's, and her T's. Why that?	85
Malvolio.	[*Reads*] 'To the unknown belov'd, this, and my	
	good wishes.' Her very phrases! By your leave, wax.	
	Soft! And the impressure of her Lucrece with which	
	she uses to seal; 'tis my lady. To whom should this be?	
Fabian.	This wins him, liver and all.	90
Malvolio.	[*Reads*] 'Jove knows I love,	
	But who?	
	Lips, do not move;	

No man must know.'
'No man must know.' What follows? The numbers   95
alter'd! 'No man must know.' If this should be thee,
Malvolio?

Sir Toby. Marry, hang thee, brock!

Malvolio. [*Reads*]
'I may command where I adore;
   But silence, like a Lucrece knife,   100
With bloodless stroke my heart doth gore;
   M.O.A.I. doth sway my life.'

Fabian. A fustian riddle!

Sir Toby. Excellent wench, say I.

Malvolio. 'M.O.A.I. doth sway my life.' Nay, but first let   105
me see, let me see, let me see.

Fabian. What dish o' poison has she dress'd him!

Sir Toby. And with what wing the staniel checks at it!

Malvolio. 'I may command where I adore.' Why, she may
command me: I serve her; she is my lady. Why,   110
this is evident to any formal capacity; there is no
obstruction in this. And the end – what should that
alphabetical position portend? If I could make that
resemble something in me. Softly! M.O.A.I. –

Sir Toby. O, ay, make up that! He is now at a cold scent.   115

Fabian. Sowter will cry upon't for all this, though it be as
rank as a fox.

Malvolio. M – Malvolio; M – why, that begins my name.

Fabian. Did not I say he would work it out? The cur is
excellent at faults.   120

Malvolio. M – But then there is no consonancy in the sequel;
that suffers under probation; A should follow,
but O does.

Fabian.   And O shall end, I hope.

Sir Toby. Ay, or I'll cudgel him, and make him cry 'O!'   125

Malvolio. And then I comes behind.

Fabian. Ay, an you had any eye behind you, you might
see more detraction at your heels than fortunes
before you.

Malvolio.	M.O.A.I. This simulation is not as the former; 130
	and yet, to crush this a little, it would bow to me,
	for every one of these letters are in my name. Soft!
	here follows prose.
[Reads]	'If this fall into thy hand, revolve. In my stars I am
	above thee; but be not afraid of greatness. Some 135
	are born great, some achieve greatness, and some
	have greatness thrust upon 'em. Thy Fates open their
	hands; let thy blood and spirit embrace them; and,
	to inure thyself to what thou art like to be, cast thy
	humble slough and appear fresh. Be opposite with 140
	a kinsman, surly with servants; let thy tongue tang
	arguments of state; put thyself into the trick of
	singularity. She thus advises thee that sighs for thee.
	Remember who commended thy yellow stockings,
	and wish'd to see thee ever cross-garter'd. I say, 145
	remember. Go to, thou art made, if thou desir'st
	to be so; if not, let me see thee a steward still, the
	fellow of servants, and not worthy to touch Fortune's
	fingers. Farewell. She that would alter services with
	thee, 150
	THE FORTUNATE-UNHAPPY.'

Daylight and champain discovers not more. This is
open. I will be proud, I will read politic authors,
I will baffle Sir Toby, I will wash off gross acquaintance,
I will be point-devise the very man. I do not now   155
fool myself to let imagination jade me; for every
reason excites to this, that my lady loves me. She
did commend my yellow stockings of late, she did
praise my leg being cross-garter'd; and in this she
manifests herself to my love, and with a kind of   160
injunction drives me to these habits of her liking.
I thank my stars I am happy. I will be strange, stout,
in yellow stockings, and cross-garter'd, even with
the swiftness of putting on. Jove and my stars be
praised! Here is yet a postscript.   165

[*Reads*]   'Thou canst not choose but know who I am. If thou
entertain'st my love, let it appear in thy smiling; thy
smiles become thee well. Therefore in my presence
still smile, dear my sweet, I prithee.'
Jove, I thank thee. I will smile; I will do   170
everything that thou wilt have me. [*Exit.*

Malvolio's 'I do not now fool myself to let imagination jade me'
(lines 155–6) is, of course, the high point of his being duped; it is
the point at which he is so fooled that he is convinced that the very
idea of folly is now out of court, and, like Lysander in the previous
scene from *A Midsummer Night's Dream* (II.ii.115–20), his position
is all the more absurd in that he now claims to be supremely rational
('for every reason excites to this ...', line 156–7). But the process of
duping differs radically from that in *A Midsummer Night's Dream*. In
the latter play the operation of the love-juice is more like a farcical
mechanism programming Lysander to folly. Here the effect of the
spurious letter is less mechanical than psychological; it works on
ground already made fertile by Malvolio's overweening egotism and
ambition. Hence the fairly elaborate build-up to his finding of the
letter dropped in his path. From his very entrance he can be heard
telling himself how much Olivia favours him (for the unspecified
'she' can be none other than his employer). Granted that 'Maria
once told me ...' suggests that the lady's maid has already begun to
say things which influence his state of mind, nevertheless what he
makes of such remarks clearly comes from his excessive readiness to
think well of himself. Whether he ever heard Olivia actually state
that 'should she fancy, it should be one of [his] complexion' is
doubtful. Later in the play, at III.iv.5–6, the audience (though not
Malvolio) hear her say that 'He is sad and civil, / And suits well for a
servant with my fortunes' (i.e. 'He is sober and diplomatic, and is a
very suitable servant for my present state of mind'), and it is just
possible that Malvolio may have heard her say something to that
effect at some time prior to II.v. But it is more likely to be a trick
that Malvolio's own memory plays on him; his deception is internal
– self-deception at least as much as external deception. If the remark
were made by Olivia, and assuming, too, that she used the very word

'fancy', the construction put on it is certainly Malvolio's own. 'Fancy' is an ambiguous word, which, in Elizabethan usage, can range from imagination to falling in love, but it is the latter meaning that Malvolio attaches to it. He is only too ready to seize on any implication in that direction.

In such a potentially gullible condition is he that his mind leaps forward to the fantasy of himself as a successful wooer become husband, and hence 'Count Malvolio' (line 32). There is perhaps an unspoken recognition that this is indeed going too far, but, if so, it is immediately squashed by the precedent he cites to himself of 'the Lady of the Strachy' who 'married the yeoman of the wardrobe' (which is perhaps, as various commentators suggest, a piece of contemporary gossip, adding a touch of topical satire to Malvolio's 'example'). What is brought to the fore by this is class distinction, and the nature of Elizabethan society, which is rigidly stratified, forbidding any climbing out of one's station, but also mobile enough to produce instances of what many would regard as the shocking breakdown of established order. In this context Malvolio becomes the detested social climber, and it is this which the hidden on-stage audience of conspirators mainly focus upon. *Twelfth Night* is a comedy of love, courtship and romantic sentiment, but the steward's fantasised courtship of his mistress has little to do with refined feeling. For him marriage is the means to social promotion (a form of ambition which, interestingly in a male-dominated society, is more disapproved of in a man than a woman) and power over those whom in the petty hierarchy of Olivia's household he has reluctantly to accept as his equals – or, in the case of Sir Toby, his superior. When he does attempt to assert his authority in II.iii, the retort of Sir Toby's that most galls him is one that firmly puts him in his place: 'Art any more than a steward?' (line 108). From the point of view of the revellers he is also a killjoy (Sir Toby continues with 'Dost thou think, because thou art virtuous, there shall be no more cakes and ale?', lines 108–10); and there may well be a political-cum-religious dimension, too, linking him to the self-righteous and anti-prelatical Puritans who, at the end of the sixteenth century, were beginning to assert their opposition to the good old days, and especially what they regarded as the moral laxity and transvestism of the theatre.

But moral values and ideology are not the core of Malvolio. Envy, resentment and self-image count for a good deal more. He craves the status and power of those above him, which is why his fantasies centre on himself as Olivia's consort and a position which allows him, not to consider his inferiors (as, by contrast, we see Olivia expressing concern and consideration for him), but to lord it over them. In his mind, too, he creates a certain kind of style which he feels to be elegant and aloof, but which strikes others as pompous and pedantic. There is, for example, a latinate fulsomeness about his language, evidenced in his dreamy, participial constructions at lines 44–6: 'Calling my officers about me, in my branch'd velvet gown, having come from a day-bed – where I have left Olivia sleeping —'. (The comedy is increased by the way the sense is left dangling in the air, without a main clause to complete it.) He also employs an inflated and affected turn of phrase which is all his own: he does not look, but gives 'a demure travel of regard' (line 50); and 'Seven of my people' (rather than one of his servants) do not hasten to carry out his orders, but 'with an obedient start, make out for [Sir Toby]' (lines 55–6). All of which makes him ripe meat for gulling. The egotism, the overweening ambition and the self-image projected in his language – all, dramatically speaking, brilliantly displayed in the passage from lines 21 to 71 – show that he is in prime condition to be duped by the device Maria has contrived. The theatre audience see and feel this for themselves, so that they, too, are ready for the letter. But to build up the comic tension further, Shakespeare also provides a counterpart for them in the persons of the on-stage con-spirators who eavesdrop on Malvolio's devastating self-revelation. The indignation and contempt expressed by Sir Toby, and the fact that he can hardly be contained by Fabian, provide both a vicarious release for the feelings of the theatre audience and a paradoxically delicious sense of anxiety that the whole hoax will be blown before it has a chance to take hold. (Witness Fabian's 'Nay, patience, or we break the sinews of our plot', line 71).

With the discovery of the letter Malvolio becomes a still more patently absurd figure of fun; the comedy draws nearer to farce. Images used by the watchers hint that he is more animal than human: as he picks up the letter Fabian speaks of him as a woodcock (traditionally regarded as the most easily duped of birds) approaching a trap (line 78), at line 98 Sir Toby disparagingly calls him a badger, and when he seems not quite to be taking the bait as intended he is first compared to a poor specimen of a hawk and then to a hound on a false trail (lines 108, 116). The jokes get coarser, too: Malvolio's reference to the supposed Olivia's handwriting incorporates (unwittingly, of course, on his part – and without the wit to grasp it on Sir Andrew's) a bawdy play on 'cut' = the female organ, and a positively gross image of Olivia urinating in 'thus makes she her great P's' (lines 81–3). And the play on the letter O at lines 123–5 implies knockabout farce as Sir Toby declares, 'I'll cudgel him, and make him cry "O!"'

In a sense this is necessary, for what happens when Malvolio reads the supposed letter from Olivia is that his psychological condition, so carefully prepared in the preceding part of the extract, is played upon to the point where it becomes a blinkering obsession, making him less and less wary of deception that may be practised on him. He becomes (and, again, the imagery, with its overtones of hunting, helps this) a beast/bird to be snared in a trap. He crosses the threshold between comedy and farce, graduating from an overweeningly ambitious character to a ludicrously gullible automaton, lacking the supple intelligence and sensitive awareness which in the well-adjusted human being would save him from skidding on the banana skin put down for him. He becomes more and more the butt of laughter – one whose preposterous behaviour the audience can laugh *at*, and whose gulling arouses few, if any, sympathetic qualms. The letter itself is cleverly composed to heighten this effect. In it he is led by large-sounding generalities (especially the grandiloquent triple parallelism of lines 135–7) to see himself, like a member of the Puritan 'elect', as singled out for peculiar favour, but also to indulge in behaviour that to any but one of his deluded imagination would be the mark of egregious folly rather than election. He is intoxicated with the prospect of being able to release all his hitherto pent-up envy and resentment by simultaneously aping the style which he takes for 'great' and giving full vent to his lust for power over his fellow-servants. Still more grossly, the translation of this suppressed mental state into words and actions is to be accompanied, most preposterously of all (it is a sign of how much he has let his guard drop that he does not immediately recognise its preposterousness) by exchanging his dark, sober garments for biliously inappropriate fashions that Olivia could not be expected to like at any time, and least of all when she is shut up in melancholy mourning for her dead brother. As with the comment at lines 22–4 on Olivia's supposedly favouring 'one of my complexion', memory again plays tricks. The letter commands him to remember who praised his yellow stockings (though, are the audience expected to believe he ever wore them before?), and repeats, 'I say, remember' (lines 144–6), which he swallows whole in his subsequent comment: 'She did commend my yellow stockings ...' (lines 157–8), suggesting even more blatantly than before that the grip on reality for which memory of particular details is an indispensable anchor has competely deserted him.

Finally, the postscript to the letter delivers the *coup de grâce* by egging him on to smile. It is Malvolio's inability to smile – his solemnity and uptight seriousness, his lack of the relaxed, 'cakes-and-ale' approach to life – which has set him at odds with Sir Toby (who, of course, carries such relaxation to excess). Now, in what he takes to be a sign of his elevation above Sir Toby, he is, in fact, being gulled into adopting the badge of easygoing cheerfulness so characteristic of his enemy; and in the process losing that very appearance of sobriety which has stood him in good stead with Olivia, notwithstanding her disapproval of his 'self-love' at I.v.85. Or, rather, the 'self-love' perversely triumphs over the sobriety, as he becomes completely the conspirators' dupe. Though in typically Puritan style he professes to attribute his good fortune to 'Jove' (cf. the substitution of the classical deity for the Christian God in *As You Like It*, II.iv.i), he is wrapped in clouds of extreme egotism which blind him altogether to the lessons of both experience and good sense. He *will* smile, he *will* do everything his imagined Olivia will have him, even though these are the very things that ought to alert him to the dubiousness of these supposed instructions. The letter has thus worked on his predispostion and inner fantasising to push him from comic reverie to what promises to be outright, farcical action totally at cross purposes with the real world in which he lives.

Brief mention should also be made of the other gull in this scene,

Sir Andrew. Although the duping is not aimed at him, and as a member of the group of conspirators taking advantage of Malvolio's gullibility he is an honorary duper rather than a dupe, the audience is reminded of his own status as fool by the limp manner in which he apes the indignation and contempt of Sir Toby, by his failure to see the blatantly bawdy implications of 'Her C's, her U's, and her T's' (line 85), and especially by the way he anticipates himself as the 'foolish knight' referred to by Malvolio at line 73. Being singled out as a fool by Malvolio links the two of them in folly. They are both would-be wooers of Olivia, and, though of quite different characters and in quite different circumstances, both are gulled into thinking they have hopes of her that are ludicrously groundless. But the odd effect of the humour is to make their respective degrees of folly impact quite differently on the audience. Malvolio seems to dig a deeper and deeper pit for himself ; Sir Andrew – though, of course, he completely lacks the audience's respect – is by contrast both ludicrous and likeable. Not to sentimentalise him (after all, he, too, is a fortune-hunter, and in other scenes a stupidly quarrelsome character who lacks the guts to go through with the quarrels he provokes), there is an almost disarming innocence in the readiness with which he recognises Malvolio's allusion as applying to himself. He manages to do this without its in any way constituting true self-knowledge. He lacks the wit to take the offence that he should – and this, of course, has much to do with his proving such an easy prey for Sir Toby. One is nearer with him, notwithstanding the class difference, to the Athenian workmen of *A Midsummer Night's Dream* and their pathetic lack of theatrical sense than to the particular brand of egotism embodied in Malvolio. Malvolio is much the cleverer of the two (but 'clever' rather than 'wise'), and also to that extent the more potentially dangerous to a society based on the good old values of 'cakes and ale'. Laughing at him the audience laugh at something which they feel a slightly anxious need to put down. Laughter at Sir Andrew can afford to be more indulgent. Many, indeed, do call him fool, but it is a folly they can live with.

*   *   *

Much Ado About Nothing, IV.i.1–62. In the church where he was to have married her, Claudio denounces Hero for what he believes to be her unfaithfulness.

Leonato.	Come, Friar Francis, be brief; only to the plain form of marriage, and you shall recount their particular duties afterwards.
Friar.	You come hither, my lord, to marry this lady?
Claudio.	No.
Leonato.	To be married to her, friar! You come to marry her. 5
Friar.	Lady, you come hither to be married to this count?
Hero.	I do.
Friar.	If either of you know any inward impediment why you should not be conjoined, I charge you, on your souls, to utter it.
Claudio.	Know you any, Hero? 10
Hero.	None, my lord.
Friar.	Know you any, Count?
Leonato.	I dare make his answer, None.
Claudio.	O, what men dare do! What men may do! What men daily do, not knowing what they do! 15
Benedick.	How now! Interjections? Why, then, some be of laughing, as, ah, ha, he!
Claudio.	Stand thee by, friar. Father, by your leave: Will you with free and unconstrained soul Give me this maid, your daughter?
Leonato.	As freely, son, as God did give her me. 20
Claudio.	And what have I to give you back whose worth May counterpoise this rich and precious gift?
Don Pedro.	Nothing, unless you render her again.
Claudio.	Sweet Prince, you learn me noble thankfulness. There, Leonato, take her back again; 25 Give not this rotten orange to your friend; She's but the sign and semblance of her honour. Behold how like a maid she blushes here. O, what authority and show of truth Can cunning sin cover itself withal! 30

	Comes not that blood as modest evidence	
	To witness simple virtue? Would you not swear,	
	All you that see her, that she were a maid	
	By these exterior shows? But she is none:	
	She knows the heat of a luxurious bed;	35
	Her blush is guiltiness, not modesty.	
Leonato.	What do you mean, my lord?	
Claudio.	Not to be married,	
	Not to knit my soul to an approved wanton.	
Leonato.	Dear, my lord, if you, in your own proof,	40
	Have vanquish'd the resistance of her youth,	
	And made defeat of her virginity —	
Claudio.	I know what you would say. If I have known her,	
	You will say she did embrace me as a husband,	
	And so extenuate the 'forehand sin.	45
	No, Leonato,	
	I never tempted her with word too large	
	But, as a brother to his sister, show'd	
	Bashful sincerity and comely love.	
Hero.	And seem'd I ever otherwise to you?	50
Claudio.	Out on thee! Seeming! I will write against it.	
	You seem to me as Dian in her orb,	
	As chaste as is the bud ere it be blown;	
	But you are more intemperate in your blood	
	Than Venus, or those pamp'red animals	55
	That rage in savage sensuality.	
Hero.	Is my lord well, that he doth speak so wide?	
Leonato.	Sweet Prince, why speak not you?	
Don Pedro.	What should I speak?	
	I stand dishonour'd that have gone about	
	To link my dear friend to a common stale.	60
Leonato.	Are these things spoken, or do I but dream?	
Don John.	Sir, they are spoken, and these things are true.	
Benedick.	This looks not like a nuptial.	
Hero.	True! O God!	

This is the climax of the Claudio–Hero plot of *Much Ado About Nothing* (and it also, later, precipitates the climax of the Benedick–Beatrice plot, leading to Beatrice's demand that Benedick 'Kill Claudio', line 287). In the main it seems tragic rather than comic; and certainly Claudio's speech at lines 24–36 is the kind of speech one would expect to find in a tragedy such as *Hamlet*, or one of the later tragicomedies (or 'problem plays') such as *Measure for Measure*, rather than the comedies of the 1590s. It shows the same preoccupation with outrages of the 'blood' (unbridled passion and animality) and the sense of sexuality (at least outside marriage, but almost sexuality *per se*) as something criminally disgusting – all in the closely related context of a bitterly perceived contrast between appearance and reality. Claudio's diatribe against 'seeming', for example, is a precursor of Hamlet's picking on his mother's use of the same word and turning it into an occasion for inveighing against 'all forms, moods, shapes of grief' which merely 'seem' (*Hamlet*, I.ii.75–86). The imagery is likewise packed with excessive disgust: the tainted (as Claudio sees her) Hero becomes 'this rotten orange' (line 26), and she 'knows the heat of a luxurious bed' (line 35, where 'luxurious' has a different meaning from its modern use, suggesting lascivious and illicit sexuality, with 'heat' and 'bed' carrying the connotation of violently climactic intercourse). Claudio is in the grip of an extreme revulsion like that which seizes Othello when he is deceived into thinking Desdemona false, and like Othello (if less eloquently) he swings, in lines 51–5, from the image of Hero as a chaste Diana, or unblown rose, to the very embodiment of sensuality in the goddess of love, Venus, or animals (on heat perhaps) raging with lust.

However, the context is still that of comedy rather than tragedy. The audience knows that the perpetrators of the plot against Hero are under arrest, and that it cannot be long before Claudio and Don Pedro come to realise how they have been deceived. Hence what Claudio does in the present scene, painful as it is, impacts on the audience as a cruel, but temporary, mistake. And the way the scene begins has light-hearted as well as serious implications. When Claudio unexpectedly replies, 'No' to the Friar's question at line 3, Leonato turns it into a verbal quibble: Claudio means that he has come to *be* married; Leonato takes it on himself to explain that the

Friar will do the marrying! Inappropriate as it might seem to indulge in such verbal nit-picking in church and at the solemn occasion of a wedding, wordplay was a standard element in Elizabethan comedies, Shakespeare's not excepted, and it might well seem to a contemporary audience that this was all part of the comic mood.

There is likewise some comic continuity in lines 14–15 with the inflated rhetoric used by Claudio at I.i.252–90 (the scene already analysed in Chapter 5, pp. 85–8). On one level Claudio's sardonic comment on Leonato's blithe assumption that the bridegroom cannot possibly know of any impediment to the wedding sounds an ominous warning of the outburst that is soon to come; on another it is pompously repetitive, and signalled as such by Benedick's essentially comic reaction: 'How now! Interjections? Why, then, some be of laughing, as, ah, ha, he!' (line 16). The editor of the Oxford Shakespeare *Much Ado About Nothing* suggests that this is an echo of the standard Elizabethan school grammar by William Lyly, which gives 'Ha, ha, he' as an example of the interjection. If so, it would underline that immature, jejune quality which seems characteristic of Claudio, and give further emphasis to the element of the ridiculous in what he says.

As already suggested, from line 25 onwards Claudio sounds more decidedly like a tragically deluded figure; but with the comment at line 62, 'This looks not like a nuptial' (and, like the mocking reference to interjections, it comes, significantly, from Benedick), the ludicrously unusual nature of this radical departure from the expected makes itself felt once more. Although Hero's exclamation, 'True! O God!' is in deadly earnest, this hint that there is a comic as well as a tragic dimension to Claudio's outburst helps to keep the scene in perspective. In addition, there is Leonato's bewildered question at line 60, 'Are these things spoken, or do I but dream?' which, for a moment at least, gives us a hint of that kind of awareness of illusion so fully explored in *A Midsummer Night's Dream*. It is immediately countered by Don John's assertion that these things are spoken, and these things are true, but that does not altogether dispel the sense of illusion. If anything, it is reinforced, for we know perfectly well that, although they are *spoken*, they are not *true*; and confirmation coming from Don John – who, as the audience know, takes perverse satsfaction in propagating evil – is counter-productive. His laconically gloomy presence on stage throughout the scene (more evident in production than perhaps it is when the text is merely read) underlines his status as the 'melancholy' malcontent whose judgement is not to be trusted; and it serves as a constant reminder that what appears so tragic is something spitefully contrived by him. He is the spectre at the feast, paradoxically throwing festive qualities into contrasting relief.

None of this means, of course, that Claudio's denunciation is likely to make the audience heave with laughter. But the slightly distancing effect of Benedick's comments and Leonato's bewilderment (helped by the studied extravagance of Claudio's language) are elements which keep the audience alert to the preposterously deluded nature of it all. Claudio remains a dupe, and his already perceived immaturity is what contributes to his over-ready susceptibility to delusion. The scene is fundamentally histrionic rather than tragic (close as it comes at times to tragedy), and the features which underline that histrionic quality are likewise the ones which help to preserve its overall function as part of the vicissitudes built into comedy.

*　　*　　*

Much Ado About Nothing, IV.ii.1–86 (1–81). Dogberry and Verges, with the help of the Sexton, examine their prisoners, Conrade and Borachio.

Dogberry.	Is our whole dissembly appear'd?
Verges.	O, a stool and a cushion for the sexton!
Sexton.	Which be the malefactors?
Dogberry.	Marry, that am I and my partner.
Verges.	Nay, that's certain; we have the exhibition to examine. 5
Sexton.	But which are the offenders that are to be examin'd?
	Let them come before Master Constable.
Dogberry.	Yea, marry, let them come before me.
	What is your name, friend?
Borachio.	Borachio. 10
Dogberry.	Pray write down Borachio. Yours, sirrah?
Conrade.	I am a gentleman, sir, and my name is Conrade.

Dogberry.	Write down Master Gentleman Conrade. Masters, do you serve God?
Conrade. *Borachio.* }	Yea, sir, we hope. 15
Dogberry.	Write down that they hope they serve God; and write God first; for God defend but God should go before such villains! Masters, it is proved already that you are little better than false knaves, and it will go near to be thought so shortly. How answer you for 20 yourselves?
Conrade.	Marry, sir, we say we are none.
Dogberry.	A marvellous witty fellow, I assure you; but I will go about with him. Come you hither, sirrah; a word in your ear: sir, I say to you it is thought you are false 25 knaves.
Borachio.	Sir, I say to you we are none.
Dogberry.	Well, stand aside. Fore God, they are both in a tale. Have you writ down that they are none?
Sexton.	Master Constable, you go not the way to examine; 30 you must call forth the watch that are their accusers.
Dogberrry.	Yea, marry, that's the eftest way. Let the watch come forth. Masters, I charge you in the Prince's name, accuse these men.
1 Watch.	This man said, sir, that Don John, the Prince's 35 brother, was a villain.
Dogberry.	Write down Prince John a villain. Why, this is flat perjury, to call a prince's brother villain.
Borachio.	Master Constable –
Dogberry.	Pray thee, fellow, peace; I do not like thy look, 40 I promise thee.
Sexton.	What heard you him say else?
.2 Watch.	Marry, that he had received a thousand ducats of Don John for accusing the Lady Hero wrongfully.
Dogberry.	Flat burglary as ever was committed. 45
Verges.	Yea, by mass, that it is.
Sexton.	What else, fellow?
1 Watch.	And that Count Claudio did mean, upon his words,

to disgrace Hero before the whole assembly, and not
marry her.   50

Dogberry.   O villain! thou wilt be condemn'd into everlasting
redemption for this.

Sexton.   What else?

2 Watch.   This is all.

Sexton.   And this is more, masters, than you can deny. Prince 55
John is this morning secretly stol'n away; Hero was in
this manner accus'd, in this very manner refus'd, and
upon the grief of this suddenly died. Master Constable,
let these men be bound and brought to Leonato's; I will
go before and show him their examination. [*Exit.*   60

Dogberry.   Come, let them be opinion'd.

Verges.   Let them be in the hands.

Conrade.   Off, coxcomb.

Dogberry.   God's my life, where's the sexton? Let him write
down the Prince's officer coxcomb. Come, bind   65
them. Thou naughty varlet!

Conrade.   Away! you are an ass, you are an ass.

Dogberry.   Dost thou not suspect my place? Dost thou not
suspect my years? O that he were here to write me
down an ass! But, masters, remember that I am an   70
ass; though it be not written down, yet forget not
that I am an ass. No, thou villain, thou art full of
piety, as shall be prov'd upon thee by good witness.
I am a wise fellow; and, which is more, an officer;
and, which is more, a householder; and, which   75
is more, as pretty a piece of flesh as any is in Messina;
and one that knows the law, go to; and a rich fellow
enough, go to; and a fellow that hath had losses; and
one that hath two gowns, and everything handsome
about him. Bring him away. O that I had been writ 80
down an ass! [*Exeunt.*

It is appropriate to match the extract from the beginning of IV.i with
this scene which follows. Both concern dupes of comedy. If,
however, classifying Claudio as 'dupe' may seem to involve some

rather special pleading, few would deny the term to Dogberry and
Verges. They are the classic dupes, or butts, of comedy. Not that
they are deceived by any practice such as that which is foisted on
Claudio; they are deceived by themselves – by their own ignorant
self-importance which makes them unable to distinguish the irrelevant from the relevant, or to use language properly, or, indeed, to see
what is plainly before their eyes. The shrewdness and efficiency of
the Sexton provides an excellent foil; he embodies the good sense
which is the implicit standard comedy brings to bear on its characters, and by which Dogberry and Verges are found so laughably
wanting. Dogberry, in particular, with his pretentious attempt to use
words which he thinks grand and impressive, but of which he does
not know the meaning, beautifully exemplies Ben Jonson's dictum,
'Speak that I may know thee.' His malapropisms (the word is taken
from Sheridan's Mrs Malaprop, but might well have been 'dogber-
ryism', from these earlier examples of verbal misappropriation), his
misplaced sense of prestige (at its most ludicrous in lines 16–18,
where the effect of his command would be to make God appear to
serve Conrade and Borachio), and his penchant for high-sounding
syntactic parallelism (which reaches the ridiculous-sublime in the
closing lines of the scene) – all these are the character of Dogberry
realised in a language unique to him. The climax of his preoccupation with his own status and dignity is the anguish with which he
wishes for the return of the Sexton to 'write him down an ass' – a
phrase in which he neatly, but unconsciously, encapsulates both his
true status as dupe and his inability to appreciate the real significance of the criminal evidence he has under his hands.

For the other – and, with regard to the play's structure, even more
important – aspect of the scene is that it shows comic incompetence
nonetheless making its contribution to the ultimately comic denouement. The Watch has, after all, apprehended Don John's villainous
henchmen, Conrade and Borachio, and thanks to the good sense
of the Sexton, the facts behind their deception are in the process
of emerging. Moreover, the very comedy of Dogberry's pompous
egotism and irrelevance helps to establish a mood which qualifies the
potentially tragic violence of the preceding and succeeding scenes.
(Isolating a passage for critical analysis should not be done without

also taking into account the way that passage dovetails with the rest of the ongoing action: the audience in the theatre – particularly the Elizabethan theatre – experience a continuous flow of words and action which encourages the modification of attitude and response by what has gone before and what spectators sense at the back of their minds is still to come.)

To call this 'comic relief', as traditional criticism has so often done, is not in itself mistaken: there is some truth in the idea that painful tension needs to be relieved if an audience's emotions are not to be overstrained. But it can be misleading in so far as it suggests that such a scene as the present one is interpolated in a purely arbitrary way, for that purpose alone. The delusions suffered by Dogberry and Verges are a kind of comically inverted, contrapuntal echo of the delusion foisted on Claudio and Don Pedro, and they form a link in the chain of delusions (including, for example, the disguised wooing of Don Pedro and the deceptions practised on Benedick and Beatrice to make each believe the other is in love with him/her) which constitute the 'much ado about nothing' that gives the play its title. Although the seriousness of some of these delusions stands in contrast to the triviality of those suffered by Dogberry and Verges, the thematic connection between them is what helps to create the necessary comic sense that, in the end, the 'ado' is indeed about 'nothing'.

The ridiculously inflated notions of status and authority exemplified by Dogberry in this scene likewise have their comically deflating link with the high political and social authority enjoyed by Don Pedro and Claudio. The one is a ludicrous parody of the other; and though it may not be subversive to the extent of undermining, or presaging the collapse of, more serious authority (as, it may be argued, is the case with the treatment of authority in a tragedy such as *King Lear*), it does help to open up a chink in the façade which has to be maintained in a hierarchical society. In this connection even such a manifest verbal howler as Dogberry's 'Dost thou not suspect my place? Dost thou not suspect my years?' (lines 68–9) makes an at least subliminal point. 'Respect' is the word he wants; but, thanks to his linguistic incompetence, 'respect' becomes 'suspect', and authority is in danger of being written down an ass.

Similarly, that Conrade the 'villain' is designated by Dogberry as 'full of piety' (lines 72–3) rather than 'impious' has its inappropriate appropriateness to the way Don John takes on the role of moral judge when he accuses Hero of dissembling and disloyalty ('The word [disloyal] is too good to paint out her wickedness', III.ii.97–8): true villainy takes on a false appearance of piety, and true piety the false appearance of villainy. The accusation subsequently made by Claudio is also redolent of villainy which is 'full of piety'; for, as we have seen in the analysis of the opening of IV.i, the deluded Claudio makes an extravagantly self-righteous denunciation of Hero's supposed disloyalty, and shows his doubtful 'piety' by doing it in the full, ceremonial context of a church wedding. He, too, is one that has 'everything hanndsome about him', and in his own way deserves to be 'writ down an ass'.

Conclusions

Misunderstandings, misconceptions and misleading appearances, accidentally run into or deliberately foisted, are the very stuff of comedy; and for Shakespeare, writing at a time when the English language was in the process of absorbing an unprecedented number of confusing, as well as enriching, new words from other languages (especially Latin), misunderstanding and misappropriation of language must also be added to the list. Comic characters are frequently the victims, or dupes, of all these things. The most obvious dupes are those who are rendered laughable by their simple, innate incompetence – like Dogberry, they are sublime in their total lack of suspicion of their own follies, or like Sir Andrew Aguecheek, pathetically funny in their sheer gullibility. Others are the ignorant victims of delusions foisted upon them from outside, though they may also, as is the case with the lovers in *A Midsummer Night's Dream*, exemplify in their puppet-like reactions the influence on human conduct, especially in matters of sex and love, of ludicrous conventions and irrational forces over which they deceive themselves into thinking they have rational control. There are still other dupes, however, who – though they may, like Malvolio and Claudio, have deception practised on them — are deceived because, fundamentally, they are deceive-able. The flaws in their own sense of righteousness, or their half-acknowledged fantasies, or their immature understanding, make them vulnerable to the tricks played upon them; and the consequences can be either riotously funny or dangerously disruptive. To be a dupe of this kind is also to be, at least potentially, a tragic figure. Nevertheless, in the world of Shakespeare's comedies tragedy does not completely take over: Malvolio remains a figure of fun, despite his capacity to suggest the partially justified malcontent, and Claudio betrays a rhetorical extravagance which, close as it comes to the rhetoric of tragedy, manages to keep him as a dupe within the frame and values of comedy. That both of these more inward dupes seem to operate on the borders of comedy and tragedy is a reminder of the mingled rather than 'pure' nature of Shakespearean comedy; but, on the other hand, that they are still kept within the overall bounds of comedy is also a reminder of the subtle way in which Shakespeare operates his comic controls.

7

Fools (2): Clever Fools

Introduction

There is another class of fools in Shakespeare's comedies who are not, strictly speaking, fools at all – though 'Fool' is what they are called, and playing the fool is what, theoretically, they spend their time doing. In fact, however, they are professionals who earn a living, invariably at the courts of kings or aristocrats, by their wits. They have to be adroit and adaptable, accommodating themselves to the way the wind blows in the draughty corridors of power – although they are not, therefore, sycophantic time-servers. On the contrary, Shakespeare's clever Fools can be remarkably outspoken. Much of their work is done in set-piece demonstrations of wit; but they are also shrewd observers of those around them, whether below or above in the social hierarchy, and, far from being really foolish themselves, they are often the sharpest exposers of folly in others.

Fools of this kind tend to appear in the later rather than the earlier comedies, and it has been suggested that this reflects a change in the personnel of Shakespeare's company of players, the Lord Chamberlain's Men (which after the accession of James I became the King's Men). In 1600 William Kempe, who played a number of comic characters, including Justice Shallow in *Henry IV, Part 2* and Dogberry in *Much Ado About Nothing*, left Shakespeare's company, and was replaced (or perhaps had already been displaced) by Robert Armin, an actor with an altogether different, less farcical, style. The latter almost certainly played Feste in *Twelfth Night* and the Fool in

King Lear; and, whether or not he played Touchstone in *As You Like It*, that, too, was a character suited to his talents.

It is in the two later comedies that one also gets references within the text to the Fool which suggest the more refined nature of the role it had become. In *As You Like It*, for example, Jaques reports to Duke Senior on his meeting with Touchstone in the Forest of Arden in terms which suggest the sharpness and acuteness of the Fool's wit:

> in his brain,
> Which is as dry as the remainder biscuit
> After a voyage, he hath strange places cramm'd
> With observation, the which he vents
> In mangled forms. (II.vii.38–42)

And in *Twelfth Night* both Olivia and Viola pay generous tributes to Feste. One occurs in the passage from I.v discussed in the analyses below, and the other in III.i, after a characteristic passage of repartee between Feste and Viola. Left to herself, Viola delivers a short speech which is almost a job description for the new kind of Fool:

> This fellow is wise enough to play the fool;
> And to do that well craves a kind of wit.
> He must observe their mood on whom he jests,
> The quality of persons, and the time;
> And, like the haggard [a tame hawk], check at every feather
> That comes before his eye. This is a practice
> As full of labour as a wise man's art;
> For folly that he wisely shows is fit;
> But wise men, folly-fall'n, quite taint their wit. (III.i.57–65)

The following analyses are, therefore, mainly taken from *As You Like It* and *Twelfth Night*, and feature, or refer to, Touchstone and Feste. The two first extracts, however, are from *A Midsummer Night's Dream*, and concern what seems to be the more Kempe-like role of Bottom. But Bottom is an interesting case of a comic character who has something in common with both a Dogberry and a Touchstone. He is a dupe (specifically of Puck), and yet also has an element of the clever fool in him (if only in his own estimation!). Properly speaking, he belongs to neither of the categories with which Chapters 6 and 7 are respectively concerned. But this makes him all the more interesting as a transitional figure between them.

Analyses

A Midsummer Night's Dream, III.i.125–86 (125–89). Bottom, having been transformed by Puck with an ass's head, sings and awakens Titania, who, also subject to Puck's mischievous magic, falls in love with him.

Titania.	I pray thee, gentle mortal, sing again.	125
	Mine ear is much enamoured of thy note;	
	So is mine eye enthralled to thy shape;	
	And thy fair virtue's force perforce doth move me,	
	On the first view, to say, to swear, I love thee.	
Bottom.	Methinks, mistress, you should have little reason	130
	for that. And yet, to say the truth, reason and love	
	keep little company together now-a-days. The more	
	the pity that some honest neighbours will not make	
	them friends. Nay, I can gleek upon occasion.	
Titania.	Thou art as wise as thou art beautiful.	135
Bottom.	Not so, neither; but if I had wit enough to get	
	out of this wood, I have enough to serve mine	
	own turn.	
Titania.	Out of this wood do not desire to go;	
	Thou shalt remain here whether thou wilt or no.	140
	I am a spirit of no common rate;	
	The summer still doth tend upon my state;	
	And I do love thee; therefore, go with me.	
	I'll give thee fairies to attend on thee;	
	And they shall fetch thee jewels from the deep,	145
	And sing, while thou on pressed flowers dost sleep;	
	And I will purge thy mortal grossness so	
	That thou shalt like an airy spirit go.	
	Peaseblossom! Cobweb! Moth! and Mustardseed!	

Enter PEASEBLOSSOM, COBWEB, MOTH, *and*
MUSTARDSEED.

Peaseblossom.	Ready.
Cobweb.	And I.
Moth.	And I.
Mustardseed.	And I.
All.	Where shall we go?

150

Titania.   Be kind and courteous to this gentleman;
          Hop in his walks and gambol in his eyes;
          Feed him with apricocks and dewberries,
          With purple grapes, green figs, and mulberries;
          The honey bags steal from the humble-bees,   155
          And for night-tapers crop their waxen thighs,
          And light them at the fiery glow-worm's eyes,
          To have my love to bed and to arise;
          And pluck the wings from painted butterflies,
          To fan the moonbeams from his sleeping eyes.   160
          Nod to him, elves, and do him courtesies.

Peaseblossom.	Hail, mortal!
Cobweb.	Hail!
Moth.	Hail!
Mustard.	Hail! 165

Bottom.   I cry your worships mercy, heartily; I beseech
          your worship's name.

Cobweb.   Cobweb.

Bottom.   I shall desire you of more acquaintance, good
          Master Cobweb. If I cut my finger, I shall make   170
          bold with you. Your name, honest gentleman?

Peaseblossom. Peaseblossom.

Bottom.   I pray you, commend me to Mistress Squash,
          your mother, and to Master Peascod, your father.
          Good Master Peaseblossom, I shall desire you   175
          of more acquaintance too. Your name, I beseech
          you, sir?

Mustardseed. Mustardseed.

Bottom.   Good Master Mustardseed, I know your patience

well. That same cowardly giant-like ox-beef hath   180
devour'd many a gentleman of your house. I
promise you your kindred hath made my eyes
water ere now. I desire you of more acquaintance,
good Master Mustardseed.

Titania.   Come, wait upon him; lead him to my bower.   185
The moon, methinks, looks with a wat'ry eye;
And when she weeps, weeps every little flower,
Lamenting some enforced chastity.
Tie up my love's tongue, bring him silently. [*Exeunt.*

In this extract there are two dupes, Titania and Bottom – both
victims of Puck's magic powers. Titania, like the lovers in this play, is
subject to the love-juice which makes her fall in love with the first
thing she sees on waking; and, interestingly, she is like the lovers in
invoking the force of love at first sight (line 129). Bottom is a dupe
by virtue of the trick played on him by Puck, i.e. his transformation
with the ass's head; but the text does not suggest that he is subject, as
Titania is, to the irrational power of love. On the contrary, it is
he who comments on the division between reason and love (lines
130–2). It is true that he loses his power to act independently: he
would like to use his 'wit' (= intelligence, good sense) to get out of
the irrational world symbolised by the wood (Shakespeare makes use
of the double meaning, in Elizabethan English, of the word 'wood',
as a noun meaning 'forest', and as an adjective 'mad'), but Titania,
with her supernatural powers, will not allow him. In no way,
however, does he lose his presence of mind or his natural self-posses-
sion. In one obvious respect that is a consequence of his being too
thick-witted to take much notice of the difference. His 'rude
mechanical' status contrasts strikingly, and with delightful comedy,
with Titania's airy refinement as a delicate, supernatural figure. As
she claims, she is 'a spirit of no common rate', and the rhymed couplets she speaks are full of delicate, imaginative effects; while Bottom
is the very embodiment of 'mortal grossness' – which Titania laughably promises to 'purge' away (lines 147–8) – and speaks in more
pedestrian prose.

Undoubtedly, the scene is designed to be played for laughs: on the one hand Titania is the romantic and imperious Queen of the Fairies who can command jewels to be fetched from the depths of the ocean, on the other Bottom is a down-to-earth working man whose mind runs on thoughts of peascods (with the inevitably bawdy associations of 'codpiece') and joints of ox-beef. On the stage, too, it is usual, at the cue given by line 189 ('Tie up my love's tongue, bring him silently') for his singing to decline into a ludicrous version of a donkey's braying, thus, allied with the grotesque appearance of the head, making the grossness grosser still. But the ease with which Bottom adapts to his totally unprecedented situation, and the instinctive courtesy with which he addresses the fairies whom Titania allocates him as his attendants, is admirable. He dignifies them with the title 'Master', or 'worship', or 'honest gentleman', (though such politeness to menials may well have seemed more ludicrous to Shakespeare's contemporary audiences than it does to us); and, besides creating a smooth, relaxed, social atmosphere, this also reveals the adroitness with which Bottom can adjust to new situations and turn them to his advantage. As elsewhere in the play, the form his adjustment takes may seem ridiculous, but in terms of his awareness and background it is both intelligent and practical. Bottom is a great survivor. The incongruities of this scene are ludicrous; but, as almost any performance of *A Midsummer Night's Dream* will testify, Bottom invariably gets the audience on his side. For comedy itself is a matter of adjusting to life, and audiences recognise in him a native genius for doing precisely that.

*   *   *

A Midsummer Night's Dream, IV.i.197–220 (197–215). Bottom, the ass's head removed, wakes from sleep, and thinks himself still at rehearsal, remembering his adventures only as a dream.

Bottom　　[*Awaking*] When my cue comes, call me, and I will
　　　　　answer. My next is 'Most fair Pyramus'. Heigh-ho!
　　　　　Peter Quince! Flute, the bellows-mender! Snout,
　　　　　the tinker! Starveling! God's my life, stol'n hence,　　200
　　　　　and left me asleep! I have had a most rare vision.

> I have had a dream, past the wit of man to say what
> dream it was. Man is but an ass if he go about to
> expound this dream. Methought I was – there is
> no man can tell what. Methought I was, and   205
> methought I had, but man is a patch'd fool, if he
> will offer to say what methought I had. The eye of
> man hath not heard, the ear of man hath not seen,
> man's hand is not able to taste, his tongue to conceive,
> nor his heart to report, what my dream was. I will   210
> get Peter Quince to write a ballad of this dream.
> It shall be call'd 'Bottom's Dream', because it hath
> no bottom; and I will sing it in the latter end of a
> play, before the Duke. Peradventure, to make it
> the more gracious, I shall sing it at her death. [*Exit.*   215

Again, Bottom shows himself laughable, but also adaptable. The confusion between dream-world and real world, which is fundamental in *A Midsummer Night's Dream*, is neatly encapsulated in the bewilderment Bottom experiences as he wakes up. At first he reacts as if in the middle of the rehearsal of *Pyramus and Thisby*, where he had made his exit as Pyramus on the line, '*And by and by I will to thee appear*' (III.i.78), and was waiting for his cue to reappear. Then he shouts the names of his fellow-actors, only to realise he is alone, and to conclude that they must have deserted him while he was asleep.

Now images of his Titania adventure seem to come back to him, but in the vague, undifferentiated form of 'dream' or 'rare vision': it was something momentous, and as he struggles to recollect it, what most strikes him is the marvellous incomprehensibility of it all. The effort shatters his syntax. He begins perhaps to say that it seemed to him he was transformed into an ass, or that he had an ass's head on his shoulders, but he cannot finish his sentences – which leaves open the alternative interpretation that he intends to say that it seemed to him that he was beloved of the Fairy Queen and had a train of fairies to do his bidding. By not being specific, however, the broken syntax has the advantage of suggesting an ambiguous state of bewilderment and elation which opens up vast and mysteriously undefined possibilities.

What is certain is that Bottom does not have any sense of shame or humiliation. The allusions to man as 'an ass', and man as 'a patch'd fool' ('patch'd' reminding the audience of the parti-coloured garment worn by the professional Fool) bring the idea of being duped, or duping, into the discourse, but clearly Bottom's self-confidence is not dented by this. It is those who would misguidedly seek to put a semantic limit to his dream who are cast by him in the role of dupes. He, on the contrary, is carried away in a quasi-religious rapture which makes him quote the Bible (lines 207–10) as he glories in the transcendent indefinableness of the experience with which he has been blessed. Of course, he *mis*quotes. An Elizabethan audience, compelled to regular churchgoing, would be entirely familar with the proper text; and even a modern, non-biblical audience can quickly spot the confusion of the senses of seeing, hearing and tasting in Bottom's version. This semi-literate corruption of the text relegates him once more to the status of dupe and the butt of comedy. Yet, uproariously funny as this may be, Bottom's enthusiasm drives him irresistibly on to imagine a higher level of reality where the dream is almost a divine revelation, to be communicated as scripture to the rest of less fortunate humanity: 'I will get Peter Quince to write a ballad of this dream ...'.

The joke here is on cheapjack accounts of wonders and miracles which are hawked around for popular consumption at fairs and other such social gatherings, and would, no doubt, be especially amusing to the more aristocratic members of Shakespeare's audience (who would also find the pun on 'Bottom' and 'bottom', intended for the groundlings, a banality that would flatter their own taste for more recondite and witty wordplay). Once again, however, Bottom's executive drive enables him to convert what is, on one level, stupidity into positive gain (literally so, in that the sale of the ballad sheets will yield a tidy little profit). It will become an addition to the forthcoming performance of *Pyramus and Thisby*, 'to make it the more gracious', and particularly so if sung at the death of the heroine. If the incongruity of this passes him by, as it blissfully seems to do, it is fully apparent to his audience, and gives them further laughs. Yet even while they laugh, they delight in the ingenuity of his invention, and recognise in him a kind of natural entrepreneur who always has an eye to the main chance and a good bargain.

If being a dupe is to be put down, this dupe is incapable of being duped, for he can never be put down. He bounces up like a cork in a stream, and sails merrily on his way, forever getting the better of people and events that would seem to get the better of him, and converting them into gain. He is a fool; but, like the professional Fool, he has a gift for living by his wits (thick-witted though he may be), and he is blessed with the special talent of turning a dream into 'a most rare vision'.

*   *   *

As You Like It, III.ii.11–75 (11–81). Corin and Touchstone debate the merits of court and country life.

Corin.	And how like you this shepherd's life, Master Touchstone?
Touchstone.	Truly, shepherd, in respect of itself, it is a good life; but in respect that it is a shepherd's life, it is nought. In respect that it is solitary, I like it very well; but in respect that it is private, it is a very vile life. Now in respect it is in the fields, it pleaseth me well; but in 15 respect it is not in the court, it is tedious. As it is a spare life, look you, it fits my humour well; but as there is no more plenty in it, it goes much against my stomach. Hast any philosophy in thee, shepherd? 20
Corin.	No more but that I know the more one sickens the worse at ease he is; and that he that wants money, means, and content, is without three good friends; that the property of rain is to wet, and fire to burn; 25 that good pasture makes fat sheep; and that a great cause of the night is lack of the sun; that he that hath learned no wit by nature nor art may complain of good breeding, or comes of a very dull kindred.
Touchstone.	Such a one is a natural philosopher. Wast ever in 30 court, shepherd?

Corin.	No, truly.
Touchstone.	Then thou art damn'd.
Corin.	Nay, I hope.
Touchstone.	Truly, thou art damn'd, like an ill-roasted egg, 35 all on one side.
Corin.	For not being at court? Your reason.
Touchstone.	Why, if thou never wast at court thou never saw'st good manners; if thou never saw'st good manners, then thy manners must be wicked; and wickedness 40 is sin, and sin is damnation. Thou art in a parlous state, shepherd.
Corin.	Not a whit, Touchstone. Those that are good manners at the court are as ridiculous in the country as the behaviour of the country is most mockable 45 at the court. You told me you salute not at the court, but you kiss your hands; that courtesy would be uncleanly if courtiers were shepherds.
Touchstone.	Instance, briefly; come, instance.
Corin.	Why, we are still handling our ewes; and their 50 fells, you know, are greasy.
Touchstone.	Why, do not your courtier's hands sweat? And is not the grease of a mutton as wholesome as the sweat of a man? Shallow, shallow. A better instance, I say; come. 55
Corin.	Besides, our hands are hard.
Touchstone.	Your lips will feel them the sooner. Shallow again. A more sounder instance; come.
Corin.	And they are often tarr'd over with the surgery of our sheep; and would you have us kiss tar? The 60 courtier's hands are perfum'd with civet.
Touchstone.	Most shallow man! thou worm's meat in respect of a good piece of flesh indeed! Learn of the wise, and perpend: civet is of a baser birth than tar – the very uncleanly flux of a cat. Mend the instance, shepherd. 65
Corin.	You have too courtly a wit for me; I'll rest.
Touchstone.	Wilt thou rest damn'd? God help thee, shallow man! God make incision in thee! thou art raw.

Corin.	Sir, I am a true labourer: I earn that I eat, get that	
	I wear; owe no man hate, envy no man's happiness;	70
	glad of other men's good, content with my harm;	
	and the greatest of my pride is to see my ewes graze	
	and my lambs suck.	
Touchstone.	That is another simple sin in you: to bring the	
	ewes and the rams together, and to offer to get	75
	your living by the copulation of cattle; to be bawd	
	to a bell-wether, and to betray a she-lamb of a twelve-	
	month to a crooked-pated, old, cuckoldly ram,	
	out of all reasonable match. If thou beest not	
	damn'd for this, the devil himself will have no	80
	shepherds; I cannot see else how thou shouldst scape.	

As You Like It is a pastoral play (but with a somewhat unconventional view of the pastoral), and this debate between Corin and Touchstone is a variation on one of the standard themes of the pastoral – the virtues of the country life versus the iniquities of the court. What Touchstone does, however, is to stand the convention on its head, using his (essentially courtly) wit to devalue the country by comparison with the court. Or so it appears. What he achieves is something more subtle than the mere reversal of pastoral's assumption that country life is simpler and purer than that of the sophisticated, but worldly court. True to his name – which suggests the capacity to examine things and find out whether they come up to the mark – he calls into question much of the sentiment surrounding pastoral idealisation of the country life; but in the process he also exposes some of the less pleasant aspects of what he nominally represents as the superior way of life of the court. Corin's role in this dialectic, like the role of the interlocutor in so many of Plato's Socratic dialogues, is to act as the sounding-board for Touchstone's probing intelligence; or, to use a less exalted analogy, he is like the 'straight man' in a modern comic duo, who feeds the clever comedian with the opportunities he needs to show off his wit. Yet here, too, the actual execution of the role goes beyond its formal purpose, and in the verbal sparring match that we see and hear Corin acquits himself much better than the standard comic stooge.

Touchstone's reply to Corin's opening question is a dazzlingly stylish performance. In fact, it is more style than substance. He adopts the pose of one sitting judicially on the fence, finding an equal tally of positives and negatives in the shepherd's life, and this is matched stylistically by the carefully contrived see-saw of his rhetoric, in which every clause naming a good quality has a balancing 'but' clause. In reality, however, he says virtually nothing, for his balancing negatives are merely the positives stated in different terms: desirable solitariness becomes vile privacy; life in the country becomes deprivation of life at court; frugality (implying a simple diet which is good for one's health) becomes meanness (which is dull and tasteless). The speech is full of repetitive formulae: 'in respect of itself ... but in respect that ...'; 'In respect that .... but in respect that ...'; 'Now in respect it is ... but in respect it is not ...'; 'As it is a ..., but as there is no ...'. All the verbal motions of a rationally considered thought-process are there, and act like a conjuror's sleight of hand; but not even a rabbit is produced from the hat. We have got no further at the end of the speech than at the beginning, except that a cleverly contrived illusion has been produced of an intelligently well-balanced mind at work trying conscientiously to weigh up the pros and cons of 'this shepherd's life'.

Then Touchstone darts out *his* question: 'Hast any philosophy in thee, shepherd?' (line 21) where, again, the word 'philosophy' suggests gravitas and deeply considered experience (though the audience knows perfectly well that it is just another device for Touchstone's wit to work on). Corin good-humouredly obliges with a series of platitudes, which are, in effect, an answer to Touchstone in his own mode: to be ill is not to be well, to lack money is to be poor; to be out in the rain is to get wet, to handle fire is to get burnt, etc., etc. His syntax is less elegant than Touchstone's. It is not a neat balancing act; simply a string of clauses providing the complement to the 'I know' of line 22. Yet there is more substance to his words than Touchstone's. They may sound unfashionably banal by comparison with the latter's verbal skilfulness, but their down-to-earth emphasis throws into relief the shepherd's greater closeness to commonplace, day-to-day living. As Touchstone sums up, 'Such a one is a natural philosopher' (line 30) (even though his pun on the word 'natural', meaning 'foolish' as well as 'pertaining to nature', gives the compliment an ambiguous flavour). What belongs to 'nature' and what belongs to 'art' is one of the most frequently debated themes in Renaissance literature. Here the contrast seems almost to be embodied in the different styles and characters of Corin and Touchstone respectively. And yet the 'natural' Corin concludes his seemingly naive 'philosophy' by a comment (lines 27–9) which implies the need for both. At first it seems that either will do: 'wit', he suggests, may come from either nature or art. But the apparent inconsistency of treating 'wit' as something that can be *learned* by nature, as well as by art, and the importance he attaches to 'good breeding' (i.e. being well brought up), underlines the point that there is still some dependence on an educative, acquiring process. Corin may well lack the sophistication of a Touchstone, but he is aware that nature and nurture must interact. If, at one level, he does indeed stand for nature, and Touchstone for art, the subtext is one of interdependence. They need to come, as they do in this scene, into dialogue with one another.

From the second half of line 30 onwards the subject of this dialogue shifts from the shepherd's life to the court. And here, so to speak, Touchstone, despite the fact he is in the Forest of Arden (and has come there of his own volition), is playing on home ground. The sophistication of his mock-judicious manner in lines 13–21 is now changed for another variety – that of the prosecuting lawyer who can twist his legal victim round his little finger; though both are pursued just as much with tongue in cheek. He begins with the shock tactics typical of the clever fool (Feste is to do much the same with Olivia in *Twelfth Night*, I.v): because Corin was never at court, he is damned. This is proved by rapidly moving argument that gives the victim no time to examine the false premises on which it is based, but is delightfully entertaining to the theatre audience, as many of John Donne's early poems are, by the ingenuity with which it invents a chain of fallacious, but plausibly logical connections. Court is only the place where a certain code of manners is practised; to call them 'good' begs all sorts of moral questions, and to assume that not to follow their example is to do the opposite of 'good' is a consequence that has no inevitability about it. But there is enough semblance of reason (plus implications, once again, about nurture and nature) for the preposterous chain, leading on to 'wickedness', 'sin' and 'damnation', to seem preposterously 'proved'.

Corin has enough sense to make the fair point that different circumstances demand different manners: 'Those that are good manners at the court are as ridiculous in the country as the behaviour of the country is most mockable at the court (lines 43–6).' He speaks of the dirtiness and rough texture of the shepherd's hands which would make courtly kissing obnoxious, only to have Touchstone maintain that mutton grease is as 'wholesome' as human sweat, and that hardness would make the hands easier to feel. To Corin's reminder that shepherds' hands, unlike the civet-perfumed hands of courtiers, are also frequently covered with the tar used to dress sheep's cuts, Touchstone likewise has the rejoinder that civet has a nastier origin than tar, being 'the very uncleanly flux of a cat' (lines 64–5). (As most editions of *As You Like It* point out, this is correct. The Everyman Shakespeare, for example, notes [p. 106] that civet is 'a musky perfume derived from the secretions of a civet cat's anal glands'.) Here Corin gives up what he perceives to be an unequal struggle: Touchstone has 'too courtly a wit' for him (line 66). And that is it; the court-honed wit of Touchstone gives him an agility that enables him to provide a plausible counter to any argument or 'instance' (example) that is cited. Yet, as he probably knows, he is starting to use arguments that, if at all closely scrutinised, would tell against his basic position that the court is superior to the country. There are decidedly unrefined aspects to court life. Beneath its claims to delicacy and sophistication there are the obnoxious realities of sweat and excreta. Touchstone scores his debating points against Corin, but in the process he proves to be as much a critical exposer of courtly pretensions as a defender of their superior refinement. That the brilliance of his 'courtly wit' should reach its climax in 'the very uncleanly flux of a cat' makes his forensic triumph a very ambiguous one. The victory of court over country, art over nature, becomes a boomerang, turning the laugh on the court as much as on the country.

That Corin gives up the contest with the simple statement, 'I'll rest', again gives Touchstone an opportunity for mock-triumph. If Corin 'rests', then he is allowing Touchstone's original assertion, 'thou art damn'd' (line 33), to stand. In which case he needs spiritual surgery ('God make incision in thee!') even more than the sheep to which he himself acts as surgeon (alluding back to line 59). He has thus shown himself to be dangerously 'raw', lacking the sophisticated awareness of those complex matters which, for a Christian (and the underlying assumptions here are all predicated on the supreme importance of damnation and salvation in the Christian religion), determine the state of his soul. What Touchstone does here is, in effect, to equate courtliness with the full, conscious awareness of things spiritual, which for every Christian is the most important aspect of his life on earth, and to reduce pastoral innocence to a condition of ignorance, which, paradoxically, imperils, rather than preserves, the soul.

This conclusion is a highly ingenious one, and arrived at by characteristically nimble chop-logic. As such, it can again be dismissed as another example of the artificiality of style scoring its suspect victories over the simple-minded matter of 'this shepherd's life'. And if one is inclined to read it that way, Corin's final rejoinder (lines 69-73) puts the case for pastoral innocence in good, plain, honest English that seems to match admirably simple language to an equally admirable simplicity of behaviour. The statements are clear and straightforward: Corin works for his living; he is nobody's parasite; he bears no grudges; and he has no envy of men who are better off than himself. Indeed, he takes delight in the good fortune which others enjoy, and he accepts contentedly any harm that may come his way. And what he takes pride in are the creative aspects of nature – seeing his ewes peacefully grazing in the fields, and his lambs sucking at the teats of their mothers. Perhaps in the whole of *As You Like It* there is no more appealing presentation of the pastoral ideal. Moreover, in the context of the country v. court debate it also scores powerful, if implicit, points against the court, where bearing grudges, backbiting, envy of favourites and malcontent resentment for lack of money and promotion are all commonplace, and where emphasis seems to be on all the negative, de-creative aspects of life. Corin's pastoral reflects the universal dream of what life *should* be, as opposed to what we daily find it disappointingly *is*.

Yet – as we have already seen, in II.iv – Corin has a master of 'churlish disposition' who 'little recks to find the way to heaven', and he himself has a very practical attitude towards what can be done with a good purseful of gold. His common man's idyll is, even in his own terms, incomplete. It is, therefore, not altogether perverse of Touchstone to leap in, as he so gleefully does, with yet another counter-argument (lines 74–81) – that it is 'another simple sin' in Corin to get his living as a kind of 'bawd', or pimp, by betraying 'a she-lamb of a twelvemonth to a crooked-pated, old, cuckoldly ram, out of all reasonable match'. This is comically exaggerated, of course; and it is comically inappropriate to judge the breeding of sheep by the same moral criteria as one does the sexual behaviour and mating of human beings. But, again, there is an undercurrent of truth. Corin's 'the greatest of my pride is to see my ewes graze and my lambs suck' needs to be set against the undeniable fact that he does, indeed, offer to get his living from the sexual intercourse of animals: the more they breed, the more money he makes, and the satisfaction he gets from seeing the resultant lambs suck comes at least in part from the contemplation of the profit he hopes to get, either from the wool he will shear from their backs, or the price he will be paid for selling them to be slaughtered. The economic basis is inescapable, and with it the risks of moral corruption. Otherwise, as Touchstone concludes, 'the devil himself will have no shepherds' – i.e. shepherds are as damnable as other men.

It is interesting that the debate ends on the word 'scape' (= 'escape'); or, to be more precise, on the inability to escape. In the exchange as a whole neither court nor country escapes. Touchstone sets himself up, nominally, as the advocate of court life against the way of life of the country, and his own style is that of the courtier, in contrast to the greater plainness and simplicity of Corin. As a critic of the country he proceeds by fantastic arguments which are amusing for their preposterousness and palpable excess of ingenuity, but which, nevertheless, succeed in exposing the partiality, if not downright sentimentality, on which the supposed appeal of the pastoral version of country life is based. However, at the same time, his defence of the court develops into an exposé of the court, and more particularly, the coarseness which underlies the assumed refinement of the court. Corin's contributions, too, score points against the court in the process of defending the virtues of the country, even though those virtues are themselves questioned as to whether they give a true and complete account of what they profess to defend. Thus the debate becomes a double process – of ludicrously overdone forensic display, and boomerang criticism undercutting what is said on behalf of both country and court. And the master showman of this process is Touchstone. It would seem that nothing he says can be taken quite seriously, and yet at the same time that none of his dazzling displays of chop-logic can quite be dismissed as mere words. He probes as much as he coruscates, and corruscates as much as he probes. He is the clever fool incarnate – a character you can never be quite sure of, as disconcertingly critical as he is entertainingly witty.

*   *   *

As You Like It, V.iv.38–97 (38–100). Touchstone appears with his rustic girlfriend, Audrey, and is presented by Jaques to Duke Senior.

Touchstone.	Salutation and greeting to you all!	
Jaques.	Good my lord, bid him welcome. This is the	
	motley-minded gentleman that I have so often	40
	met in the forest. He hath been a courtier,	
	he swears.	
Touchstone.	If any man doubt that, let him put me to my	
	purgation. I have trod a measure; I have flatt'red	
	a lady; I have been politic with my friend, smooth	45
	with mine enemy; I have undone three tailors;	
	I have had four quarrels, and like to have fought one.	
Jaques.	And how was that ta'en up?	
Touchstone.	Faith, we met, and found the quarrel was upon	
	the seventh cause.	50
Jaques.	How seventh cause? Good my lord, like this fellow.	
Duke Senior.	I like him very well.	
Touchstone.	God 'ild you, sir; I desire you of the like. I press in	
	here, sir, amongst the rest of the country copulatives,	
	to swear and to forswear, according as marriage	55
	binds and blood breaks. A poor virgin, sir, an ill-	

	favour'd thing, sir, but mine own; a poor humour	
	of mine, sir, to take that that no man else will. Rich	
	honesty dwells like a miser, sir, in a poor house; as	
	your pearl in your foul oyster.	60
Duke Senior.	By my faith, he is very swift and sententious.	
Touchstone.	According to the fool's bolt, sir, and such dulcet	
	diseases.	
Jaques.	But, for the seventh cause: how did you find the	
	quarrel on the seventh cause?	65
Touchstone.	Upon a lie seven times removed – bear your body	
	more seeming, Audrey – as thus, sir. I did dislike	
	the cut of a certain courtier's beard; he sent me	
	word, if I said his beard was not well cut, he was	
	in the mind it was. This is call'd the Retort	70
	Courteous. If I sent him word again it was not	
	well cut, he would send me word he cut it to	
	please himself. This is call'd the Quip Modest.	
	If again it was not well cut, he disabled my	
	judgment. This is call'd the Reply Churlish.	75
	If again it was not well cut, he would answer	
	I spake not true. This is call'd the Reproof Valiant.	
	If again it was not well cut, he would say I lie.	
	This is call'd the Countercheck Quarrelsome.	
	And so to Lie Circumstantial and the Lie Direct.	80
Jaques.	And how oft did you say his beard was not well cut?	
Touchstone.	I durst go no further than the Lie Circumstantial,	
	nor he durst not give me the Lie Direct; and so we	
	measur'd swords and parted.	
Jaques.	Can you nominate in order now the degrees of	85
	the lie?	
Touchstone.	O, sir, we quarrel in print by the book, as you·	
	have books for good manners. I will name you the	
	degrees. The first, the Retort Courteous; the second,	
	the Quip Modest; the third, the Reply Churlish;	90
	the fourth, the Reproof Valiant; the fifth, the	
	Countercheck Quarrelsome; the sixth, the Lie with	
	Circumstance; the seventh, the Lie Direct. All these	

you may avoid but the Lie Direct; and you may
avoid that too with an If. I knew when seven   95
justices could not take up a quarrel; but when the
parties were met themselves, one of them thought
but of an If, as: 'If you said so, then I said so'.
And they shook hands, and swore brothers. Your
If is the only peace-maker; much virtue in If.   100

Here again the courtliness, or mock courtliness, of Touchstone is to
the fore. As in the scene with Corin, he is also in the company of
one of the rustic characters, Audrey; but the social context is more
complicated, for the presence of Duke Senior – formerly a ruling
aristocrat who presided over his own court, and even now, though
exiled, the acknowledged head of those courtiers who have chosen
exile in the Forest of Arden with him – places him in a position
where he is effectively both at court and in the country. Among the
rustics Touchstone lords it as a superior figure (this is implicit in the
scene already examined, III.ii, and still more evident in III.iii and
V.i, where the gulf between him and Audrey and William is farcically exaggerated); but vis-à-vis Duke Senior and Jaques he is socially
inferior, and though not dependent on their patronage, as he was
previously on that of Duke Frederick (Celia's father), with regard to
them he is much more in the position of the professional Fool who
must 'perform' for the benefit of the court.

   This dual role, and somewhat ambivalent situation, manifests
itself in the above extract. Jaques calls him 'the motley-minded gentleman' whom he has so often met in the forest, and who 'hath been
a courtier, he swears'. Although this is well intended, and Jaques is,
as it were, using his influence with Duke Senior to recommend
Touchstone, the coupling of 'motley-minded' with 'gentleman' is
double-edged. 'Gentleman' gives him social standing, but 'motley-
minded' suggests the professional entertainer's role, with a parti-
coloured suit and a parti-coloured mind that compromises him
socially.

   Similarly, the reference to his having been a courtier is qualified
by 'he swears'. Jaques, while vouching for him, is leaving open the
possibility that his word may not be entirely reliable. And clearly

Touchstone is sensitive to this, for his immediate response is to offer himself for 'purgation' (i.e. testing – with overtones both of blood-letting to purge of disease, and bodily evacuation to get rid of excrement). The evidence he then proceeds to give of his appropriately courtly qualifications is, of course, typically satirical, reducing the business of being a courtier to: dancing, flattering ladies, being both a hypocitical friend and a flattering enemy, ruining tailors by never paying their bills, conducting a quarrel, and (at least potentially) fighting a duel. Needless to say, if this were not satirical, it would *dis*qualify rather than qualify him, especially in the the eyes of someone like Duke Senior. But Touchstone knows his audience: he instinctively appreciates that lightly carried mockery of false courtiership will endorse his own claim to courtly knowledge far more effectively than a display of supposedly good courtier's manners. Moreover, adeptly executed – as it is by Touchstone – this piece of mockery also enables him to pave the way for an item from his professional repertoire which will show his courtly wit in dazzling action. For the claim to have 'had four quarrels' and being 'like to have fought one', with its unfinished implication that only one of the four got as far as the risk of a duel, and even that one was somehow averted, simply asks to be queried – as it duly is, by Jaques. Likewise, the reference to the 'seventh cause' (line 50) is a bait – intended as another lead-in to the anecdote to follow – which Jaques obligingly swallows.

However, Touchstone delays still further, opportunistically seizing the occasion provided by Jaques's 'Good my lord, like you this fellow' to execute a digression which will both whet his audience's appetite still more, and, in the guise of explaining, capitalise on the oddity of his appearing as 'courtier' in such strange company as that of the extremely rustic Audrey. As Touchstone makes sufficiently clear (in his punning play on the word 'like', at line 53), he wishes to be in good favour with the Duke, and with regard to his choice of Audrey for his mate, he does this on the basis of a two-way insurance: if Audrey looks inappropriately inferior, he's only doing what everybody else does, i.e. answering to basic sexual drives. On the other hand, by choosing a plain country wench he is preferring simple, unadorned virtue to more sophisticated vice – an alternative explanation which he contrives to bolster with the proverbial wisdom implied in lines 58–60 (that the true moral riches of chastity are to be found in poor, or ugly-seeming, surroundings). Such sententiousness does, apparently, have its desired effect on the Duke – perhaps because it chimes in with that taste for pastoral moralising which he has demonstrated at the beginning of II.i. But Touchstone's insurance means that he can also, if necessary, fall back on his role as the courtier whose knowledge of the world tells him that 'marriage binds and blood breaks'. In that role his moralising could be construed as sophisticated guying of pastoral common-places, and he would not, then, have forfeited his claim to be regarded as a courtly wit.

What Touchstone means is thus ambiguous – and, quite possibly, deliberately so. It is part of his own ambiguous status, as both 'clever' and 'Fool', that this should be so. He cannot afford to let himself be too easily pinned down. The cryptic nature of his comment at line 62 is perhaps further evidence of this. Here he picks up the word 'swift' in the Duke's 'he is very swift and sententious' (61) and makes it the pretext for a curious reference to 'the fool's bolt' [= arrow] and 'such dulcet [sweet] diseases'. Various commentators have produced various explanations for these words (of the latter phrase Dr Johnson was honest enough to say quite frankly, 'This I do not understand'). What does seem clear is that the fool's arrow flies very fast – so fast that one has to be very quick-witted to follow it; but it is an arrow, i.e. a kind of weapon, and as such it is pointed and capable of wounding. The reference to disease may also suggest that the arrow is poisoned; but, if so, the qualification 'dulcet' seems to take the nastiness of the sting out of it. Perhaps the implication here, as in so much of what Touchstone says, is that his satire – notwithstanding its sharpness, and the overtones of worldliness, bawdiness and even cynicism which often accompany it – is not ultimately a destructive weapon. It is still adapted to his desire of the 'like', and is an accom-modation to the real rather than the corrupt.

At line 64 Jaques brings Touchstone (and, of course, the theatre audience) back to the suspended interest in 'the seventh cause'. Here the Fool at last displays his professional slickness (but with an inter-jection to Audrey which comically highlights her contrasting gawki-

ness). He adopts a formula of challenge and reply which is made to
sound technically impressive, so that the trivial provocations of
which the quarrel consists are given an inflated air of importance. As
most commentators point out (referring to such books as William
Segar's *The Booke of Honor and Armes* and Vincentio Saviolo's
Practice of the Sword and Dagger), all this is a parody of the contemporary Elizabethan manuals which found a market among insecure
newcomers to London and its sophisticated society who wished to
be instructed in supposedly correct behaviour. The repetitive rhetorical structure and the labels attached to each phase of the quarrel,
which are made to sound fashionably foreign by the use of post-
positioned adjectives ('Retort *Courteous*', 'Quip *Modest*', etc.), seem
to impose order and authority on an essentially silly process; and the
carefully constructed impression that there is a definable point at
which one can stop (i.e the 'Lie Circumstantial') purports to reassure
the novice – a coward at heart, but bent on giving a macho impression of courage and manliness – that actual blood need never be
shed. When asked by Jaques if he can nominate the degrees of the
lie, Touchstone reels off his labels in neatly numbered sequence to
give what must sound in the theatre like a brilliant *tour de force*, and
is a further confirmation of what he mockingly, yet revealingly, calls
quarrelling 'in print' and 'by the book'. Then, to cap his performance, he produces, like a conjuror pulling a rabbit out of a hat, his,
again, essentially verbal device for ensuring that quarrelling remains
at the level of words, and never gets translated into action. 'If'
becomes the means for making everything purely suppositional; it
retrieves the show of honour from the test of deeds, and it acquires
the 'virtue' of a political peacemaker.

All this is a tribute both to Touchstone's own verbal skill and his
knowledge, as a 'gentleman' belonging to the courtly centre, of what
is and is not the done thing. It is designed to tickle the fancy of those
like the Duke and his followers who are confident enough not to
need such didactic aids to proper conduct, and are amused by the
pretensions of those who do. It exposes the hollowness beneath the
verbal code, but leaves the code – for those who pay more than lip-
service to it – intact. Yet the cleverness is also brittle. Touchstone, in
a sense, becomes the verbal sparring-partner whose underlying inse-

curity he so adeptly satirises. As the presence of Audrey suggests – she is given no lines to speak in this scene, but there she is on stage; and one of the things that distinguishes performance of a play from reading is that silent presence can have its effect as well as the speaking of cunningly contrived words – he is a man of the flesh as well as of wit, and linked to rustic plainness as well as courtly sophistication. His ambivalent social position makes him dependent on the very verbal devices that he so cleverly parodies, and, paradoxically, his consummate ability to expose the mere wordiness of the degrees of the lie highlights the wordplaying nature of his own way of life.

*   *   *

Twelfth Night, I.v.47–92 (47–94). Feste proves his mistress, Olivia, to be 'the fool'. Malvolio also stands by.

Feste.	The lady bade take away the fool; therefore, I say again, take her away.
Olivia.	Sir, I bade them take away you.
Feste.	Misprision in the highest degree! Lady, 'Cucullus 50 non facit monachum'; that's as much to say as I wear not motley in my brain. Good madonna, give me leave to prove you a fool.
Olivia.	Can you do it?
Feste.	Dexteriously, good madonna. 55
Olivia.	Make your proof.
Feste.	I must catechize you for it, madonna. Good my mouse of virtue, answer me.
Olivia.	Well, sir, for want of other idleness, I'll bide your proof. 60
Feste.	Good madonna, why mourn'st thou?
Olivia.	Good fool, for my brother's death.
Feste.	I think his soul is in hell, madonna.
Olivia.	I know his soul is in heaven, fool.
Feste.	The more fool, madonna, to mourn for your 65 brother's soul being in heaven. Take away the fool, gentlemen.

Olivia.	What think you of this fool, Malvolio? Doth he not mend?
Malvolio.	Yes, and shall do, till the pangs of death shake him. 70 Infirmity, that decays the wise, doth ever make the better fool.
Feste.	God send you, sir, a speedy infirmity, for the better increasing your folly! Sir Toby will be sworn that I am no fox; but he will not pass his word for 75 twopence that you are no fool.
Olivia.	How say you to that, Malvolio?
Malvolio.	I marvel your ladyship takes delight in such a barren rascal; I saw him put down the other day with an ordinary fool that has no more brain than 80 a stone. Look you now, he's out of his guard already; unless you laugh and minister occasion to him, he is gagg'd. I protest I take these wise men that crow so at these set kind of fools no better than the fools' zanies. 85
Olivia.	O, you are sick of self-love, Malvolio, and taste with a distemper'd appetite. To be generous, guiltless, and of free disposition, is to take those things for bird-bolts that you deem cannon bullets. There is no slander in an allow'd fool, though he do nothing 90 but rail; nor no railing in a known discreet man, though he do nothing but reprove.
Feste.	Now Mercury endue thee with leasing, for thou speak'st well of fools!

In this passage Feste, a professional Fool like Touchstone, gives an example of his wares (as Touchstone does in the previous extract from *As You Like It* in his degrees of the lie speech), but also becomes the object of discussion by Olivia and Malvolio. To take his professional performance first: he has already – a few lines earlier than this extract begins – taken a considerable risk when Olivia, seemingly not in the mood for badinage, has told her attendants to 'take the Fool away', and he has attempted to turn the tables on her by telling them to 'Take away the lady'. Here he repeats the joke, knowing that it is likely to prompt an indignant reply, but still confident that he can stick to his position (implicitly, that she, not he, is the fool) because he has the wit to prove it. That 'proof' is, of course, hardly convincing in itself; but tone, and undertones, are what matter in this game of words. The superficial play is on the question of who is the 'fool', Feste or Olivia herself; but the more relevant point, as far as Feste is concerned, is to deflect from himself the inappropiate implications of foolishness, and to get Olivia to snap out of her excessive indulgence in grief, and see that as a kind of folly. On the first point, Feste's Latin tag (meaning 'it's not the hood that makes the monk') is his way of saying that the persona he has to adopt as Fool, and the traditional motley wear, should not lead anyone (and this includes the theatre audience) to assume that he himself is an idiot. On the second point, what he wants to say to Olivia must both hit home and be entertaining. It is a delicate balance which is required; and in achieving this he clearly enjoys the advantage of being able not only to rely on the 'safe passage' customarily accorded the Fool, but also the indulgent tenderness of Olivia. He twice calls her 'good madonna', on which the editor of the Macmillan *Twelfth Night* comments: 'Feste seems to hint that she puts on a "Madonna" act – she is too good to be true. He mocks her saintliness and her parade of grief, both of which he thinks suspect'; and the Oxford editors suggest that the word is chosen because its Italianate/ Catholic overtones 'will antagonize the puritan Malvolio'. There are elements of truth in both these comments – and the latter, in partic- ular, reminds us that in performance the presence of Malvolio on stage, and the political-cum-religious prejudices of the Elizabethans in the auditorium, also help to condition the significance of what Feste says. But the motherly suggestions of 'madonna', coupled with the quite obviously affectionate 'Good my mouse of virtue' (line 57–8) (where 'mouse' is a term of endearment, not contempt) , indi- cate a touch of softness as well, which, though it is conditioned by household hierarchy on Olivia's side and professional asperity on Feste's, helps to create a specially poised relationship between the two. If the 'proof' is to be made, it has to be done, as Feste claims he can do it, 'dexteriously' (line 55); and the overtones of the scene suggest that these are what make it possible.

'Madonna', as in the editorial comment mentioned above, has religious overtones, and these are lightly played upon by Feste in other parts of his dialogue with Olivia. His Latin tag hints at the life of the monk; when he asks leave to interrogate her it is with the word 'catechize' (with its suggestion of a priest taking children through the catechism); and then at the climax of his questioning he speaks of the great last things – death, heaven and hell. This does not mean that the comedy suddenly becomes deeply solemn and serious. But it is characteristic of Feste (and this distinguishes him from that other professional Fool, Touchstone) that even when he seems to be jesting light-heartedly deeper implications are not far beneath the surface. Here he makes his point that Olivia's prolonged mourning for her dead brother is excessive, and inconsistent with Christian belief in life after death – ergo, she is the fool; but he himself is not such a fool as to think that grief is a mere act of folly. If he is mocking her extravagance (as most critics say), he is also (as few seem to recognise) consoling her by reminding her that her brother has exchanged temporal life for eternal bliss. Which is perhaps why Olivia does not take the offence that might otherwise be expected of her.

Instead of rebuking Feste she turns to Malvolio with a couple of questions, the second of which ('Doth he not mend?') seems to imply a degree of approval. What Olivia really thinks is left open to interpretation; but the suggestion that she is given pause for thought, that there are contradictory reverberations going on in her mind, is highly probable. Her turning to Malvolio – with his known degree of seriousness – would seem to suggest that she is interested in the response of someone who will not merely dismiss the deeper implications. What he does, however, is to take what the Fool says both too seriously and too narrowly. Olivia's 'mend' becomes perverted by him from 'improve' to 'get worse', and the reference to death in the preceding dialogue is distorted into an image of Feste's becoming ever more addicted to his folly till the prospect of death finally (but too late) sobers him up. He cites the standard Christian notion that 'infirmity' can have a beneficially arresting effect (in the form, for example, of deathbed repentance); but his tone suggests decidedly un-Christian feelings of anger and resentment. He is incapable of the mercurial shifting between light and shade, mockery and consolation, which characterises the relationship between Feste and Olivia. The complex issues surrounding the idea of what it is to be a 'fool' elude him; he is more the one-dimensional Puritan. This makes Feste's jesting reversal of his words (at line 73) singularly appropriate: Malvolio, rather than the Fool, is the one who needs the sobering effect of 'infirmity' to make him better appreciate the true nature of 'folly' – some psychological jolt is needed (and does this look forward to what is to happen to him later in the play?) to help him to 'mend' and become a better adjusted inhabitant of the comic world of *Twelfth Night.*

Feste's poise, so far, is a nimble demonstration of what it is to be the well-balanced inhabitant of that world. But the second half of his response (lines 74–6) suggests that he, too, loses his cool under Malvolio's sarcasm. His reference to Sir Toby – who, he claims, will vouch for him, and scorn Malvolio as a merely foolish, not a wise, 'fool' – reveals both the insecurity and the fragility of judgement that makes him depend on Olivia's notoriously drunken uncle for support. Although Sir Toby may well be a more appealing character than Malvolio, he, too, needs sobering up; and Feste's alliance with him belongs to an aspect of 'folly' which is perhaps less defensible than the Fool appreciates.

However, Malvolio's further response (lines 78–85) is so extreme that it makes the weakness in Feste's position seem negligible by comparison. Feste has already shown enough inventiveness to make the 'barren' in 'barren rascal' manifestly unfair; and the insult to Olivia implicit in Malvolio's wondering that she takes delight in the Fool's performance discredits both the steward's judgement and humanity. It is this which provokes Olivia to a short, but trenchantly accurate, criticism of Malvolio; and also to a defence of the satirical role of clever Fools in general. The terms she uses at lines 87–8, 'generous [liberal-minded], guiltless [with a clear conscience], and of free disposition [magnanimous]', suggest an aristocratic ideal which can sustain dignity with humanity and a sense of humour – one that understands what true comedy is about. The individual possessed of these qualities is confident enough not to be riled by the relatively harmless shots that Malvolio takes for cannon balls, especially, Olivia implies, when they come from the Fool who, by custom, is granted the privilege to mock. She takes her stand, that is, on customs and habits of mind that have become a kind of instinct in good society – her rebuke to Malvolio implying that his self-conscious rectitude (or pose) needs adjusting by tact and imagination. The very formally balanced sentence at lines 89–92 has an elegance matching the claim she makes; its equation of the Fool's gibes with the more circumspect man's strictures assumes the capacity to take criticism, not as carping, but as civilised acceptance of the fallibility of all human beings. In practice, of course, it seems that the Fool does have to watch his step, and Malvolio, who would appear to be the specific example in this scene of 'a known discreet man' much given to reproving, is not altogether found guiltless of railing. But it is part of Olivia's generosity that to some extent she glosses this over in her counsel of perfection (in the process, modifying the harshness of the previous sentence directed at Malvolio); and it is part of Feste's instinctive adjustment of the ideal to the real that in thanking her (line 93) he ironically invokes Mercury – as the god of deception – to give her the gift of lying. He knows that she is giving him the benefit of the doubt; but genuinely appreciates her voicing of the usually unspoken assumptions on which clever foolery is based.

*   *   *

Twelfth Night, V.i.10–45 (10–46). An exchange between Feste and Orsino, who is on his way to seek an interview with Olivia.

Orsino.	How dost thou, my good fellow?
Feste.	Truly, sir, the better for my foes and the worse for my friends.
Orsino.	Just the contrary: the better for thy friends.
Feste.	No, sir, the worse.
Orsino.	How can that be?
Feste.	Marry, sir, they praise me and make an ass of me. Now my foes tell me plainly I am an ass; so that by my foes, sir, I profit in the knowledge of myself, and by my friends I am abused; so that, conclusions to

15

	be as kisses, if your four negatives make your two	20
	affirmatives, why then, the worse for my friends	
	and the better for my foes.	
Orsino.	Why, this is excellent.	
Feste.	By my troth, sir, no; though it please you to be one	
	of my friends.	25
Orsino.	Thou shalt not be the worse for me. There's gold.	
Feste.	But that it would be double-dealing, sir, I would	
	you could make it another.	
Orsino.	O, you give me ill counsel.	
Feste.	Put your grace in your pocket, sir, for this once,	30
	and let your flesh and blood obey it.	
Orsino.	Well, I will be so much a sinner to be a double-dealer.	
	There's another.	
Feste.	Primo, secundo, tertio, is a good play; and the old	
	saying is 'The third pays for all'. The triplex, sir,	35
	is a good tripping measure; or the bells of Saint	
	Bennet, sir, may put you in mind – one, two, three.	
Orsino.	You can fool no more money out of me at this throw;	
	if you will let your lady know I am here to speak with	
	her, and bring her along with you, it may awake my	40
	bounty further.	
Feste.	Marry, sir, lullaby to your bounty till I come again.	
	I go, sir; but I would not have you to think that my	
	desire of having is the sin of covetousness. But, as	
	you say, sir, let your bounty take a nap; I will awake	45
	it anon. [*Exit.*	

At one level this exchange is simple enough: Orsino wishing to gain access to Olivia, who has frequently denied him, thinks that Feste may be able to help him to this end; and Feste, seeing in the wealthy Duke an opportunity for making some extra money, gains his attention with a bit of professional fooling. Each has his own purpose in mind – the one able, and not unwilling, to pay, the other wishing to augment his precarious income; and they end by striking some sort of a bargain.

But more goes on than this basically commercial transaction. Not that its commercial nature should be lightly dismissed: even in the romantic comedy of wooing, to which this situation belongs, money has a significant part to play, and as far as Feste is concerned (compare, for example, his somewhat similar exchange with Viola at the beginning of III.i) his wit is something by which he has to earn his living. 'Gold' (line 26), 'money' (line 38) and no less than three references to 'bounty' (lines 41–5) are all words which underline this fact. Moreover, Feste's reference to 'profit' (at line 18), though the word is not used there primarily in its commercial sense, already hints at a link between morality and money which is realised in his subsequent begging (to give it, as it is not given in the text, its more bluntly unvarnished name). The relationship between Feste and Orsino concerns much more than the cash nexus, but payment for services rendered is something that neither party loses sight of.

Another aspect to that relationship is class, as the very first line implies. Affable though Orsino is, he is the Duke, Feste the Fool (or 'clown', or 'jester'), whom he addresses as 'fellow', and to whom he uses the second-person singular pronoun 'thou'. Feste replies with the respectful 'sir' (which is repeated again at lines 14, 16, 18, 24, 27, 30, 35, 37, 42, 43 and 45), and later, when he uses the personal pronoun it is the more deferential second-person plural 'you'. He knows his place vis-à-vis Orsino; and though in some ways he can appear to be impertinent (as in the scene already examined with Olivia), he is careful not to overstep the social mark.

This does not, however, preclude Feste's being provocative. Indeed, it is part of his technique for gaining attention – as he shows by opening the dialogue with the paradoxical assertion that he is the better for his foes and the worse for his friends. Orsino corrects him (whether because he actually thinks that Feste has slipped up, or because he realises that this is what he is being prompted to say, is open to opinion), but Feste's emphatic repetition of 'the worse' leads on to a witty resolution of the paradox. This is done in a way that we have now come to recognise as a trademark of Feste's, involving an inversion of the usual expectations of folly coupled with tacit criticism of courtly insincerity. It is the flattery of his 'friends' which makes an ass of him, and the plain speaking of his enemies which redeems him morally by helping him to the 'profit' of self-knowledge. Feste, of course, performs a verbal sleight of hand by substituting 'friends' who are false for friends who are true; but in the process he enhances the implied criticism that one needs to be on one's guard – particularly in the courtly world where verbal skills such as his are at a high premium – against duplicity and double-dealing. The dazzling flourish with which he ends his sentence ('so that ... for my foes') quickly glances at other aspects of doubleness which have significance for *Twelfth Night* as a whole – namely, that a lady's 'no, no' may equal 'yes', just as in strictly logical grammar two negatives equal a positive; with the result that the triumphant repetition of the original proposition, 'the worse for my friends and the better for my foes', now becomes part of a revelation that the world is full of contradictions. Orsino finds this 'excellent'; for him, apparently, it is simply an entertaining verbal display. Feste, however, only too aware of its more disturbing implications, rejects the very praise he has elicited, and is bold enough to include Orsino in the now decidedly ambiguous category of 'friends'.

The remainder of this exchange between Feste and Orsino is taken up with Feste's ingenuity in doubling the fee that he has earned from the Duke, and then attempting to treble it. Again, it is his skill in wordplay that he relies on to accomplish this. But his exploitation of the double meaning of words is done in such a way that the moral debate also continues. At line 27, for example, 'double-dealing', as well as being a term for doing the same thing (i.e. tipping) twice, also becomes an invitation to two-facedness, or duplicity – which, as Orsino jokingly recognises, is evil advice; and at line 30 'grace' embraces both the correct form of address for a duke ('your grace') and an invitation to forget the Christian imperative of being in a state of grace (i.e. the need to resist sin) and to give way to the temptations of 'flesh and blood'. Orsino again shows his nobleman's complaisance, and his appreciation of Feste's wit, by allowing himself to be cajoled into being enough of a 'sinner' and 'double-dealer' to hand over a second coin. It is, of course, part of the joke that tipping twice over would normally be thought of as virtuous generosity, and it is precisely because the Duke *is* generous that he can laughingly allow himself to be treated as if he were a 'sinner'. Likewise at lines 34–5 Feste's attempt to get a third tip hinges on wordplay that has to do with the sin of gambling: he invites the Duke to imitate the dice-player who thinks that a third throw of the dice will enable him to recoup his previous losses (to be 'third time lucky'), and the reference to 'the bells of Saint Bennet' (a church on the other side of the Thames from the Globe, where these lines were probably first spoken) reinforces the Christian moral sanctions which are here being wittily subverted. And, finally, at line 44 Feste's reference to his 'desire of having' and 'the sin of covetousness' serves to link the very concepts which he professes to separate, and his references to sleep at lines 42 and 45 (implicit in 'lullaby', 'nap' and 'awake') carry a subtext of the need for moral vigilance and wakefulness in a world of sinful neglect.

Such a teasing-out of the implications in what looks like a fairly light-hearted, bantering exchange between Feste and Orsino must inevitably sound heavy-handed. In the theatre the whole thing is played at speed, in what must seem an entertainingly flippant rather than a morally earnest manner. The quick flash of the repartee (within *Twelfth Night* as a whole so different in style from the didactic pomposity of Malvolio) dazzles and scintillates like a verbal fireworks show. But even to follow the jokes the audience have to keep their wits about them. The words must be listened to *as* words, and in that process they reverberate with morally ambivalent meanings which set up a kind of contrapuntal subtext. Feste is far from teaching a moral lesson (if he has to take sides, he belongs with Sir Toby Belch, who opts for 'cakes and ale' rather than virtue); but his mind plays all the time – even if it seems frivolously – with Christian concepts and moral values. He plays the innocent Fool, but he lives in a world where sinning, whether it be duplicity, gambling or greed, is rife, and with which he has to come to terms. Accordingly, his expressions are loaded with the implications of that world; and the provocative exploitation of them forms the stock-in-trade of his professional foolery. The 'bounty' of *his* wit never succumbs to the 'lullaby' that soothes the innocent child, and though it may appear to take a moral 'nap' it is perpetually on the qui vive and widely 'awake'.

Conclusions

This chapter began with the foolery of Bottom, a character who shares many characteristics with the duped fools of Chapter 6, and it ended with the sophisticated wit of Feste, who embodies the comic spirit and yet seems inward with the morally corrupt world that Shakespeare was to explore in his tragedies. In between came the foolery of Touchstone, a courtier who finds himself in the country, but is completely *of* neither the courtly nor the pastoral worlds. Properly speaking, it is he and Feste who represent 'the clever Fool', for there is no pretence that either of them is a dunce. On the contrary, they are astute characters who use their insight and imagination, and their often ruthlessly probing wit, to expose the folly of those around them. They are professional Fools, appropriately garbed with cap and bells, but they dupe others rather than suffer duping themselves. Indeed, they are granted the privilege, as 'licensed fools', to say provocative things and voice criticisms which, coming from the mouths of ordinary characters, would be deemed worthy of whipping or imprisonment (which is not, however, to say that they themselves do not live dangerously at times). None of these things applies to Bottom; but he shares with the 'clever Fool' a poise and adaptability which makes him nobody's ass. That he actually does wear the head of an ass for much of his time in *A Midsummer Night's Dream* may seem to class him as one more of the 'dupes', but that can also be regarded as his version of the fool's garb, which, in the case of the professional Fools, Touchstone and Feste, takes the form of cap and bells and parti-coloured suit. His appearance belies his native wit and capacity for survival. For, like the other two, he is an opportunist – an essentially comic character who survives (in contrast to the tragic character, who is destroyed) in whatever circumstances he is placed, and survives, not because he is too thick-witted (like a Dogberry or a Verges) to know any better, but by the exercise of his wit. The foolery of these clever fools is a positive quality – a nimbleness that saves them from being the dupe of others; and, more particularly in the case of Touchstone and Feste, a foolery that is the living, analytical enemy of mere foolishness.

Methods of Analysis (Chapters 6 and 7)

The methods used in other chapters apply yet again here, with this difference – that a more than usually heightened awareness is needed of linguistic devices and their tonal implications.

In *A Midsummer Night's Dream* note the inconsistencies between, for example, Lysander's situation in II.ii and the claims he makes for the rationality of his change of allegiance. But also look for the possible ambiguity of effect such seeming inconsistency might have – as when Bottom, in III.i, comes out with a sensible comment on the division between reason and love which shows him to be less of a fool than his ass's head makes him look.

In *Twelfth Night* the exaggerated expressions and pompous language of Malvoio are tell-tale indications of his inflated self-image; and they are matched by the style of the decoy-letter, which is designed to lure him to pushing what are at least plausible possibilities to impossibly foolish and extravagant behaviour.

In *Much Ado About Nothing*, IV.i.1–62 Claudio's extravagant language is also a clue to his loss of a sense of proportion and decorum in denouncing Hero, as he does, in the very church where he was to have married her. Another, but perhaps not unrelated, kind of pompous extravagance is exhibited by Dogberry in IV.ii.1–86.

Above all, however, analysis of scenes involving the clever fools, Touchstone and Feste, calls for exceptionally alert attention to possible discrepancies between what is being said and the way in which it is said. For example, in *As You Like It*, III.ii.11–75 the balanced style of Touchstone's anatomy of 'this shepherd's life' needs to be held in conjunction with the lack of substance behind it; and – as an interesting counterweight – Corin's seemingly banal style, yet honest, rustic substance, has implications for the underlying debate about nurture v. nature.

Both Touchstone and Feste are much given to quibbling with words, and one has, therefore, to be on guard for sometimes strained punning on different senses (which may not be the same as those in modern usage) and exploitation of different shades of meaning. (See, for example, Feste's play on 'double-dealing' and 'grace' in his exchange with Orsino in *Twelfth Night*, V.i.10–45.) Even such apparently trivial matters as the use of the personal pronouns 'thou' and 'you' can be of significance; and certainly the tonal implications of a word like 'madonna' in Feste's exchange with Olivia at I.v.47–92 need to be analysed.

The use of argument and false argument (chop-logic) also need to be given special scrutiny. Here paraphrase may often be useful – aided by appropriate reading of the notes in a good edition of the text – to ensure that the full, intricate process of an argument and its implications are properly followed. (Paraphrase, however, should only be a means to the end of clarifying Shakespeare's meaning to oneself; it should never be allowed to become a substitute for the exact words of the text.)

Suggested Work

Analyse *A Midsummer Night's Dream*, IV.i.184–96 ('These things seem small and undistinguishable ... And by the way let us recount our dreams'). Read this passage in conjunction with the preceding part of the scene in which Oberon commands Puck to restore all the enchanted characters to their normal states of mind (leaving Demetrius, however, in love with Helena). How does this extract convey the lovers as still poised between their confused, duped condition and the recovery of normal rationality? Consider, in particular, the use of imagery and the balancing of positive against negative, affirmation against question.

Analyse *Much Ado About Nothing*, II.iii.201–23 ('This can be no trick ... I do spy some marks of love in her.') This is the soliloquy in which Benedick reveals the effect on him of the trick played by Don Pedro, Claudio and Leonato to make him believe that Beatrice loves him. How does the syntax aid the impression of a debate going on in the speaker's mind? Does the speech, and its relationship to what has gone before, make him look a fool? How does it compare with the duping of Malvolio in *Twelfth Night*, II.v.21–158 (analysed in Chapter 6)? (Compare Benedick's 'This can be no trick' with Malvolio's 'I do not now fool myself to let imagination jade me.')

In *As You Like It*, V.i.10–55 ('It is meat and drink to me to see a clown ... God rest you merry, sir') consider how Touchstone bamboozles William. Analyse the mock-reasoning he employs at lines 37–41 and the comic tirade at lines 44–53, and show, in particular, how Touchstone shows off his superior comand of words and syntax. What are the parts played by Audrey and William in all this?

Analyse the dialogue between Viola and Feste (the Clown) at *Twelfth Night*, III.i.1–33 ('Save thee, friend, and thy music! ... her corrupter of words'). How does Feste play on such words and phrases as 'live by', 'wanton', 'reason' and 'care'? Is he right in describing himself as Olivia's 'corrupter of words'? What is Viola's role in this extract? How does it contrast with William's role in the *As You Like It* passage mentioned above?

8

Manlike Women

Introduction

A remarkable feature of Shakespeare's comedies is the prominence given to women. It may almost be said that if men dominate the tragedies, it is women who dominate the comedies. This is all the more surprising in the context of Elizabethan society, where the orthodox view was that women were subordinate to men. In the biblical story of Adam and Eve it was Adam who was created first, and Eve was created out of one of his ribs as a helpmeet to him. As Milton expresses it (writing in the latter half of the seventeenth century, but voicing doctrine unchanged from the sixteenth), although both man and woman reflected the 'image of their glorious Maker', they were not equal – Adam was formed for 'contemplation' and 'valour', Eve for 'softness' and 'sweet attractive grace'; his obedience was due directly to God, hers to God via him: 'He for God only, she for God in him' *(Paradise Lost,* IV.295–9). That Queen Elizabeth was on the throne from 1558 to 1603 undoubtedly enhanced the status of woman: many poets, including Spenser and Sir Walter Raleigh, praised her lavishly, and in *A Midsummer Night's Dream,* II.i.155–63 Shakespeare followed what had become a contemporary fashion for elevating the Virgin Queen to the status of 'imperial vot'ress'. But this did not necessarily apply to women in general. To refer to *A Midsummer Night's Dream* again, as we have already seen in the analysis of I.i.22–82 (Chapter 5, pp. 72–7), it was still a commonplace idea that an unmarried daughter owed complete allegiance to her father; and once married, her husband became her lord. Modesty and self-effacement were also the marks of respectable womanhood; as in the time-honoured ritual of courtship, where the intiative is taken by the man, a woman's part was to respond rather than dispose. And yet Shakespeare's comic heroines frequently behave in direct contradiction of these conventions. Often it is the women who take control of events (notably so with Rosalind in *As You Like It*); and it is the women who seem to possess not only greater intuitive awareness than the men, but also more common sense and emotional maturity. The fact that in the Elizabethan theatre it was boys who played the parts of women (though, ironically, this itself was due to the prevailing convention that it was immoral for women to appear on the stage) goes some way to explain the 'manliness' of Shakespeare's heroines; and the frequency of situations in which the boy-actor plays the part of a girl who disguises herself as a boy also adds an intriguingly androgynous – some would say, ambivalent – dimension. But the depth and richness which Shakespeare gives to his comic heroines goes far beyond considerations of theatrical expediency. Characters like Beatrice, Rosalind and Viola are not merely pert boys in petticoats. Just as Touchstone and Feste use their supposed 'folly' as a stalking-horse under the cover of which they shoot their wit, these boy-represented heroines reveal manlike qualities which challenge conventional ideas of womanhood.

Analyses

Much Ado About Nothing, II.i.24–70 (24–72). Beatrice engages in banter with her uncle, Leonato, against the background of the marriage proposal which it is expected that Don Pedro will be making to her cousin Hero. The latter and her uncle, Antonio, are also present.

Beatrice.	I could not endure a husband with a beard on his face; I had rather lie in the woollen.	25
Leonato.	You may light on a husband that hath no beard.	
Beatrice.	What should I do with him? Dress him in my	

apparel, and make him my waiting gentlewoman?
He that hath a beard is more than a youth, and he that
hath no beard is less than a man; and he that is more   30
than a youth is not for me, and he that is less than a
man I am not for him; therefore I will even take
sixpence in earnest of the berrord [bearward], and
lead his apes into hell.

Leonato.   Well then, go you into hell?   35

Beatrice.   No; but to the gate, and there will the devil meet me,
like an old cuckold, with horns on his head, and say
'Get you to heaven, Beatrice, get you to heaven;
here's no place for you maids'. So deliver I up my
apes and away to Saint Peter for the heavens; he   40
shows me where the bachelors sit, and there live
we as merry as the day is long.

Antonio.   [*To Hero*] Well, niece, I trust you will be rul'd by
your father.

Beatrice.   Yes, faith; it is my cousin's duty to make curtsy, and   45
say 'Father, as it please you'. But yet for all that,
cousin, let him be a handsome fellow, or else make
another curtsy and say 'Father, as it please me'.

Leonato.   Well, niece, I hope to see you one day fitted with
a husband.   50

Beatrice.   Not till God make men of some other metal than
earth. Would it not grieve a woman to be over-master'd
with a piece of valiant dust, to make an account of
her life to a clod of wayward marl? No, uncle, I'll none:
Adam's sons are my brethren; and, truly, I hold it a   55
sin to match in my kindred.

Leonato.   Daughter, remember what I told you: if the Prince
do solicit you in that kind, you know your answer.

Beatrice.   The fault will be in the music, cousin, if you be not
wooed in good time. If the Prince be too important,   60
tell him there is measure in every thing, and so dance
out the answer. For, hear me, Hero: wooing, wedding,
and repenting, is as a Scotch jig, a measure, and a
cinquepace; the first suit is hot and hasty, like a Scotch

jig, and full as fantastical; the wedding, mannerly 65
modest, as a measure, full of state and ancientry;
and then comes repentance, and, with his bad legs,
falls into the cinquepace faster and faster, till he sink
into his grave.

Leonato. Cousin, you apprehend passing shrewdly. 70
Beatrice. I have a good eye, uncle; I can see a church by
daylight.

Before considering the content of this passage it is worth taking a
quick look at the style. Leonato and Antonio are somewhat laconic.
Three of their comments are introduced by 'Well', which is a filler,
making no substantial contribution to what is said, but conveying a
note of reserve, and perhaps disapproval. Both rely, too, on slightly
oblique formulae ('I trust you will ...'; '... remember what I told
you ...', '... in that kind ...', '... you know your answer'). These imply
that Hero has been privately schooled, and is being reminded not
only of what has been said, but also of her duty to obey. Hero's
silence, as so often in this play, speaks of her submissiveness, and
perhaps of the tight rein she keeps on her feelings.

Beatrice, by contrast, is voluble, even to the point of noisiness.
Her imagination is vigorously at work expressing itself in metaphor
(lines 54, 59–60), elaborate simile (lines 62–9) and witty adaptation
of proverbial sayings (e.g. the notion that old maids lead apes in hell,
line 34) – all of which tend towards the satirical debunking more
usually associated with young gallants than gentlewomen. She also
makes use of neatly shaped syntax (as in the adroitly balanced 'a
beard / more than a youth': 'no beard / less than a man' of lines
29–30, and the balancing of the antithetical pronouns 'you' and 'me'
against each other in lines 46–8), and such aural effects as alliteration and similar endings.(e.g. 'wooing, wedding, and repenting' and
'mannerly modest, as a measure', lines 62–6). These more elegant
devices seem to contain and abate the pertness of her wit, giving her
nonconformity an air of civility and accomplishment which, though
it does not blunt the cutting edge of her tongue, suggests that she is,
for all that, not prepared to sacrifice her status as a well brought-up
young woman.

Beatrice's style matches what she says. Though scoffing at marriage (to the extent that her uncle is clearly anxious that she will make herself ineligible), she is nevertheless much preoccupied with the qualities that make for a good husband. With seeming perversity, she will have neither a beardless nor a bearded man – the one is too callow for her, the other too old. She can crack the standard joke about unmarried women leading apes in hell, but she firmly rejects the idea of hell (and, jocular though it may be, the wearing of horns – the tediously reiterated Elizabethan way of mocking men whose wives are unfaithful to them – is for her asssociated with the devil). Her verbal sparring with the bachelors – who obviously resemble the witty Benedick – is to go on in heaven, and does not compromise her maidenhood. It remains implicit with her that she will not lose her virginity outside marriage: wit and honour maintain an equilibrium.

When Antonio raises the question of a daughter's obedience to her father (lines 43–4), although this concerns Hero rather than Beatrice herself, Beatrice is forward enough to speak out what the quiet Hero would not dream of saying. Although accepting all that the words 'duty' and 'curtsy' in line 45 imply, Beatrice firmly asserts the woman's right to take only a man who is attractive to her. Just as the 'you' and 'me' of lines 46–8 are held in stylistic balance, so the rights of the daughter are put in equal scale (if not more so) with those of the father. And when it comes to the question of a wife's obedience to her husband (whom the wedding service would require her to honour and obey), she speaks of the relation between Adam's sons and daughters, which is one of equality, rather than the subordination of Eve to Adam. The preceding lines 52–4 are, it is true, predicated on the assumption of the mastery of the man; they do not directly challenge that conventional precedence. But the scoffing personifications, 'valiant dust' and 'wayward marl', are a reminder that man (and woman, too) is but clay; and if the wife has to submit, it will only be to a man who has earned the right to command by his essential courage and dignity.

Beatrice's elaborate figure, based on music – with puns on the answering of one voice to another in part-song (line 59) and the keeping of time (line 60) – which leads into three kinds of dancing (lines 62–9), again suggests, as music invariably does in Shakespeare, the principle of order; but she shifts the burden from Leonato's emphasis on filial obedience to criticism of a wooer who is excessively importunate ('important', line 60) and does not give the woman proper time and leisure to consider her position. For Beatrice takes a realistic rather than romantic view of marriage. Without disparaging it, and without losing the nimble way with words that is an essential chracteristic of her comic verve, she sketches in three stages of marriage – precipitate wooing, decorous wedding ceremony, and post-marital disharmony – which give full weight to its seriousness for woman. Hero's father and uncle are far too much preoccupied with the social and political considerations (the more so as they are, at this point in the play, under the mistaken apprehension that Don Pedro is wooing for himself). Their view is both selfish and exclusively male. Beatrice rapidly touches in an image of the whole spectrum of what marriage can all too easily become for a woman. The vividness of her contrast between the stately 'measure' and the increasingly giddy 'cinquepace' makes the possibility of subsequent disenchantment graphically immediate, and the final word of her peroration, 'grave', seals the passage from headlong wooing to mortal repentance.

Beatrice does, as Leonato says, 'apprehend passing shrewdly' (line 70), but less in the shrewish spirit he suggests than with the acumen that 'shrewdly' can also mean. Her final comment is a claim that she can see what is plain enough to anyone; but the truth is that she sees what others, either wilfully or ignorantly, do not see. Hers is the clear-sighted common sense vital to comedy, and a necessary corrective to the narrower interests of the men, not only in this scene, but frequently throughout *Much Ado About Nothing* and Shakespearean comedy generally.

*   *   *

As You Like It, III.v.35–69. Rosalind (dressed as the boy, Ganymede) steps forward to interrupt a scene between Silvius and Phebe in which the latter is scornful of Silvius's protestations of love for her.

Rosalind.	Who might be your mother,	35
	That you insult, exult, and all at once,	
	Over the wretched? What though you have no beauty –	
	As, by my faith, I see no more in you	
	Than without candle may go dark to bed –	
	Must you be therefore proud and pitiless?	40
	Why, what means this? Why do you look on me?	
	I see no more in you than in the ordinary	
	Of nature's sale-work. 'Od's my little life,	
	I think she means to tangle my eyes too!	
	No, faith, proud mistress, hope not after it;	45
	'Tis not your inky brows, your black silk hair,	
	Your bugle eyeballs, nor your cheek of cream,	
	That can entame my spirits to your worship.	
	You foolish shepherd, wherefore do you follow her,	
	Like foggy south, puffing with wind and rain?	50
	You are a thousand times a properer man	
	Than she a woman. 'Tis such fools as you	
	That makes the world full of ill-favour'd children.	
	'Tis not her glass, but you, that flatters her;	
	And out of you she sees herself more proper	55
	Than any of her lineaments can show her.	
	But, mistress, know yourself. Down on your knees,	
	And thank heaven, fasting, for a good man's love;	
	For I must tell you friendly in your ear:	
	Sell when you can; you are not for all markets.	60
	Cry the man mercy, love him, take his offer;	
	Foul is most foul, being foul to be a scoffer.	
	So take her to thee, shepherd. Fare you well.	
Phebe.	Sweet youth, I pray you chide a year together;	
	I had rather hear you chide than this man woo.	65
Rosalind.	He's fall'n in love with your foulness, and she'll	
	fall in love with my anger. If it be so, as fast as she	
	answers thee with frowning looks, I'll sauce her	
	with bitter words.	

Rosalind's long speech breaks itself into four sections, according to the person to whom she addresses herself. From lines 35–48 she speaks to Phebe, lines 49–56 to Silvius, lines 57–62 to Phebe again, and the last line to Silvius. The simplest way to analyse it therefore is to take it section by section.

In the first section she steps forward, in the character of the young man Ganymede, prompted by high indignation at the treatment Phebe is handing out to Silvius. By questioning who Phebe's mother might be she is, in effect, rebuking her for being unfeminine in her haughty attitude towards Silvius (the conventional line being that a true daughter of a true woman would be much more meek and sympathetic). At lines 37–40 she likewise treats Phebe as unjustified in her rejection of Silvius because she is no beauty (she could go to bed in the dark, as that would be the best way of hiding her plainness), and therefore, again on the conventional assumption, has nothing to be so proud about. On the face of it, this suggests that Rosalind goes along unquestioningly with accepted notions of what is appropriately feminine behaviour. But the condemnation of Phebe is clearly overstated – line 36, for example, with its studiedly similar sound values (in*sult*, ex*ult*, *all at once*) and its exaggeration of Phebe's tone, so that she sounds like a braggart warrior triumphing over a fallen foe, is a deliberate travesty of Phebe's manner. (At lines 8–9 – which Rosalind would have overheard – Phebe had told Silvius, ' I would not be thy executioner; / I fly thee, for I would not injure thee.') Moreover, it is highly unlikely that Phebe is as plain as Rosalind/Ganymede claims: as the disdainful shepherdess of pastoral she is probably very attractive, in a conventionally pretty way. Rosalind's indignation is overdone – to shock Phebe into more reasonable behaviour. And with this deliberate exaggeration also goes her apparent adoption of conventionally feminine assumptions. As a woman disguised as a young man, bursting in, with very little excuse, on the lovers' scene, she is herself behaving very unconventionally. Consequently, her use of convention can be seen more as a convenient stick with which to beat Phebe than as a reflection of her own private feelings.

In a triple sense 'Rosalind' is playing a part: he/she is a boy-actor playing Rosalind, who is playing Ganymede, who is here playing the

part of an onlooker compelled by 'his' conventionally minded indignation to intervene in the scene between Silvius and Phebe. To add
to this complicated irony, Ganymede's anger gives 'him' an unexpected sexual appeal to Phebe, who – though she does not as yet say
anything – is clearly (as implied by lines 41–4) gazing at the seeming
young man with undisguised admiration. As soon as she realises this
Rosalind/Ganymede rebuffs Phebe, referring sarcastically to her
appearance in terms which emphasise (interestingly, as also happens
in Shakespeare's Sonnets when he is speaking of the so-called 'dark
lady') how little it conforms to accepted Elizabethan standards of
fair-haired, white-skinned beauty. The 'young man' now becomes an
Adonis figure rejecting the advances of Venus, but with very different motivation from the love-scorning Adonis of legend (and,
again, as portrayed in one of Shakespeare's earlier poems, *Venus and
Adonis*). The disguised Rosalind now not only wants to bring Phebe
down off her pedestal, but also to discourage a love which is based
on a complete misapprehension of her true gender. The first section
of this speech thus ends with further scoffing at the scoffer (Phebe)
who has till now held the stage, and an even more dramatically complicated relationship between Rosalind and Phebe.

With section 2 the 'young man's' mockery turns on Silvius, and,
once more, male disguise enables Rosalind to be more outspoken
than she would be able to be in her female character. She grossly
debunks Silvius's unrequited love by reducing it to the image of the
fog-bearing south wind puffing out its cheeks (as represented in contemporary maps) 'with wind and rain'; and not only can she tell
Silvius that he is more handsome as a man than Phebe is as a
woman, but she can also make the – from a conventional point of
view, highly immodest – suggestion that the sexually deluded choice
which causes him to take a merely plain woman for a ravishing
beauty results in the begetting of ugly babies. To rub still more salt
in this wound, she tells him that the portrait he creates of Phebe is a
merely subjective illusion, and in so doing she radically undermines
the assumption on which romantic love is based. In the Neoplatonic
philosophy of love, what the lover worships as beauty in his mistress
is a reflection of the real and eternal Idea of Beauty, and is capable of
becoming a stepping-stone to the realisation of that ultimate Beauty.

Rosalind/ Ganymede, however, degrades Silvius's love to the status of a distorting mirror which, instead of reflecting things truly, produces a mere illusion, and in the process deceives with malicious flattery. Love is thus turned inside out, and Silvius ironically becomes an aider and abetter of Phebe's egotistical self-deception.

When, in section 3, Rosalind returns to Phebe, it is to pursue this theme of self-deception further. She becomes almost sternly didactic, ordering Phebe to follow the traditional injunction: *nosce teipsum* – 'know thyself', but with an unusually practical basis in market values. This was already hinted at in line 43, with the reference to 'nature's sale-work'. Now her 'Sell when you can' (60) is much more explicit; it make no bones about the assumption that marriage is at bottom a matter of supply and demand, and that a plain woman cannot pick and choose, but must snap up what offer comes her way. The rhyming couplet at lines 61–2 heightens the crispness and sharpness of what she says, and the triple play on the word 'foul' (embracing ugliness, culpability and ill-mannered behaviour) makes the stinging wit still more prominent.

There is a studied crudeness here which belongs to the macho character Rosalind puts on to suit her persona as Ganymede; but its deliberately exaggerated commercialism also serves to make a point about relations between the sexes which convention and romantic sentiment tend to gloss over. In a world where it is accepted that a woman has to depend on a man for subsistence and protection, and economic power rests with the man, women are indeed like goods in a market where similar wares are also up for sale. Consequently, they refuse a reasonable bid at their peril, running the risk of being left unsold at the end of the day. This is not a view with which Rosalind herself can be identified. Elsewhere (for example, in the passage already analysed from IV.i) she shows awareness that more complex issues are at stake. But, crude as it is, it is an important substratum which the manlike 'Ganymede' is able to voice in a way that would not be open to the feminine Rosalind.

The last section of the speech is addressed to Silvius again. Brief and dismissive, it is somewhat comically high-handed in its assumption that the speaker has power to set Silvius and Phebe right, and then pair them off with each other. (Yet in that respect it anticipates what Rosalind does in Act V in quite serious vein.) It sets the seal on Rosalind's creation of a cockily 'Ganymede' version of herself.

In what remains of the passage we see Phebe falling head over heels with this persona. She is charmed by the somewhat impertinent youth's 'chiding' almost, it seems, in perverse opposition to the dogged devotion she gets far too easily from Silvius. And we hear Rosalind – having summed up the situation with one clause directed to Phebe ('He's fall'n in love with your foulness'), and one to Silvius ('and she'll fall in love with my anger') – decide to use the 'Ganymede' role with which Phebe has become infatuated as a means of giving the shepherdess a taste of her own medicine. The metaphor, 'sauce her with bitter words', carries a double meaning: (1) it suggests that Rosalind will be deliberately rude so that Phebe is made to suffer as she makes Silvius suffer (and so, presumably, learn to become more sympathetic); and (2) that the comic situation, already a tasty dish, will be further spiced up by the insolent tone 'Ganymede' will adopt towards Phebe. Both meanings are appropriate – the first points to the corrective role which Rosalind's disguise enables her to adopt, and the second to the heightening of the comedy which Shakespeare is able to bring about by this device. Either way, it is the liberation of the masculine element in Rosalind which secures the effect. She becomes almost an androgynous character, capitalising on both the sympathetic awareness traditionally associated with the woman, and the scoffing pertness associated with the adolescent male.

*   *   *

Twelfth Night, II.ii.15–39. Malvolio has just left the stage, having been sent to return a ring which Viola is supposed to have left behind after her interview with Olivia in I.v. However, Viola – the speaker in the following soliloquy – knows that this was not the case.

> I left no ring with her; what means this lady?   15
> Fortune forbid my outside have not charm'd her!
> She made good view of me; indeed, so much

That methought her eyes had lost her tongue,
For she did speak in starts distractedly.
She loves me, sure: the cunning of her passion   20
Invites me in this churlish messenger.
None of my lord's ring! Why, he sent her none.
I am the man. 'If it be so – as 'tis –
Poor lady, she were better love a dream.
Disguise, I see thou art a wickedness   25
Wherein the pregnant enemy does much.
How easy is it for the proper-false
In women's waxen hearts to set their forms!
Alas, our frailty is the cause, not we!
For such as we are made of, such we be.   30
How will this fadge? My master loves her dearly,
And I, poor monster, fond as much on him;
And she, mistaken, seems to dote on me.
What will become of this? As I am man,
My state is desperate for my master's love;   35
As I am woman – now alas the day! –
What thriftless sighs shall poor Olivia breathe!
O Time, thou must untangle this, not I;
It is too hard a knot for me t' untie!
                                        [*Exit.*

There are some obvious similarities between this and the previous passage from *As You Like It*. In both the heroine is disguised as a boy, and in both her male disguise causes her to become the object of another woman's love. Viola, however, is more anxious about her disguise than Rosalind, and she is more markedly compassionate towards Olivia than Rosalind is towards Phebe. This can be explained – in part at least – because Viola is here musing to herself, whereas Rosalind was interacting with other characters. Something like the witty pertness typical of 'Ganymede' is to be found in other scenes in *Twelfth Night* where Viola is required to play up to her role as 'Cesario'; and as it is the boyishness of the disguised Rosalind which attracts Phebe, so it is that quality in 'Cesario' which causes Olivia to fall in love with him/her. But left to herself Viola is more

Viola than Cesario, and more acutely conscious of the problems her disguise causes – both for herself and others. There is also more dramatic development in her speech, as she dwells on those problems, and becomes more aware of the predicament she has got herself into. The very situation which has brought her into the presence of Olivia – i.e. her being made the reluctant messenger of Orsino's love – is a painful one for her, and this soliloquy involves a deepening of the suffering which that entails.

Viola begins with puzzlement as to what all this fuss about leaving behind a non-existent ring means. With typically quick, intuitive insight, however, she guesses at the reason . She rapidly focuses on the misleading nature of her appearance: 'Fortune forbid my *outside* have not charm'd her!' (line 16) – the use of the word 'outside' heightening the contrast between what 'Cesario' is to others and what Viola (still in that costume and hence showing the same 'outside' to the theatre audience) is now saying in her own person. Lines 17–19 elaborate the effect of her 'outside' as she recalls the way Olivia had behaved at their interview. She enters feelingly into the mental turbulence which the false image must have caused, and the poetry increases in intensity as she does so, producing the comic, yet affecting, words of line 18. (Commentary may paraphrase these as: 'It seemed to me that what she saw so disturbed her that she was temporarily unable to speak coherently'; but the bizarre image of 'eyes' which somehow had the capacity to have 'lost' a 'tongue' communicates that sense of disturbance far more graphically.) After this (comparatively) lengthy flashback, the speech returns to the present in the short sentence, 'She loves me, sure', and the swift, elliptically expressed interpretation of the significance of Malvolio's message – it is a cunning device prompted by passion to give me enticement under the pretence of rejecting a gift which I never, in fact, brought. The colloquial stresses of line 22, cutting across what has up to now been a fairly regular iambic rhythm, act out Viola's astonishment and scorn, and the heavy stress on 'I' at the beginning of line 23 dramatically underlines the shift from what is supposed to concern Orsino to what Viola now suspects to be aimed at herself. In the second half of line 23 the rapid change from the conditional 'If' to the declarative ''tis' reflects the instantaneous hardening of that suspicion into truth, and the pitiful 'Poor lady', which immediately follows in the next line, shows how soon that realisation turns scorn into compassion – beautifully, yet succinctly, crystallised in 'she were better love a dream'.

Lines 25–30 are less dramatically urgent, and slightly sententious in form. But they serve, nonetheless, to suggest a process of reflection which is deepening Viola's immediate experience into something of wider validity. The complications and disadvantages of disguise in general are now being brought home to her by the predicament into which her use of it has thrown Olivia; and, as the latter part of this speech makes clear, Viola is also becoming more conscious of the trap that it has sprung for herself. The 'pregnant [= subtle, resourceful] enemy' would appear to be a reference to Satan; and although this is not, presumably, to be taken as a deeply serious moral comment, the conception of disguise as a double-edged weapon that can be used by the devil counterbalances its use as a means of liberation. The latter aspect of disguise is what predominates in Rosalind's use of it in *As You Like It*, and is perhaps the aspect that was uppermost in Viola's mind when she originally took it on; but now she is coming to see how treacherous it can be. That it is coupled, in lines 27–30, with a more conventional acceptance of the supposed frailty of women, also suggests some undermining of Viola's confidence. Again, it is as well to remember that this is not Viola putting on a boyish act of bravado towards others, but musing with herself. It is as if she feels a guilty reaction against her own flouting of gender protocol by adopting boy's disguise, and thus finds herself mouthing the more orthodox strictures against it. Certainly, this is one way of accounting for the almost pat quality and somewhat banal rhyming of lines 29–30. Here is the manlike woman reverting to a rather more womanish version of womanliness.

But with the more colloquial 'How will this fadge [work out]?' of line 31, and the mock self-pity of 'I, poor monster' (32), Viola seems to snap out of her conventionally moralising frame of mind. She engages once more with her particular situation, rather than generalised moral sentiment, as (in lines 31–3) she reviews the criss-cross of affections which she sees developing; and she retains enough sense of humour to distance her emotion with a slightly ironic choice of verbs in 'fond' and 'dote'. ('Fond' here has a different emphasis from modern English 'to be fond of': it carries a hint, like 'dote', of foolishly excessive love.) She is puzzled – as the repeated question at line 34 indicates; and she gives the sense of hovering uncertainly on the brink of both tragedy and comedy as she weighs up the gender implications of her present situation. The balanced phrasing, 'As I am man ... As I am woman ...' is the stylistic counterpart of this hovering: in her disguise as 'Cesario' she cannot attract the heterosexual love from Orsino which her femaleness desires, since she would have to have the 'outside' of a female to do this, and, given Viola's 'inside' nature as a woman, Olivia's equal desire for a heterosexual love is equally doomed to frustration. (That this formulation also carries the subtext of possible homosexual relationships adds to the intriguing nature of the parallelism – along with the ever-present ambiguity, in the Elizabethan theatre, presented by a 'man' who is a 'woman' actually being a boy-actor.)

Viola's position now is such that she can satisfy neither Olivia's desire, nor her own – a situation potentially tragic for both of them. But, at the same time, she seems to relish the poised absurdity of this comic equation. The very phrasing of line 37 ('What thriftless sighs shall poor Olivia breathe!') both sympathises with the frustration in store for Olivia, and laughs at the waste of breath. Similarly, the self-pity Viola expresses for her own dilemma vis-à-vis Orsino is countered by her choice (as already noted) of such words as 'poor monster' and 'fond'. Sympathy and mockery, tragedy and comedy, female and male roles – each of these dualities seems an aspect of the poised opposites of which Viola's situation is composed. Her conclusion, therefore, is that it is something which *her* actions cannot resolve. The resolution lies with Time: 'O Time, thou must untangle this, not I; / It is too hard a knot for me t' untie!'

With this scene-ending couplet (it is followed by Viola's *Exit*) we are on the verge of issues which must be reserved for the chapter devoted to 'Endings'. But it is worth remarking here and now that Viola's sense of how things can be resolved is different from Rosalind's in *As You Like It*. Rosalind takes charge and virtually becomes the stage manager of her play's ending. And that she is able to do so derives from her androgynous man–woman state. However, that Viola feels differently is also due to her androgynous state. This may seem paradoxical, but the difference lies in the emphasis placed on the possibilities opened up for each heroine by her adoption of male disguise. It may be liberating, but it may also be 'a wickedness'. Moreover, as analysis reveals, to whichever end of the scale the emphasis moves, there always seems to remain some recognition of the other. In this, as in so many other respects, Shakespearean comedy is not a straight piece of string, but a fascinatingly tangled knot.

Conclusions

It has to be admitted that to call such heroines as Beatrice, Rosalind and Viola 'manlike women' is potentially misleading. They are not blusteringly domineering, macho characters, as the phrase might perhaps suggest. In so far as Beatrice cultivates a style of apprehending 'passing shrewdly', and Rosalind, in her disguise as 'Ganymede', adopts a rather boyish bravado, they do approach these supposedly manlike qualities; but these tend to be manners deliberately employed for particular ends. For example, Beatrice, despite her pose as scourge of men and mocker at marriage, is intensely interested in the qualities that make for a good husband and what the married state means for a woman, not just at the artificial stage of courtship, but when all the excitement of the wedding is over. As a corollary to this, on the other hand, Rosalind/Ganymede takes Phebe to task for ignoring the underlying commercial and competitive aspects of marriage which dictate that a woman must know her bidding price in the market. The 'manlike' persona that each adopts is something which enables them to speak in such terms, as the Elizabethan conventions of womanliness would not.

Implicit in this more forcible way of speaking out on issues discouraged by convention is, it may be argued, a fundamental dissatisfaction with the role allotted to woman in a male-orientated society. This is an argument in tune with late twentieth-century feminism, and has some degree of validity. Which is not, however, to say that it is what Shakespeare consciously intended (if we can ever know what his intentions were); nor that it is the meaning that contemporary audiences would have found in these comedies. As we have seen, Beatrice is careful, even at her most outspoken moments, to preserve a feminine decorum, expressing her criticism of the 'Father, as it please you' stance expected of a woman, not by aggressive rejection, but by balancing it with an equally important 'Father, as it please me'.

In this respect, the case of Viola is also very interesting. She benefits, like Rosalind, from the privileges accorded to the pert and witty young male by adopting disguise as a boy; but she also finds disguise 'a wickedness' in that it prevents her from exercising those womanly charms which are her birthright, and which, in more conventional circumstances, she would find it much easier to deploy. The tone of her speech in *Twelfth Night*, II.ii is thus complex and varied, at times 'boyish', at times pathetically (or even approaching the tragically) 'womanish'.

The theatrical conditions requiring a female role to be played by a boy-actor also add to the complexity of the 'manlike' qualities Shakespeare gives these heroines. Because the audience knows that they are actually boys, they can get away with saying and doing things that might not be accepted from women as such. Just as the Fools use their 'folly' as a stalking-horse under which they shoot their wit, so the heroines use their androygnous natures to be more provocative than might otherwise be possible. Yet they do play the parts of women who – to step outside the comedies for a moment and quote from Cleopatra, the most complex of all Shakespeare's tragic heroines – are but women 'and commanded / By such poor passion as the maid that milks / And does the meanest chares [tasks]' (*Antony and Cleopatra*, IV.xv.73–5). That is to say, they combine the amusingly, and provocatively, 'manlike' with a quite conventional version of the womanly, to produce characters who are uniquely male *and* female.

9

Odd Men Out

Introduction

Shakespearean comedy is a synthesis of many elements, many moods and many different kinds of characters and atmosphere. It is also hardly ever pure comedy or farce, and, as we have already seen, it can border on the tragic. Likewise, there are characters who do not 'fit in' – who seem outside the normal range of comic figures, but who, in doing so, greatly enrich the sense that these plays are perpetually open to new possibilities of meaning and value.

Each of the four plays on which this study focuses has its odd men out. (They are, incidentally, all men; the women may be unusual and distinguished, but their difference from the other characters among whom they move never creates the sense that they do not belong to the same comic world.)

Puck in *A Midsummer Night's Dream*, though the agent of Oberon's comic activity, administering the love-juice at his master's behest, has almost an independent addiction to mischief. When he anoints the eyes of the wrong lover he takes an amoral delight in the chaos he has inadvertently created: his attitude is summed up by the twin statements, 'Lord, what fools these mortals be!' and 'those things do best please me / That befall prepost'rously' (III.ii.115 and 120–1).

In *Much Ado About Nothing* the odd man out is Don John, whose addiction is to villainy. When he hears that Borachio can foil the proposed marriage of Claudio to Hero, his reaction is: 'Any bar, any

cross, any impediment, will be med'cinable to me ... and whatso-
ever comes athwart his affection ranges evenly with mine' (II.ii.4–8).
The metaphor contained in the word 'med'cinable' suggests the
curative, life-affirming spirit of comedy; but, perversely, Don John's
'medicine' is poison. His is a melancholy, malcontent nature which
can feed only on destruction.

But neither of these figures is as interestingly developed as Jaques
in *As You Like It* or Malvolio in *Twelfth Night*. These are the two
'odd men out' on which this chapter will focus. In the first,
Shakespeare explores the melancholy already adumbrated in Don
John, but, singling it out from the decreative viciousness of the latter,
makes of it an altogether more original principle of critical curiosity,
which subsists on the borderline of comedy. In Malvolio, as the
name suggests (it means 'ill will'), he experiments with the 'humour',
or type, character that Ben Jonson was beginning to popularise in his
satirical comedies – a character dominated by one particular obsession which is carried to a self-defeatingly farcical excess. But
Shakespeare does not stop short there; he becomes interested in the
different sense of values on which Malvolio's life is based, and introduces him into the comic world of *Twelfth Night* as a risible killjoy
who nevertheless has his own kind of dignity and self-justification.

Analyses

As You Like It, II.i.29–68. Jaques himself does not speak in this
passage, but one of Duke Senior's attendant lords gives an account of
what he overheard Jaques saying in the Forest of Arden.

First Lord.	To-day my Lord of Amiens and myself
	Did steal behind him as he lay along 30
	Under an oak whose antique root peeps out
	Upon the brook that brawls along this wood!
	To the which place a poor sequest'red stag,
	That from the hunter's aim had ta'en a hurt,
	Did come to languish; and, indeed, my lord, 35
	The wretched animal heav'd forth such groans

That their discharge did stretch his leathern coat
Almost to bursting; and the big round tears
Cours'd one another down his innocent nose
In piteous chase; and thus the hairy fool,   40
Much marked of the melancholy Jaques,
Stood on th' extremest verge of the swift brook,
Augmenting it with tears.

Duke Senior.   But what said Jaques?
Did he not moralize this spectacle?

First Lord.   O, yes, into a thousand similes.   45
First, for his weeping into the needless stream:
'Poor deer,' quoth he 'thou mak'st a testament
As worldlings do, giving thy sum of more
To that which had too much'. Then, being there alone,
Left and abandoned of his velvet friends: 50
''Tis right;' quoth he 'thus misery doth part
The flux of company'. Anon, a careless herd,
Full of the pasture, jumps along by him
And never stays to greet him. 'Ay,' quoth Jaques
'Sweep on, you fat and greasy citizens;   55
'Tis just the fashion. Wherefore do you look
Upon that poor and broken bankrupt there?'
Thus most invectively he pierceth through
The body of the country, city, court,
Yea, and of this our life; swearing that we   60
Are mere usurpers, tyrants, and what's worse,
To fright the animals, and to kill them up
In their assign'd and native dwelling-place.

Duke Senior. And did you leave him in this contemplation?

Second Lord. We did, my lord, weeping and commenting   65
Upon the sobbing deer.

Duke Senior.   Show me the place;
I love to cope him in these sullen fits,
For then he's full of matter.

A feature which makes this passage different from all those which
have been previously analysed is that it reports the principal char-

acter instead of showing that character in his own person. What Jaques is quoted as saying is, presumably, the equivalent of his speaking himself – though one has to allow that it could be subject to the distortion which a reporter inevitably puts on anything he reports. However, assuming that the First Lord's memory is accurate, we have both the words Jaques utters and the impression he creates on those who overhear him. The latter is an important aspect of the passage, since, clearly, Jaques is an object of considerable interest to those around him, not least the Duke. That we have this report is due to the fact that two of the courtiers took the trouble to pursue him, when he thought himself to be alone, and to eavesdrop on him; and it is not unreasonable, given what the Duke says at lines 66–8, to assume that they did this because they knew that his behaviour and comments would be something out of the ordinary, and especially intriguing to their leader. The implication is that this is one of several such episodes, which are typical of the peculiar brand of melancholy (or 'sullen fits' as the Duke calls them) affected by Jaques. On such occasions he is known to be 'full of matter', i.e. full of interesting, if perhaps eccentric, things to say. (That he also speaks them aloud, even when alone, does not mean that he is mentally unstable, but is part of the convention of the soliloquy – in this speech in particular, a convention which the audience happily accepts, as otherwise they would have no idea what Jaques was thinking.) His reputation, in other words, goes before him. He is known, and tolerated, as an odd man out, one of the fashionably melancholy men of his day whose values and attitudes are fascinatingly out of the ordinary.

How far this special relationship between Jaques and those around him influences the style of the report delivered by the First Lord is also an interesting question. When – as the Duke expected (and very probably hoped for) – Jaques drew a moral from the spectacle of the deer's weeping into the stream, he somewhat blatantly personified the animal, treating it as if it were capable of human emotions, and imagining a moral context for its behaviour, and that of the other deer, which is drawn from human society. In his account the First Lord seems to present the deer in similar terms. The wounded deer comes to the same spot as Jaques – a spot picturesquely described as one where the root of an 'antique' oak *peeps out* at the woodland stream (line 31) – in order to *languish* and heave forth *groans* (lines 35–6), very much as if it were a sentient human being; and the sentimental account of the way these groans stretch his leather *coat* almost to bursting point, and the tears run down his *innocent nose* (lines 36–9), strongly suggests that the deer as hunter's quarry has become injected with the qualities of a human being victimised unjustly by a ruthless society. (In lines 39–40 there is even a peculiar double-take whereby the tears rolling down the cheeks of the victimised deer/human being are imaged as hounds engaged in headlong pursuit of their quarry – which becomes a '*piteous* chase [hunt]' only in the sense that it arouses pity in the eyes of the beholder, much as the plight of the hunted deer excites pity in the First Lord's own narrative.)

When we come to the report of Jaques's comments, we find that what is implicit in the narrative now becomes more explicit. To begin with he seems to be critical of the deer, for the first of his 'thousand similes' is to compare its adding needless tears to the stream with a worldly minded person who makes a will, not with a view to rewarding those who are in genuine need, but to get favours from rich people (who will be told, of course, that they are his heirs). But when the deer is considered as one abandoned by his 'velvet friends', Jaques's comparison is with the man who, meeting with misfortune, finds that those who previously claimed friendship now desert him. (And here 'velvet' suggests not only the smooth skin of the deer, but also the idea that such friends are to be had only while comfort and prosperity last.) Now the deer has become a victim, and the next comparison develops this into the broader notion of the citizen-deer whose ill luck has brought bankruptcy on him. His former friends (now no longer merely 'velvet', but repulsively 'fat and greasy'), untouched by care themselves, sweep past, unwilling even to speak to him. However, what connects both deer as will-maker and deer as victim is Jaques's criticism of a society in which the ruling traits are selfishness, greed and ruthless disregard of the suffering of others.

This would appear to be an attack on the commercial values of those London citizens in Shakespeare's day whose pursuit of profit through trade was making them significant rivals to the traditional rulers represented by crown and aristocracy. But the First Lord goes on to say (at line 59) that Jaques's satire embraces country and court as well as city, and (at lines 60–3) includes even the way of life adopted by Duke Senior in the Forest of Arden. The paradoxical feature of the latter criticism is that it treats the Duke and his followers, who have been extirpated from their place at court by the usurpation of Duke Frederick, as themselves equally culpable 'usurpers, tyrants, and what's worse' by killing the animals and displacing them from the forest habitat which is naturally and rightfully theirs. Although it would be anachronistic to see this as an Elizabethan anticipation of twentieth-century animal rights campaigning, it does suggest that Jaques does not merely take sides with the old (embodied in the liberal aristocracy of Duke Senior) against the new (embodied in the vilified 'citizens'), but is prepared to direct his criticism even at the unexamined assumptions of his own side.

The passage under examination ends with Duke Senior asking to be taken where Jaques is. His appetite has been whetted by what has been reported, and he is keen to hear more. This reflects interestingly – and perhaps favourably – on the Duke, for the attack on his own supposed 'tyranny' seems to rouse his further attention rather than resentment. Elsewhere, however, he reveals scepticism of Jaques's status as a critic. In II.vii, for example, where Jaques expresses his wish to be given the freedom to speak out which is traditionally given to the Fool, claiming that in the process he would 'Cleanse the foul body of th' infected world' (line 60), the Duke is less sympathetic. He reveals that Jaques himself has, in the past, been a sensual libertine, and, far from using this satirical freedom as a curative medicine, he would infect the world with his own mental diseases: 'And all th' embossed sores and headed evils / That thou with licence of free foot hast caught / Wouldst thou disgorge into the general world' (II.vii.67–9). And in his encounter with Rosalind (at IV.i) Jaques's claim that he has developed a form of melancholy uniquely his own, as if this makes him in some way intellectually superior to other men, is dismissed by her with a brisk mockery that leaves him quite deflated.

These (and other passages) create an extended context in which

Jaques's moralising on the deer in II.i must ultimately be judged. Among other things, they suggest that his stance as critic is not altogether a detached one. For example, his very attraction to the plight of the deer may well be a form of self-pity: the deer as odd man out from the herd may be an imaginative projection of his own image of himself as the melancholy odd man out from all the norms of human society, whether associated with country, city or court. At this moment, however, in the unfolding of the play (the audience has not yet seen Jaques on the stage, and this report of the First Lord's acts as a kind of 'trailer' for his subsequent appearance) he represents an unusual, intriguing figure, who promises, not only novelty and variety, but the possibility of a quite different scale of values from those on which comedy is normally based. Or, at least, a widening of the range of comedy to include questionings and probings that will not allow assumptions to be taken for granted. As the Duke's appetite is whetted for more, so is the audience's; they, too, are prepared for 'sullen fits', which may nevertheless be 'full of matter'.

*   *   *

Twelfth Night, IV.ii.17–60 (17–59). With Sir Toby and Maria egging him on in the background, Feste, disguised as the priest Sir Topas, comes to visit Malvolio in his supposed madman's prison.

Sir Toby.	To him, Sir Topas.
Feste.	What ho, I say! Peace in this prison!
Sir Toby.	The knave counterfeits well; a good knave.
Malvolio	[*Within*] Who calls there? 20
Feste.	Sir Topas the curate, who comes to visit Malvolio the lunatic.
Malvolio.	Sir Topas, Sir Topas, good Sir Topas, go to my lady.
Feste.	Out, hyperbolical fiend! How vexest thou this man! Talkest thou nothing but of ladies? 25
Sir Toby.	Well said, Master Parson.
Malvolio.	Sir Topas, never was man thus wronged. Good Sir Topas, do not think I am mad; they have laid me here in hideous darkness.

Feste.	Fie, thou dishonest Satan! I call thee by the most 30 modest terms, for I am one of those gentle ones that will use the devil himself with courtesy. Say'st thou that house is dark?
Malvolio.	As hell, Sir Topas.
Feste.	Why, it hath bay windows transparent as barricadoes, 35 and the clerestories toward the south north are as lustrous as ebony; and yet complainest thou of obstruction?
Malvolio.	I am not mad, Sir Topas. I say to you this house is dark. 40
Feste.	Madman, thou errest. I say there is no darkness but ignorance; in which thou art more puzzled than the Egyptians in their fog.
Malvolio.	I say this house is as dark as ignorance, though ignorance were as dark as hell; and I say there was 45 never man thus abus'd. I am no more mad than you are; make the trial of it in any constant question.
Feste.	What is the opinion of Pythagoras concerning wild fowl? 50
Malvolio.	That the soul of our grandam might haply inhabit a bird.
Feste.	What think'st thou of his opinion?
Malvolio.	I think nobly of the soul, and no way approve his opinion. 55
Feste.	Fare thee well. Remain thou still in darkness: thou shalt hold th' opinion of Pythagoras ere I will allow of thy wits; and fear to kill a woodcock, lest thou dispossess the soul of thy grandam. Fare thee well.

Although Malvolio is, indeed, the odd man out in *Twelfth Night* – and earlier scenes have shown the mixture of killjoy seriousness, egregious pomposity and overweening ambition that makes him so – here, paradoxically, it is he who seems in tune with common-sense orthodoxy and Feste whose behaviour represents ludicrous eccentricity. But Feste, of course, is playing the part of Sir Topas, a bizarrely fictional parish priest supposedly come to exorcise, if he can, the demon who has possession of the, likewise supposedly, mad Malvolio. It is a deliberately topsy-turvy situation, invented by Maria to put the crowning touch to the elaborate hoax by which she deluded Malvolio into believing that Olivia was in love with him, and in consequence conducting himself in a way that could be construed as madness.

Sir Toby's initial exhortation to Feste, 'To him, Sir Topas', is like the setting-on of a dog to worry an opponent; it sets the tone for what follows. Not that Feste snaps like a terrier. In his disguise as the priest (and especially bearing in mind that he uses the name of the comic knight, Sir Topas, in Chaucer's *Canterbury Tales*) he, no doubt, adopts a pompously parsonical voice and manner, and his use of the standard salutation of visiting priests ('Peace in this prison!') immediately wins Sir Toby's applause. But he is there to tease and torment Malvolio, not to comfort him; and the more he exaggerates this farcical role, the more he succeeds in his purpose.

As the stage direction at line 20 suggests, the audience does not see Malvolio himself; only his voice is heard – from off stage, or from behind the closed curtains of the inner stage, or perhaps, via a trapdoor, from beneath the platform-stage. This enables Feste to be seen and heard in his actual person of Fool by Sir Toby and Maria (plus the theatre audience as well) while being heard by Malvolio solely in his 'Sir Topas' character. The very conditions of the stage performance thus add to the 'odd-man-out' effect; they emphasise the sociable, interactive role of Feste/Sir Topas, and heighten by contrast the sense of Malvolio as an alien figure cut off from normal human society.

Similarly, in accordance with this double level of theatrical presentation, Malvolio and Feste, though nominally engaged in dialogue with each other, are, on the farcical level, completely at odds. From the darkness of his prison Malvolio shouts, 'Who calls there?' only to receive a reply, both parts of which are deliberately falsified by the speaker: Feste is not 'Sir Topas the curate' [= parish priest], and he knows that Malvolio is not 'the lunatic'. In his desperate plight, however, Malvolio snatches at the straw of 'Sir Topas's' appearance, repeating his name three times, and pleading with him to become an intercessor with 'my lady'. Malvolio refers, of course, to his employer, Olivia, but 'Sir Topas', addressing his words to the evil spirit which he pretends has taken possession of Malvolio, treats 'lady' as an indication of sexual obsessiveness. As Sir Toby delightedly recognises, this is a hit which is doubly comic when aimed at the strait-laced Malvolio (and it may also, for the Elizabethan audience, have had comic associations with Catholic worship of the Virgin Mary, which to a Puritan would be still more abominable). However, the gibe seems to pass over Malvolio's head. He is entirely preoccupied with the darkness of his prison and the wrong that has been done him. Here he has truth on his side, and he speaks of it in a plain, straightforward way (which contrasts, significantly, with the inflated style characteristic of him in earlier scenes). 'Sir Topas', however, professes the opposite: what is objective truth to Malvolio he sees as the deceitful work of Satan; and to the acutely felt suffering of Malvolio he opposes the image of himself as a mild-mannered Christian who carries meekness and reasonableness to the ridiculous degree that he 'will use the devil himself with courtesy'. Nevertheless, in a pretended effort to convince Malvolio that the house is not dark he invents a nonsensical language of fashionable-sounding jargon (lines 35–8) which, if it means anything at all, confirms the opaqueness ('transparent as barricadoes') and blackness ('lustrous as ebony') of the windows, and places them in a self-contradictory ('south north') direction which is tantamount to admitting their non-existence. And to Malvolio's simple repetition, 'I say to you this house is dark', he retorts with a mixture of moral cant ('there is no darkness but ignorance') and biblical allusion (to Exodus 10:21–3) designed to obfuscate rather than clarify the situation. In a final attempt to keep hold on stable, meaningful reality Malvolio calls on the supposed priest to put any sensible question to him so that he can demonstrate his sanity with what are obviously sensible answers. What he gets, however, is a question about Pythagoras's eccentric theory of the transmigration of souls; and when he answers with a standard summary and example, followed by the orthodox Christian refutation (lines 51–2 and 54–5), he is confounded by Sir Topas's bizarre upholding of 'th' opinion of Pythagoras' as if it were an essential article of the faith.

This combination of inventive nonsense and linguistic babble is typical of the method employed by Shakespeare's 'clever Fools' to baffle ignorant inferiors; and as such it gets plenty of laughs. But its use here on Malvolio is something different. In common-sense terms Malvolio stands up to it very well (as the usual victims of the Fools do not); and, despite the degrading circumstances in which he is placed and the intellectual verbiage which is flung at him, he manages to retain a modicum of dignity (as shown for example, in what he says at lines 44–7 and 54). Feste's brilliant execution of Maria's strategy to deceive Malvolio into thinking that black is white and white is black creates fantastic comedy, but it does not succeed to the extent that the earlier letter strategy had done. What that scene had to work on was the potentiality for illusion already existent in Malvolio. What the present scene reveals is that, despite all the tricks played on him, Malvolio is capable of maintaining his own validly independent grip on reality. His voice, which comes from that dark, invisible off-stage area suggested by 'Within', is poised against the bizarre inventions of Feste/Sir Topas intended to ridicule him as the lunatic odd man out. In the event, however, the beleaguered voice succeeds in holding its own against its opponent, and in so doing achieves some sort of justification. Laughably misled as he is, and subjected to ridicule as the odd man out, Malvolio attracts both sympathy and respect. To that extent, the second stratagem practised upon him helps to adjust the balance of the first; he emerges, not merely as dupe, but as victim, with a case (even if a minority case) against those who victimise him.

Conclusions

As the last sentence of the preceding analysis implies, in Shakespearean comedy we can often discern a 'majority case' and a 'minority case'; and, broadly speaking, it is the business of comedy to reinforce the 'majority case' against the 'minority' one. In *Twelfth Night* the majority case is that represented by the idea of tolerant festivity suggested by the play's title, with its allusion to the twelve days of feasting and relaxed discipline which follow Christmas –

backed up by the permissive-sounding, alternative title: 'What You Will'. In the contest between Maria, Sir Toby and Feste on the one hand, and Malvolio on the other, it is the sociable 'cakes and ale' of Sir Toby which capture the audience's allegiance, and the killjoy rectitude of Malvolio which becomes the butt of comedy. Malvolio is an isolationist, egotistical figure at odds with the easygoing merriment, the generosity and the community spirit of his opponents. He does not share the values which make possible the play's traditionally happy ending (indeed, he opts out of that ending), and the comedy therefore singles him out for ridicule as the odd man out.

In *As You Like It* it is Jaques who opts out. The very first report of him concerns one of his characteristically 'sullen fits' (as Duke Senior calls them) when he has separated himself from the community of his fellow-courtiers-in-exile, and finds in a similarly herd-abandoned deer a symbol for his own isolation. Jaques is not as offensive a character as Malvolio, and he is not subjected therefore to the same baiting and exposure (though there are scenes in which he is made to look something of a fool by Touchstone and Rosalind, and even by Orlando). But the oddity of his odd-man-out status is exemplified in the minority view he takes of the community's widely practised – and, it would seem, unthinking acceptance of – deer-hunting, and the morals he draws from the herd's abandonment of one of its wounded members. His position probably seemed more comically bizarre to the original Elizabethan audiences of *As You Like It* than it does in the late twentieth century, and, although his criticisms of a self-seeking, commercially minded society might well have accorded with aristocratic attitudes to the customs and values of the newly rich citizens of the day, his self-indulgence and his sentimentality still make him seem a legitimate object of laughter. Moreover, as a 'humorous' cultivator of discords he is clearly a potential spoiler of the harmony towards which the comedy is ultimately directed.

Nevertheless, not only is the pleasure of finally harmonising concords, as in a piece of music, made greater by the cacophony of discords encountered on the way, but also the sense of the play's fullness and humanity is enhanced by the accommodation it gives to attitudes and values outside the majority ones to which the comedy conforms. This saves the social basis on which the comedy itself is erected – the 'majority case' to which the 'minority' one is opposed – from becoming too tight and restrictive a container. The admission of elements of uncertainty, variations of light and shade, and even destructive, anti-social traits that threaten the tolerant norms to which the comedy implicitly appeals – all these help to protect the comedy from becoming a tyranny to itself. Odd men out, it may be said, are a prophylactic against complacency; they inoculate a comedy against its own necessary, yet potentially harmful, sense of what its destiny should be.

10

Set Pieces

Introduction

In some respects Shakespeare's plays are more like opera than modern plays, and especially films and television productions. As in opera, where action may be suspended while a singer performs an aria which the audience enjoys virtually for its own sake, so in Shakespeare a character may be given a passage to speak – and also, as it happens, a song to sing —which stands almost on its own and can be enjoyed by the audience as a verbal tour de force in its own right. The relation of such passages to the rest of the play may vary, some seeming more relevant than others; but it is part of the entertainment which Shakespeare's plays provide (and particularly his comedies) that relevance to the rest of the action is not necessarily the overriding criterion. The ideas may be interesting in themselves, the bravura performance of the actor a source of admiration and delight, and – something truer perhaps for Elizabethan audiences than for modern ones – the skilful construction of the language and the adroit display of rhetorical qualities to be enjoyed as much for their own sake as for what they contribute to the development of the play as a whole. This chapter is devoted to the analysis of three such passages, two of them 'set-piece' speeches, from *A Midsummer Night's Dream* and *As You Like It*, and the other a song sung by Feste in *Twelfth Night*.

Analyses

A Midsummer Night's Dream, II.i.155–69. Oberon tells Puck about
the flower, 'Love-in-idleness', which has the power to make people
fall in love.

> That very time I saw, but thou couldst not,   155
> Flying between the cold moon and the earth
> Cupid, all arm'd; a certain aim he took
> At a fair vestal, throned by the west,
> And loos'd his love-shaft smartly from his bow,
> As it should pierce a hundred thousand hearts;   160
> But I might see young Cupid's fiery shaft
> Quench'd in the chaste beams of the wat'ry moon;
> And the imperial vot'ress passed on,
> In maiden meditation, fancy-free.
> Yet mark'd I where the bolt of Cupid fell.   165
> It fell upon a little western flower,
> Before milk-white, now purple with love's wound,
> And maidens call it Love-in-idleness.
> Fetch me that flow'r ...

There is some relevance to the rest of the play here, for the flower
which Puck is instructed to fetch is to become an important instrument of the plot, causing the lovers to fall in love with the wrong
person and so bringing about the cross-wooing on which much of
the comedy depends. But the description is much in excess of what
is need for the purpose of the plot; and, in particular, lines 157–64
could be omitted without any loss to the business in hand. Yet the
loss in aesthetic pleasure, and – for Elizabethan audiences – in political significance, would be great. For, as most (but not all) commentators agree, Shakespeare is here probably paying a graceful
compliment to Queen Elizabeth I, the Virgin Queen, who found it
expedient to fend off various suitors for her hand in marriage.

Of course, elaborating 'Love-in-idleness' in this way does usefully
underline the importance of the flower; but the the way the under-
lining is done draws attention to itself. Expectations of something

special are heightened by the distinction Oberon makes between what he has the power to see and Puck has not. This enables him to act as an intermediary for the audience, too; he opens up the hidden world of the gods for them, and provides imaginative reality for the unreal. The delay in his sentence structure, which holds back what Oberon 'saw' in line 155 until line 157, creates pleasurable suspense, and the contrast, in the intervening line 156, between 'cold moon' and more ordinary 'earth', together with the as yet undefined act of 'flying', intensifies the curiosity and wonder of the audience. When the unknown being is at last named as 'Cupid' this suspension heightens the effect of his appearance, and the position of 'Cupid' at the beginning of the line, with stress on the first syllable instead of the second, adds metrical emphasis as well. Then the doubling of this unusual stress with two heavily marked syllables, 'all arm'd', thrills with a sense of unexpected aggressiveness, and apprehension, too, as the god bends his bow and takes deliberate aim at an unspecified 'fair vestal'. What is highlighted now is the opposition between erotic love and chastity; and a little drama is enacted, within this virtually self-contained aria, between the seeming defencelessness of the virgin and the supernatural power of the love-god. An intriguing additional piece of information about the virgin is slipped in at line 158, to the effect that she is 'throned by the west' – which implies that she is regal, and that she rules over some land to the west of Cyprus, where Cupid and his mother, Venus, live. But the significance of this is left temporarily in abeyance while the destructive impetus begun by Cupid's 'certain aim' (line 157) is transmitted through the twanging, alliterative line 159 ('And loos'd his love-shaft smartly from his bow') to the histrionic exaggeration of the next line in which the force of the divine arrow is said to be enough to 'pierce a hundred thousand hearts'. Calmness and restraint are restored, however, as Oberon furthers what he has so far been able to see with a new aspect of that seeing in the poised, metrically regular line, 'But I might see young Cupid's fiery shaft' (line 161). The use of 'young' now makes the 'all arm'd' Cupid seem less devastatingly mature; and though 'fiery' reminds us of the emotional burning that his arrow can produce, it is followed immediately by another effectively chosen word, 'Quench'd' (placed, again, at the beginning of the line, and thus counterbalancing the 'Cupid' of line 157) which both in sense and sound seems to douse that raging fire. The previously mentioned 'cold moon' also comes in to aid this act of quenching, reinforced by the still more suggestive properties of 'chaste beams' and 'wat'ry'; and the 'fair vestal' now significantly changes character to 'imperial vot'ress', moving – in another beautifully controlled, and metrically regular, line, hinged on two alliteratively balanced phrases – 'In maiden meditation, fancy-free' (line 164). Now the new, and different, suggestion of power associated with 'imperial' not only provides a more than adequate opposing force to that of Cupid, but also simultaneously identifies this vestal votaress as none other than Queen Elizabeth and her throne 'by the west' as that of England. The whole is thus a triumphant and adroitly handled piece of poetic rhetoric, at once afffirming the superior, 'quenching' power of chastity over erotic desire, and complimenting the virtuous-cum-politically-astute Queen of England.

The remainder of the passage is a winding-down from this exalted height, and a transition back to the immediate dramatic business in hand. For the third time Oberon recounts what he has seen, varying the verb this time, however, to 'mark'd' (line 165). He noted that Cupid's arrow fell on 'a little western flower' – 'western' now reduced from its grand association with the throne to something that suggests a more humble wild flower native to England (so merging with the natural vegetation characteristic of *A Midsummer Night's Dream*, and echoed, for example, in the homely names of Titania's attendant fairies). The flower's transformation from 'milk-white' to 'purple with love's wound' (as if tinged with blood) also indicates a level of vulnerability below that of 'the imperial vot'ress', and again aids the return to the play's normality (as does the notion of transformation itself). And finally we link up with the ongoing action again as Puck is told, 'Fetch me that flow'r'. The set-piece aria is completed, and the splendour of the music modulated to suit the more quotidian needs of the play.

*   *   *

As You Like It, II.vii.139–66. Jaques compares human life to a play.

All the world's a stage,

And all the men and women merely players;   140
They have their exits and their entrances;
And one man in his time plays many parts,
His acts being seven ages. At first the infant,
Mewling and puking in the nurse's arms;
Then the whining school-boy, with his satchel   145
And shining morning face, creeping like snail
Unwillingly to school. And then the lover,
Sighing like furnace, with a woeful ballad
Made to his mistress' eyebrow. Then a soldier,
Full of strange oaths, and bearded like the pard,   50
Jealous in honour, sudden and quick in quarrel,
Seeking the bubble reputation
Even in the cannon's mouth. And then the justice,
In fair round belly with good capon lin'd,
With eyes severe and beard of formal cut,   155
Full of wise saws and modern instances;
And so he plays his part. The sixth age shifts
Into the lean and slipper'd pantaloon,
With spectacles on nose and pouch on side,
His youthful hose, well sav'd, a world too wide   160
For his shrunk shank; and his big manly voice,
Turning again toward childish treble, pipes
And whistles in his sound. Last scene of all,
That ends this strange eventful history,
Is second childishness and mere oblivion;   165
Sans teeth, sans eyes, sans taste, sans every thing.

This passage is even more obviously than the one from *A Midsummer Night's Dream* surplus to the needs of the plot. It has a slight pretext in that Duke Senior has just made the remark that he and his fellows in the Forest of Arden are not the only unhappy ones: 'This wide and universal theatre / Presents more woeful pageants than the scene / Wherein we play in' (lines 138–9). But if it has a dramatic purpose it is to fill the gap while Orlando goes to find Adam; and this seems to be confirmed by the fact that as soon as it is finished Orlando re-enters with Adam. And yet this is one of the best known, and most popular, speeches in *As You Like It*. If it is a 'filler', it is a highly successful way of occupying a gap in the action.

We have found the musical analogy of an operatic aria a convenient way of analysing Oberon's speech on the 'fair vestal'. On similar lines the appropriate analogy here would be a theme and variations. Duke Senior's cue indicates what the theme is – one of the most frequently used in Shakespeare, and of immediate interest to the audience because it relates to the place they are in at the moment: the theatre. (The Editor of the Everyman edition of *As You Like It* also reminds us [p. 92] that the words 'Totus mundus agit histrionem' [all the world plays the actor] were displayed as the motto of the Globe Theatre, where this play was first performed.)

Another analogy would be that of the extended conceit, frequently used by Shakespeare and also in the literature of his day. A metaphor is established – in this case, the idea that the whole world can be regarded as 'a stage' – and then, over a considerable number of lines, the possible implications of this master-idea are ingeniously teased out. Given that the world is a stage, who are its actors ('players')? Answer: all the men and women who inhabit it. What are their entrances to, and exits from, this stage? Answers: their births and deaths. However, in the professional theatre one actor plays many different roles in the course of his career. How can this be applied to inhabitants of the world-stage? Answer: the human being's characteristics change as he/she progresses from childhood, throughout adulthood, to old age, and he can therefore be said to play a similarly varied string of roles. A play is customarily divided into Acts – how does this apply? Answer: there are seven major phases in man's life (but here we stretch the usual five Acts of drama) which can be regarded as the Acts into which the play of his life can be divided.

The danger of this method is that, if it is spelt out in too pedestrian a manner, it can become tedious. When, therefore, Jaques gets on to specifying the seven Acts, he avoids repeating the theatrical metaphor too often, contenting himself with just one or two reminders (as at line 157, 'And so he plays his part', and line 163, 'Last scene of all'). Yet there remains a 'theatrical' quality to each of the ages in that they are slightly caricatured, painted in colours that make them seem somewhat larger than life, as do the make-up, clothing and histrionic gestures of the professional actor on the public stage (more particularly, the Elizabethan stage, where realism was less assiduously cultivated than on the modern stage). In addition, this is a speech by Jaques, the 'odd man out' and rather affected satirist who can be expected to give his own, slightly cynical twist to whatever observations he makes. Accordingly, the baby is not a picture of innocent bliss, but a creature wailing like a cat and being sick all over its nurse; the schoolboy, though he does have a 'shining morning face' (because thoroughly scrubbed by his mother?) goes reluctantly to his lessons, 'whining' and creeping as slowly as a snail; and the lover is absurdly passionate, and writes ridiculously mournful verses on a trivial subject like the eyebrow of his mistress. (This latter, however, is in tune with the mockery directed elsewhere in Shakespeare's comedies at the moodiness and exaggerated eulogy found in so much conventional love poetry of the day.)

In the fourth and fifth ages the technique is varied again and becomes more like that of the written 'characters', or brief portraits, coming into vogue at the time. Thus, the soldier is both heard (swearing strange oaths that he has picked up abroad) and seen (with his supposedly fierce-looking beard, trimmed to resemble a leopard's whiskers), and characterised as tetchily quarrelsome and obsessed with his 'reputation' to the point of foolhardy rashness in battle. (Courage is devalued, and, though 'honour' is mentioned, it becomes more like the 'honour' analysed by Falstaff in *Henry IV*, Part I, V.i.127–40.) By contrast, the portrait of the middle-aged Justice of the Peace becomes one of pot-bellied self-indulgence and tedious moralising illustrated with 'modern' (i.e. banal, commonplace) examples – the archetypal bore.

With the sixth age the element of caricature becomes still more marked, and it is accompanied with a sinister note of decay. The underlying theatrical metaphor also contributes to this effect, for the 'pantaloon' alludes to the *pantalone* of Italian *commedia dell'arte*, a pantomime-like figure of fun guying the physical and mental deterioration which accompanies the onset of old age. An elaborate description makes him look the part, and the very sound of his shrill, enfeebled voice is onomatopoeically rendered in lines 161–3.

The curtain falls with the seventh, and final, Act. The decay highlighted in the sixth age now becomes all-encompassing; and the wheel also comes full circle in that infancy is re-enacted as 'second childishness'. But the most striking feature is deprivation, strikingly embodied in the remorseless repetition of the last line, where the use of the French 'sans' for the English 'without' tellingly foregrounds a catalogue of qualities noteworthy only for their absence.

The speech as a whole is itself a brilliant performance. It does not require the audience's enthusiastic approval. If the *Midsummer Night's Dream* 'aria' almost seems to call for a burst of applause like that which follows an aria in traditional opera, the chilling climax of this verbal tour de force is more likely to be met with stunned silence. But the differentiation of the episodes (or Acts) – individualised, and yet linked by an underlying and unifying astringency of manner – arouses admiration for the ingenuity with which the theme and variations are executed; and the rhetorical flourish of the last line (which, incidentally, also distorts the iambic pentameter to such an extent that here every single syllable seems to get an emphatic stress) concludes 'this strange eventful history' with terrific panache. It is an astutely theatrical treatment of the theme of theatre, and one that is appropriately adjusted to the histrionic nature of the 'melancholy' Jaques.

*   *   *

Twelfth Night, II.iv.50–65. Feste sings a song at Orsino's bidding.

> Come away, come away, death; 50
> And in sad cypress let me be laid;
>   Fly away, fly away, breath,
> I am slain by a fair cruel maid.
> My shroud of white, stuck all with yew,
>   O, prepare it! 55

My part of death no one so true
    Did share it.

    Not a flower, not a flower sweet,
On my black coffin let there be strown;
    Not a friend, not a friend greet   60
My poor corpse where my bones shall be thrown;
A thousand thousand sighs to save,
        Lay me, O, where
Sad true lover never find my grave,
        To weep there!   65

This song is a set piece in a more explicit way than the other two
passages analysed in this chapter, as it is specifically commanded by
Orsino. It is one which he has heard before, and likes because 'it is
silly sooth, / And dallies with the innocence of love, / Like the old
age' (II.iv.45–7). These words help to place it as something rather
old-fashioned and in keeping with the Duke's taste for the sad and
sentimental treatment of love; and Feste, who knows his patron,
provides just what is asked for. The original musical setting has not
survived, but one imagines that it would consist to a large extent of
those 'dying falls' Orsino praises in his opening speech.

Rhetorically, it relies mainly on figures of sound rather than
metaphor, as 'silly sooth' [innocent, or simple, truth] would lead the
audience to expect. With the exception of 'prepare it' and 'share it'
(lines 55 and 57) the rhymes are monosyllabic, but avoid any sharp,
epigrammatic effect; and the sense of musical chiming is increased
by assonantal connections which have an effect close to internal
rhyme (e.g. 'slain'/'maid', line 53; and 'bones'/'thrown', line 61).
Frequent 's's' and 'd's' and open vowels create a whispering, sighing
effect; and the soft 'f's' of lines 52–3, 58 and 60 and the liquid 'l's' of
51–3, 58–9 and 63–4 smooth and soften the sound.

Repetition is a major device, here used not so much for emphasis
as to create a seductive, incantatory effect. It is also integral to the
structure of the stanzas: the first and third lines of each stanza
consist of repeated phrases, related to each other by the imperative
mood and recurrence of 'away' in stanza 1, and the 'Not a' formula

and alliteration in stanza 2. The parallelism of 'My shroud of' and 'My part of' (lines 54 and 56), echoed, with slight variation, in 'My poor corpse' and 'my bones' (line 61), add further to this incantatory effect. On the other hand, 'thousand thousand' (line 62) *is* repetition for emphasis, and provides a contrast (which would, no doubt, be heightened by the musical setting) of considerable tonal value.

On the semantic level, words associated with pain, grief, sadness and death predominate. 'Death' itself occurs twice, as does 'sad'; and there are single examples of 'slain', 'cruel', 'shroud', 'black', 'coffin', 'corpse', 'bones', 'sighs', 'grave' and 'weep'. The 'cypress' in line 51 may refer to branches of cypress strewing the corpse, or to the coffin being made of cypress wood; but either way the funereal associations are significant, as are the associations of the other tree mentioned, 'yew'. 'Flower' and 'flower sweet' are negatived; they are not to be part of the scene. But their mention, along with the act of strewing (also negatived, line 59), nevertheless brings pastoral/elegiac associations into play which, like the similarly negatived 'Sad true lover' of line 64 who is not to 'weep there', modifies the would-be starkness of the scene.

Without the actual music, of course, the full effect of this set-piece cannot properly be gauged; but it would, no doubt, enhance the aesthetic pleasure, making the beautiful sounds and associations already analysed still more beautiful. For this is a song of pain and grief which have been converted into essentially musical and literary pain and grief. Death is sentimentalised. And there is one other element in the song which should be mentioned, though it is present only as a somewhat subdued undertone. The supposed 'I', the persona, who sings this song is there in the recurrent use of the first person singular: 'I', at line 53 (echoing the sound of 'Fly ... fly' in line 52); 'me', at lines 51 and 63; and six uses of 'my', at lines 54, 56, 59, 61 (twice), and 64. And this 'I' sees himself as uniquely 'true' (lines 56-7). He professes the wish to spare friends, and save mourners from sighing their thousands of sighs; and he wishes to be exempt from any other true lover weeping at his grave. But all this, in fact, focuses attention on himself; it is a self-regarding fantasy of unique devotion and unique isolation that he indulges in. Even the mistress who fails to requite his love, and is supposedly causing his death, is present only in line 53 (a line which is a peculiarly good example, metrically at least, of Orsino's beloved 'dying fall'). Everything is turned in on the persona's own woebegone state.

Primarily, then, this song is a professional set piece, made for, and performed to, the order of Orsino, and also enjoyed by the audience – as modern audiences enjoy broken-hearted pop songs. But in the very adroitness Feste shows in suiting his wares to the customer there is also implicit a criticism of the persona projected in the song – a persona who, it is not difficult to see, holds up a mirror to Orsino himself. To that extent Feste's song is not only an interpolated 'aria', but something which can be connected to the dramatic context as a whole.

Conclusions

Each of these passages gives the actor an opportunity to display his talents, and gives the audience the opportunity to enjoy a pleasing combination of verbal technique and histrionic performance. They are memorable, and yet not necessarily integral to the plays in which they appear. (Just how relevant they are to the rest of the play varies; and can be a matter of critical opinion.)

A recurrent comparison in the analyses has been the enjoyment of an aria in an opera, where, though it may well have links with the rest of the work, the music and performance have a virtually independent status, enjoyed as such by the audience, and may even be given applause which interrupts and suspends the rest of the action. While no such reception is to be expected to the set-pieces in Shakespearean comedy, the assumption is that the audience can take pleasure in them for their own sake. This is perhaps a more justified assumption with regard to Elizabethan than to present-day audiences, since the modern demand for realism – strongly aided and abetted, as it is, by cinema and television – tends to dicourage attention to art *as* art. Shakespeare belonged to a different age, and one in which there was intense consciousness of the new and exciting things happening to the language. The difference should not, however, mean that such passages are inaccesssible to us. Listening (though perhaps more deliberately than is customary for us) to the sound, structure and choice of words can make this pleasure retrievable. And when this is done, a valuable dimension is added to our enjoyment of the plays.

Methods of Analysis (Chapters 8, 9 and 10)

In these chapters, as in each of the previous ones, the basic tools of analysis – attention to diction, imagery, rhetoric and syntax – have again been used; and in the discussion of set pieces in Chapter 10 they have been especially prominent. But consideration of 'manlike women' and 'odd men out' has called for attention to social as well as linguistic features. Not that these are to be considered as separate, unrelated categories. In *As You Like It*, for example, Rosalind's 'market' imagery in the passage from III.v.35–69 conveys important implications for the condition of women and their place in the marriage stakes; and the overtones of the word 'velvet' in II.i.29–68 reinforce Jaques's criticism of the fickleness of commercially minded friends. Careful attention to tone and rhythm in *Twelfth Night*, II.ii.15–39 also helps to make clearer the changes of perception and accompanying changes of attitude which occur as Viola appreciates the special predicament that disguise and proxy wooing have brought on both Olivia and herself.

Dramatic situation and the actual sights, sounds and on-stage movements as the text of the play is put into performance in the theatre also need to be taken fully into account. The 'madness' scene in *Twelfth Night*, IV.ii.17–60 is a particularly good example of how these features affect interpretation and audience response. It must always be remembered that the printed words are in essence a script to be filled out and made a living reality in the theatre. As stressed in Chapter 8, this includes keeping oneself aware of the importance of disguise and its triple effect when a boy plays a girl playing a boy.

Also in these chapters – as in earlier ones, but still more emphatically here – analysis must keep itself alert to shifting effects of light and shade in situations that move from comedy to near-tragedy and back again. The distinction made in Chapter 9 between 'majority' and 'minority' values needs to be kept in mind (i.e. the distinction between characters and assumptions which reinforce comedy's emphasis on good sense and those which imply different standards). And even within 'majority' cases there may well be subdivisions in which a 'minority' position significantly modifies the 'majority' one. This qualification is especially important with regard to the treatment of marriage, and makes for complex attitudes in such characters as Beatrice, Rosalind and Viola which analysis needs to take into account if the plays' overall sense of balance is not to be falsified.

Suggested Work

Analyse the songs, 'Sigh no more, ladies' (*Much Ado About Nothing*, II.iii.57–69) and 'It was a lover and his lass' (*As You Like It*, V.iii.14–31). What are their qualities as set-piece performances? (Discuss, for example, their use of imagery and refrains.) What thematic connections may they be said to have with rest of the plays in which they appear?

Analyse *A Midsummer Night's Dream*, II.i.32–57 ('Either I mistake your shape and making quite, ... A merrier hour was never wasted there'). What does this passage tell the audience about Puck, as seen by the Fairy and by himself? To what extent does Puck's love of mischief accord with the play's overall sense of values, and to what extent does it make him an odd man out? (Pay particular attention to the farcical and realistic elements in the anecdotes retailed by both characters.)

Analyse *As You Like It*, I.i.123–40 ('Charles, I thank thee for thy love to me ... and thou must look pale and wonder'). Consider the use made of such words as 'love', 'young', 'underhand', 'natural', 'disgrace' and 'grace'. How does the syntax contribute to the would-be civilised, but hypocritical, effect of Oliver's speech? Is this a speech which would qualify Oliver to be added to the list of the odd men out in Shakespeare's comedies (compare him, for example, with Don John in *Much Ado About Nothing*); and, if so, how does this speech square with what happens later in the play?

Analyse *Twelfth Night*, I.ii.21–61 ('Know'st thou this country? ...

Only shape thou thy silence to my wit'). Consider the value to the audience of the information which is conveyed in these lines about Orsino and Olivia, and the significance of Viola's response to what she hears. Details worth looking at include: the implications of 'noble' (line 25), 'What great ones do the less will prattle of' (line 33), 'leaving her / In the protection of his son' (lines 37–8), 'nature with a beauteous wall / Doth oft close in pollution' (lines 48–9), and the references to Viola being presented as a eunuch (what becomes of her singing?) and to 'time' in the final couplet.

11

Endings

Introduction

Endings are important in all kinds of drama, but in none more so than in comedy, which in its simplest definition is a play with a happy ending. All four of the plays here under discussion have happy endings, but – to adapt George Orwell – some are happier than others. It is part of the inclusiveness, the freedom from rules and rigid conventions which is typical of the mixed nature of Shakespearean comedy, that the degree of happiness in the endings of some plays should be more muted than in others, that some notes should be in the sadder, minor key rather than the cheerful, major key, and that certain characters should seem to share less fully in the general happiness than the majority – or even deliberately dissent from the overall comic happiness.

As individual passages do not necessarily serve the purpose of examining these varied kinds of ending, this chapter must differ in method from its predecessors. Instead, each of the final Acts of the four chosen plays will be discussed in chronological sequence, pausing for detailed analysis where this is helpful, but concentrating in the main on the way the action is directed to its conclusion, and on the degree to which the happiness is all-inclusive. Each play will be seen to have its own particular combination of features, making for its own, unique kind of ending, ranging from the multiple and universally satisfying ending of *A Midsummer Night's Dream* to the more mixed ingredients of the fair-and-foul-weather ending of *Twelfth Night*.

A Midsummer Night's Dream

A Midsummer Night's Dream is unique among these four comedies in that a provisional ending has already been reached by the conclusion of Act IV. The confusion among the lovers has been sorted out, Titania has been released from her enchantment, and Bottom has been restored to his human shape. The way is thus clear for the wedding celebrations which constitute the happiness towards which the comedy is aimed. What has not been accomplished, however, is the performance of the Athenian workmen's play, so far glimpsed only in rehearsal; and it is this burlesque version of *Pyramus and Thisby* to which the bulk of Act V is devoted.

The story of Pyramus and Thisby entails more variation on the theme of illusion which has been dominant throughout the play so far. It is Pyramus's misreading of the significance of Thisby's blood-stained mantle which leads him to kill himself, and this in turn leads to Thisby's suicide. Through illusion Hero and Helena had both been caused great pain, and Demetrius and Lysander had been brought close to murder; but for them the play had worked out to avoid a tragic result. On one level, then, the misfortunes of Pyramus and Thisby exemplify the unhappy ending of tragedy, in contrast to comedy's happy averting of tragedy in the preceding plot. But, of course, the patent burlesquing of the Pyramus and Thisby story, and the ridiculous notion of theatrical illusion on which the inexpert Athenian actors work, turns 'tragedy' into uproarious comedy. Their play thus becomes a reinforcement (though in a different mode) of the triumph of comedy.

This is confirmed by the climax of *Pyramus and Thisby* as performed by Flute/Thisby and commented on by the stage audience. Thisby finds the body of Pyramus, stabs herself, and, with the words, '*Thus Thisby ends; / Adieu, adieu, adieu*', according to the stage direction, 'Dies' (V.i. 337–8). Theseus comments, 'Moonshine and Lion are left to bury the dead' (line 339). But Bottom, the 'dead' Pyramus, leaps up, asking, in language which embodies his characteristic confusion of the senses: 'Will it please you to see the Epilogue, or to hear a Bergomask dance between two of our company?' (lines 342–4). To which Theseus replies (lines 345–51):

No epilogue, I pray you; for your play needs no excuse. Never excuse; for when the players are all dead there need none to be blamed. Marry, if he that writ it had played Pyramus, and hang'd himself in Thisby's garter, it would have been a fine tragedy. And so it is, truly; and very notably discharg'd. But come, your Bergomask; let your epilogue alone. [*A dance.*

The banter here turns death into little more than a verbal quibble. On the principle of *de mortuis nil nisi bonum* (of the dead only good should be spoken), and on the assumption that an epilogue is only added to a play to defend it from adverse criticism, Pyramus and Thisby and the play in which they have 'died' need no excuse. Theseus jokes about the ineptitude of the anonymous playwright's deserving a tragic death; but this, too, is a way of saying what a fine farce the potentially 'fine tragedy' has inadvertently become – thanks to the notable discharging of it by Bottom and his fellow actors. Burlesqued unhappy ending equals comic happy ending; and the appropriate rounding-off of this is not defensive epilogue, but joyful dancing. Hence Theseus's preference for the 'Bergomask' (probably a blatantly rustic version of the dance, and, as such, one more under-lining of the way the Athenian workmen, with happy unawareness, knock the stuffing out of pomp and circumstance).

Notwithstanding, there is an Epilogue to *A Midsummer Night's Dream*, preceded by a double coda. After the end of the Bergomask Theseus observes that 'The iron tongue of midnight hath told twelve' (line 352), and orders the lovers to bed. His metaphor for the booming of the bell which tolls the hours sounds for a moment an ominous note – only, however, to emphasise once more its conver-sion into happiness. The 'palpable-gross play' to which he and the lovers have just been witnesses has had the opposite effect: it has 'well beguil'd / The heavy gait of night' (lines 356–7). Moreover, that 'heavy gait' has another context; it signifies how slowly the evening would otherwise seem to have passed for young people eager to perform the rites of love.

For the human beings, then, the play ends on the happiest note of potential procreation. But the fairies have yet to have their say. The first of them to enter is Puck. His speech (lines 360–79) takes up the burden of night once more, and its first fifteen lines are full of the wildness and horrors traditionally associated with darkness: 'the hungry lion roars', the wolf howls, the screech-owl 'Puts the wretch that lies in woe / In remembrance of a shroud', and graves let forth their ghosts. This, as Theseus had forewarned, is 'fairy time' (line 353), and the fairies run 'From', not towards, the presence of the life-giving sun, 'Following darkness like a dream' (line 375) – a phrase which is a virtual summary of *A Midsummer Night's Dream* itself in its dark and dream-enfolded first four Acts. But Puck's syntax swerves at last to the climax that 'we fairies ... Now are frolic' (lines 372–6), and the declaration that nothing shall disturb 'this hallowed house' (line 377). Superstitious horror is converted to a simple cleansing action: 'I am sent with broom before, / To sweep the dust behind the door' (lines 378–9).

This is the cue for Oberon and Titania, 'with all their Train', to enter. Their power is limited to the hours of darkness ('until the break of day', line 390), but their actions are such as to emphasise yet again the reversal of night's ominous associations. They sing to 'bless this place' (line 389), and Oberon, their leader, gives his sanction to the acts of procreation for which the human beings have gone to their beds. The 'issue' there to be created is to be 'fortunate' (line 395) and free from any 'blots of Nature's hand' (line 398). All is to be blessed ' with sweet peace' (line 407); and the owner of this palace 'Ever shall in safety rest' (line 409). Supernatural power itself is sanctified and used to perfect the happy ending.

Is there need, then, for Puck's final speech (lines 412–27)? Is it not true that this play, like its play-within-the-play, 'needs no excuse'? The answer, in part, is that it is for himself and his fellow performers that Puck intercedes with the audience. Their inherently fallible humanity remains, and the possibility that they may not have performed as well as they might is a failing to be excused by the applause of the audience. But Puck's characterisation of the actors as 'we shadows' (line 412) also suggests a further dimension to the Epilogue. It constitutes a transition from the imaginative world of the play and its elaborately sophisticated exploitation of different levels of illusion to the prosaic world of ordinary daytime reality – the level on which Puck, though still calling himself 'Puck', has become a player speaking to his fee-paying customers, and promising, if he has not succeeded in giving them the value they seek, to make up for it next time. His last couplet is thus one more bit of word-play, 'Give me your hands' (line 426) – a plea both for fellowship and applause – which, in rhyming 'friends' with 'amends', bids for a happy ending, not only to the fictional play, but also to the acting company's relationship with its patrons.

Much Ado About Nothing

The ending of *Much Ado About Nothing* is another example of modulation from tragedy back to comedy; but in place of the nocturnal dream-world giving way to daylight reality, the device of masking and unmasking is employed.

By the beginning of the final scene (V.iv), as indicated by the opening question of the Friar, 'Did I not tell you she was innocent?' (line 1), Hero's name has been cleared; and Leonato, with his scheme already laid for marrying Claudio to a fictitious niece (who will prove to be the bride he has already married, but now believes to be dead), is anxious to confirm the 'innocence' of the Prince and Claudio, too. 'Some fault' remains with Margaret, but this is mitigated by its being 'against her will' (line 5). And the true villain, Don John, was reported, at the end of V.ii, to have fled Messina. Antonio is thus able to strike the required note for the restitution of comedy with his statement (at line 7), 'Well, I am glad that all things sorts so well' – the first colloquial 'Well' and the last happy-ending, adverbial 'well' neatly enfolding the 'all things' about which there has been so much ado in the preceding scenes.

The stage is then set for the charade-wedding and discovery which will be this play's version of the expected ending of a comedy in 'the state of honourable marriage' (line 30). With the entrance of Don Pedro and Claudio the action proceeds with slightly stiff formality towards this ceremony, the only alien notes being those of Claudio's 'I'll hold my mind were she an Ethiope' (line 38; which confirms his resolve to go through with the arrangement, but hardly suggests enthusiasm) and the hostility apparently shown by

Benedick. The look on the latter's face prompts Don Pedro to dub it an unseasonably 'February face, / So full of frost, of storm, and cloudiness' (lines 41–2); but this is in the mode of comic exaggeration – as is Claudio's mocking reference to Jove's wooing Europa in the shape of a bull (lines 43–7) as way of alluding to Benedick's love for Beatrice. Benedick's not very witty reply (lines 48–51) suggests some lingering resentment; but its shift into rhyme, and its macho manner, echo the tone of the earlier banter between them, hinting that their quarrel is now less earnest than it was.

The next stage direction reads, '*Re-enter* ANTONIO, *with the* Ladies *masked*'. Masking is necessary for the device of the false marriage; but it is also a reminder of the earlier masked ball in which Don Pedro's wooing on Claudio's behalf was misconstrued, and it is analogous to the impersonated wooing of Margaret by Borachio which led to Claudio's rejection of Hero. But this ritual masking and mistaking is to be one which reverses the harm done by previous false appearances. It climaxes in words that deliberately emphasise both similarity and difference:

Claudio.	Give me your hand; before this holy friar
	I am your husband, if you like of me.
Hero.	And when I liv'd I was your other wife; [*Unmasking.*
	And when you lov'd you were my other husband.
Claudio.	Another Hero!
Hero.	Nothing certainer.
	One Hero died defil'd; but I do live,
	And, surely as I live, I am a maid.
Don Pedro.	The former Hero! Hero that is dead!
Leonato.	She died, my lord, but whiles her slander liv'd. (lines 58–66)

Choosing the masked Hero, Claudio is again deceived, but his deception now undoes the harm he did when previously he was tragically deceived. Though there is continuity, too, in that the masked figure is the true Hero, whom it has been necessary to mask with death only because her 'slander' lived. Life and death are thus intricately interchanged. Through her masked death Hero undoes her killing by dishonourable masking, and replaces the false life of her slander by the true life of her virginal self. This causes 'amazement' among the onlookers, which, however, the Friar assures them he can 'qualify' (line 67) after the religious significance of this masking ritual has been celebrated in the chapel towards which he ushers them all.

To balance things out, there remains the effecting of the union between Beatrice and Benedick, to accompany that between Hero and Claudio. For this purpose Beatrice also has to unmask – which she does at line 73. For her, however, the unmasking is not a matter of returning from supposed death, but of emerging from an embattled stance towards the male sex, and Benedick in particular, to a more marriageable disposition. To a large extent the trick played upon both her and Benedick in II.iii and III.i has done this already. But since that has its basis in misrepresentation, there has to be a psychological unmasking which will confront the pair with the reality of their love for each other and bring it on to the conscious level. The means for accomplishing this involves, paradoxically, a temporary return to their mutually scoffing state: in the questioning that takes place between them at lines 73–83 they reveal to each other the nature of the tricks played on them, and try to deny that they are really in love (or, more precisely – and revealingly perhaps – they say that they love 'no more than reason'). But evidence is produced against them in the form of the love sonnets each has written to the other – which is comically appropriate poetic justice, since they have both been fierce critics of such poetic sentiment. For a while both maintain the same mocking attitudes: Benedick will take Beatrice, only ' for pity', and she will take him only to save his life, 'for I was told you were in a consumption' (lines 93–6); but their words concede their love, and their mouths are eventually stopped by Benedick's kiss. Their wit is revealed in its true colours, not as the mark of fundamental hostility, but as an expression of abundant vitality, heightened and intensified by each other's very presence. And the unmasking of this truth is sealed by Benedick's brilliant speech in response to Don Pedro's mocking 'How dost thou, Benedick the married man?' (line 98) – a speech delivered with all the panache of his previously inconoclastic wit, now directed against the power of scoffing itself:

I'll tell thee what, Prince: a college of wit-crackers cannot flout me out of my humour. Dost thou think I care for a satire or an epigram? No. If a man will be beaten with brains, 'a shall wear nothing handsome about him. In brief, since I do purpose to marry, I will think nothing to any purpose that the world can say against it; and therefore never flout at me for what I have said against it; for man is a giddy thing, and this is my conclusion. (lines 99–104)

In the same bantering mode the quarrel between him and Claudio is converted into renewal of their friendship, and all – or nearly all – is harmonised as Don Pedro, who looks 'sad' (which may mean no more than 'solemn'), is told to find himself a wife also. One last discordant note seems to be struck as a Messenger enters with news of Don John's arrest; but Benedick dismisses that with a promise to devise 'brave punishments for him', which sounds more like a set of practical jokes than drastic retribution. His, and the play's, concluding words are: 'Strike up, pipers' – words put into action with a general dance which, to set the final symbolic seal to the process of comic reversal, is now unmasked.

As You Like It

The ending of *As You Like It*, with its multi-layered effect and rounding off with an Epilogue, has some resemblance to that of *A Midsummer Night's Dream*; and in ending with a dance it echoes both that play and *Much Ado About Nothing*. The odd-man-out role played by Jaques, and the interruption caused by the late entrance of Jaques de Boys, may also seem to build on the note of discord created by Don John's arrest. But the overall effect is something quite different. In its use of structure and tone, *As You Like It* is one of the most interesting and experimental of Shakespeare's comic endings.

What might be called the major ending of *As You Like It* occurs at V.iv.103–44. There are important modifications to follow, but this is the main substance of its 'happy ending', in which complications are smoothed out, problems resolved, divided persons reunited, and tensions eased.

The tone is set by solemn music, and the suggestion of supernatural blessing created by the appearance of Hymen, the god of marriage, leading in the brides, Rosalind and Celia – who are no longer in their woodland disguises, but dressed as themselves. Hymen's first words make the significance of all this explicit: 'mirth' is felt in heaven when the reconciling motions of comedy on earth are completed; odds are made even, and all come together in a divinely sanctioned atonement (lines 103–4).

The presence of a god on the stage also underscores the impression of ceremony and convention. We are not here concerned with realism, but with that formalised operatic effect to which the Elizabethan theatre lends itself more readily than the modern stage. Accordingly, it is not only the visual with which this passage is concerned, but also – and perhaps more significantly – the aural. The use of music has already emphasised this, but much is also owed to the transparently artificial structuring of the verse. Almost the whole passage is in rhymed couplets, thus setting it off from the rest of the play, which has as its norm either prose or the unrhymed pentameters of 'blank verse'. The exceptions are lines 111–13 (which, however, by virtue of their repetition, are still more artificially marked) and the verse spoken by Hymen. Through the use of shorter, more varied line-lengths and some alternated rhymes (e.g. AABCCB for lines 102–7 and 119–24) this creates an effect of inset lyrics, which precede, and match, the ABABCC of his actual song at lines 135–40.

The sense thus created of formality and decorum is enhanced still further by the syntactic shapeliness of the language. For example, Rosalind's sentence to Duke Senior, 'To you I give myself, for I am yours' (line 110) corresponds exactly with what she says to Orlando; and the two men's replies have a like correspondence to each other:

Duke Senior.   If there be truth in sight, you are my daughter.
Orlando.   If there be truth in sight, you are my Rosalind.
                                                        (lines 112–13)

To the theatre audience, previously aware – as most of the onstage characters were not – that the Duke is actually Rosalind's father, and

Orlando the man she loves, there is no surprise here; but this is the moment when perception dawns on those to whom she is speaking, and the linguistic parallelism both heightens and controls their astonishment. Understanding simultaneously dawns on Phebe, and her realisation that the boy 'Ganymede' she loves is in fact a woman is made more dramatically effective by use of the same formula, but with the nouns inverted and the line contracted to six syllables, and with the addition of a brief, rhyming farewell: 'If sight and shape be true, / Why then, my love adieu!' (lines 114–15).

Rosalind next adapts the conditional clause to confirm her relationships to the Duke and Orlando ('I'll have no father / husband, if you be not he', lines 116–17), but to add confusion for Phebe ('Nor ne'er wed woman, if you be not she', line 118). This, however, is the cue for Hymen to step forward, and 'bar confusion' by exercising his divine function as marital god and sorting the characters into appropriate pairs. This he does with another syntactically parallel formula ('You and you ...'), which he varies, however, to suit the different conditions of the partners. Orlando and Rosalind, Oliver and Celia are given conventional blessings; Phebe is told she must knuckle down to reality; and Touchstone and Audrey are told that they are to enjoy the concord-in-discord of 'winter to foul weather'. If there is an echo here of the harshness to which conventional pastoral has had to adapt earlier in the play (e.g. 'the icy fang / And churlish chiding of the winter's wind' at II.i.6–7), it is only in comically light-hearted vein. And likewise, if Phebe, unlike the rest, seems not to be getting what she has freely chosen, harmony is restored at line 144 when she tells Silvius, 'Thy faith my fancy to thee doth combine'. Momentary discords serve only to make the overall harmony of Hymen's blessing, and the song in his praise ('Honour, high honour, and renown, / To Hymen, god of every town!', lines 139–40), still more pleasing to the ear.

The words just quoted from Phebe might seem to round this harmony off, and so signal the end of the play. But the end is not yet reached. At this point the stage direction reads: '*Enter* JAQUES DE BOYS'. Nothing has been seen of him before. The introduction of a new character so late in the play goes against all rules of dramatic construction; but this seems to worry Shakespeare no more than the

sudden appearance of a supernatural being (Hymen) at the beginning of the passage already discussed. After briefly announcing
himself : 'I am the second son of old Sir Rowland' (line 146; those
members of the audience with exceptionally good memories might
recall Orlando's opening speech and its statement that 'My brother
Jaques he [Oliver] keeps at school, and report speaks goldenly of his
profit', I.i.6–7), he goes on to tell the happy news of Duke
Frederick's astonishing volte-face. Making for the Forest of Arden
with the intention of putting an end to the happy-go-lucky life of
his banished brother, Frederick fell in with 'an old religious man'
who persuaded him to repent, become an anchorite, and restore the
dukedom to its rightful owner, Duke Senior. Such a tale is no more
realistically probable than what the audience has just seen and heard,
but it is something which can be accepted precisely because it
accords with the general mood of ordered artificiality that has been
created. In that sense it is a continuation and extension of the
Hymen passage. Like the messenger who bears it, however, this story
brings with it a reminder of the world outside Arden. It picks up the
minor notes of discord associated with Touchstone and Audrey (and
perhaps with Phebe), and though, like them, it is absorbed into the
larger harmony, it also reverberates with deeper echoes of such
things as vengeance, sin, repentance and the felt need for restitution
– things which, again, are contained, but have greater potentiality to
worry and disturb.

   The speech from Duke Senior (lines 160–73) which follows
Jaques de Boys's news is one that furthers the larger harmony. Its
keynotes are welcome, restoration of what has been lost, and the call
to dancing; and its conclusion ('you brides and bridegrooms all, /
With measure heap'd in joy, to th' measures fall', lines 172–3) neatly
combines the multiple meanings of 'measure' as the correct, filling
quantity of food and drink, as stately dance, and as regularity, or
order. In this way it seems to focus all the themes which we have
now come to recognise as characteristic of the happy ending of
comedy. Yet, once more, this is not quite where Shakespeare chooses
to leave his audience. At this point Jaques – not the newly introduced brother of Orlando, but the one we have been familiar with
since the beginning of Act II – steps forward to reveal that what has

most excited his interest has been the usurper's conversion, and that he intends to join Duke Frederick, for 'Out of these convertites / There is much matter to be heard and learn'd' (lines 178–9).

This very different reaction suggests a contrast, not only between Duke Senior and Jaques, but also between the two Jaques's we now have on the stage. Jaques de Boys brings news of evil turning to good; the other Jaques turns away from that happy prospect to investigate the state of mind of the man who has repented of his evil. (The identical first name also tempts one to suggest that they are the obverse and reverse of the same coin, except that in performance the new arrival's first name remains unspoken.) And what follows this is a speech from the melancholy Jaques which seems rather like a duplication of the confusion-barring speech of Hymen at lines 119–34. Like Hymen he takes upon himself the authority to 'bequeath' rewards – to Duke Senior his 'former honour', to Orlando 'a love that your true faith doth merit', to Oliver 'land, and love, and great allies', and to Silvius 'a long and well-deserved bed'. His words to Touchstone likewise echo the 'winter' note in Hymen's speech but not so light-heartedly: 'And you to wrangling; for thy loving voyage / Is but for two months victuall'd' (lines 185–6); and his conclusion, on his own behalf, is, once more, an emphatic turning away from happiness and dancing: 'So to your pleasures; / I am for other than for dancing measures' (line 187).

In form also there is a resemblance between this speech and Hymen's (and, it is worth noting, Rosalind's words at lines 110–18 as well). Rhyme is discarded (and there is a reversion to the standard ten-syllable line), but the same 'You ... You ...' formula is employed, and the same distribution of words to each addressee in turn. Yet the effect is not one of mere (and possibly otiose) repetition. Jaques, unlike Hymen, does not include the female characters in his 'You', and his words to Touchstone forecast quarrelling and possibly the break-up of his marriage to Audrey. Moreover, his final words are another reminder of that anti-social element in his character that make him the play's odd man out, and they are reinforced by his subsequent refusal, even at Duke Senior's request, to 'stay'. He suits his action to his words, departing before the dance begins, and letting it be known that he will return to the 'abandon'd cave' (line

190). Repetition is there, but it is repetition in a minor key, qualifying and discomposing (though not destroying) the happy rounding-off that the comedy would otherwise seem to be getting.

Jaques makes his exit; the Duke emphasises in his final couplet the ritual nature of the ending ('We will begin these rites, / As we do trust they'll end, in true delights' (lines 191–2)); and the dance is performed. But, as in *A Midsummer Night's Dream,* there is something else to come – the Epilogue. Counterpoising Jaques's exclusively male-oriented speech, this is spoken by the principal female character, Rosalind – a point foregrounded in her opening words: 'It is not the fashion to see the lady the epilogue ...' Other marked differences are that it is in prose, and that it stands outside the fictional structure of the rest of the play. 'Rosalind' now speaks in her own person, not as the supposed daughter of Duke Senior, but as the actor playing that role in the comedy of *As You Like It* (though the fiction is still maintained that 'she' is a woman).

The change from verse to prose underlines that this is a move on to a different level of reality, as does the direct mode of address to the theatre audience and the slightly flirtatious distinction made between its male and female members. All along the performance has worked – as all theatrical performances must – on the tacit assumption that the audience will give a ready ear and a sympathetic response to the enacted fiction which constitutes the play; but now, at the conclusion of the performance, that implicit relationship will become explicit and take the form either of applause or, if things have not gone well, of boos and hisses. The actor concedes that the play ought to be able to stand by itself, and that, strictly speaking, the epilogue is superfluous (''tis true that a good play needs no epilogue'). Nevertheless, adroit public relations may make a difference to the reception; and, with a reference to the mutual attraction between the sexes ('I charge you, O women, for the love you bear to men' and 'I charge you, O men, for the love your bear to women') 'Rosalind' pleads that 'the play may please'. She also offers the ambiguous bribe of a kiss – ambiguous because she would give it if she 'were a woman', and to 'as many of you as had beards that pleas'd me, complexions that lik'd me, and breaths that I defied not'. The stratagem here wins applause because of the way it teasingly plays with gender issues, and because none of the men, at any rate, wants to admit lacking good beards, complexions and breaths. Its effect is akin to that of a modern stand-up comic who relies on winning over members of the audience by establishing a particular kind of intimacy with them. In the case of *As You Like It,* however, the 'comic' who performs this Epilogue is also a boy-actor who has played one of its leading roles. Hence a bridge is neatly constructed from the ficitional level of the play as such, with characters supposedly male and female, to the actual level of those actors, all male, who are entertaining an audience on whom they are are dependent for their very existence.

As You Like It, then, has virtually four endings rather than one. The first, the 'Hymen' ending, belongs to the world of romantic courtship in which, after dangers and vicissitudes, true lovers are united; and the second, the 'Jaques de Boys' ending, belongs to a variation which might be called heroic romance, in which evil is overcome and enemies reconciled. The third – the melancholy Jaques ending – rehearses a sardonic version of these two (but especially the first) in which the assumption of all-inclusive happiness is, if not entirely rejected, at least slyly undermined. And the last ending, which actually does bring the comedy to its conclusion, is the Epilogue, effecting a transition from the make-believe convention in which actors are assumed to be the fictional characters they represent, to the never-quite-to-be-forgotten reality of theatre itself, in which the performers depend on the response of the audience if the ending is to be a happy one for them also. Together these four constitute a sophisticated, multiple ending in which the conventions of comedy are duly complied with, but also questioned, and the fictional nature of theatrical performance is both exposed and exploited.

Twelfth Night

The conclusion of *Twelfth Night* is the most complicated of the endings analysed in this chapter. Like that of *A Midsummer Night's Dream* it extends over the whole of the final Act, but is much more concerned with plot. From V.i.44 onwards confusions and anxieties grow in intensity as the mistakes resulting from Viola's disguise as 'Cesario', and her close resemblance to her brother Sebastian, pile one upon another. Antonio, arrested as an old enemy of Illyria, is denied by Viola, whom he mistakes for Sebastian; and Olivia, entering at line 91, newly wedded, and similarly mistaking 'Cesario' for Sebastian, produces the Priest (line 144) who has just performed the ceremony as 'proof' that they are man and wife. With the entrance of Sir Andrew (line 166) and Sir Toby (line 182) the timid 'Cesario' is again mistaken for the formidable adversary who has given them both 'a bloody coxcomb'. And not until Sebastian's entrance (line 201), when sister and brother are for the first time both present on the stage together, revealing, in Orsino's words, 'One face, one voice, one habit, and two persons!' (line 208), is this dilemma resolved. What follows is a concentrated enactment of a typically romantic denouement, as Viola and Sebastian regale each other with the family details (including the serio-comical recollection that 'My father had a mole upon his brow' [line 234]) which confirm their relationship to each other; Sebastian reveals himself to Olivia as her true husband; and Orsino – recognising the woman's love in what he has hitherto taken to be a boy's devotion, and alluding to the original shipwreck from which all these confusions take their beginning – claims his share, too, 'in this most happy wreck' (line 258).

As disguise and misconceptions give way to knowledge of things as they are – a knowledge, of course, already vouchsafed to the theatre audience, and thus placing them in a secure and privileged position – everything seems set for the comic finale. But there remains the disillusioning of the deluded Malvolio, last seen in IV.ii, horribly baited in the madman's prison. It is at this point (line 278) that his letter to Olivia is produced. At her command Feste begins to read it, which he does in the farcically distorted fashion he deems appropriate to a madman's 'vox' [voice]; but Olivia decides that the letter must be allowed to speak for itself, and so the reading is transferred to Fabian:

'By the Lord, madam, you wrong me, and the world shall know it. Though you have put me into darkness and given your drunken cousin rule over me, yet have I the benefit of my senses as well as your ladyship. I have your own letter that induced me to the semblance I put on, with the which I doubt not but to do myself much right or you much shame. Think of me as you please. I leave my duty a little unthought of, and speak out of my injury.

THE MADLY-US'D MALVOLIO.' (lines 291–8)

Here there is still illusion and misunderstanding. Malvolio has yet to be disabused of his conviction that he has been ill-treated with the knowledge and approval of Olivia, but the fault for that cannot be laid at his door. He writes as one who feels himself seriously wronged, and there is a plainness and directness in what he says which cuts right across the romantic denouement which precedes it. The hostility to Olivia is misguided; the threat to 'shame' her vindictive; and his bluntness (even more to Elizabethan than to modern ears) shocking – as, in effect, he concedes with 'I leave my duty a little unthought of'. But he speaks out of his 'injury', and that excuses much.

The trick played on him was on one level a practical joke, which he brought on himself and was richly deserved; and as such it should be something, along with the blame he attaches to Olivia, that he is capable of forgiving and forgetting. With his entrance at line 314, bearing the letter that first deceived him, this would seem to be about to happen. The action appears to be moving on to a different plane (a point underlined by Malvolio's speaking in verse for the first and only time in the play). But his speech is essentially a reiteration of his grievances; and even when Olivia explains that the handwriting is Maria's, not hers, he shows no sign of relenting. Instead, he stalks from the scene exclaiming: 'I'll be reveng'd on the whole pack of you' (line 364). This is the odd man out, very much with a vengeance. His words isolate him completely from the rest of the characters; and, though Orsino's 'Pursue him, and entreat him to a peace' (line 366) suggest some attempt to mollify their effect, they echo with a bitterness that gives Malvolio the aura of a potentially tragic character.

However, the manner of Malvolio's exit must not be allowed to distort the overall effect of the ending. Between the reading of his 'madman's' letter and his entrance at line 314 there are important gestures of reconciliation between Olivia and her long-resisted suitor, Orsino, which smoothly convert him from lover to brother-in-law, and between Orsino and Viola/Cesario, which convert the latter into her 'master's mistress' (line 313). And following Malvolio's speech there is Fabian's speech (also in verse) confessing the plot, and pleading that 'no quarrel nor no brawl' be allowed to 'Taint the condition of this present hour' (lines 343–4). These are all in the true comic vein, and help to create a very different atmosphere. If they are offset by Feste's taunting reminder to Malvolio of the words in the original letter which so misled him, this, in turn, is balanced by the sympathetic words of Olivia (at lines 356 and 365). Taken all together, harmony prevails in spite of Malvolio's notes of discord.

But there remains the epilogue – which in this case is a song, sung by Feste. Commentators are divided as to whether this is a folk song, a song composed by someone else (Robert Armin, the actor who played Feste, has been suggested), or by Shakespeare himself. Whichever way, it is a surprising, and somewhat puzzling, choice. The most obvious link with the rest of the play is via the drunken carousing of Sir Toby and his companions; but the 'wind and rain' refrains, with their haunting suggestion of continual storm ('For the rain it raineth every day'), recall the shipwreck theme which is sounded at the beginning of the play and, as well as being mentioned again at V.i.258, recurs in Sebastian's allusion to his supposedly lost sister as one 'Whom the blind waves and surges have devour'd' (line 221) and Viola's answering reference to her brother's 'watery tomb' (line 226).

It is a drunkard's song, and a melancholy one. It traces the development of man from childhood to manhood in a sequence that seems to treat the innocence of the 'little tiny boy' as at worst doubtful and, at best, short-lived. Experience is much more to the fore, with its shutting of the gate ''Gainst knaves and thieves', its 'swaggering' that proves useless in marriage, and its bouts of wild drinking that end in drunken debauchery. And the world-weariness of 'A great while ago the world begun' – although qualified by a reference (faintly echoing Rosalind's Epilogue) to the relation between actors and audience in 'we'll strive to please you every day' – seems to be the keynote, not only of the last stanza, but of the song as a whole. Just how it will affect the audience will depend on the music to which it is set, and the manner in which Feste sings it; but there is an unmistakable resemblance to the set-piece cynicism in Jaques's *As You Like It* speech on 'All the world's a stage'. The mood is one of disillusionment verging on tragedy (words from this same song, it is perhaps worth mentioning, are quoted in *King Lear*); and, along with the bitter exit of Malvolio already discussed, it is curiously at odds with the impression of social cohesion and renewed vitality towards which the play as a whole moves. The major theme of the ending is thus the predictably comic one of happiness achieved, or restored, but discordant notes, and an underlying sense of potential tragedy, create a disturbing minor theme.

Conclusions

The endings of all four of these plays are directed towards the traditionally happy resolution expected of comedy. They are aware of the convention, and fulfil it in ways that signal its artificiality without necessarily undermining the optimistic assumptions on which it is based, or the pleasurable sense of well-being it communicates to the audience. But, viewed in chronological order, they also reveal an increasing emphasis on satirical or melancholy elements which complicate and disturb the serenity of the happy ending. The expected framework is provided, but accompanied by a growing sense that greater complexity exists outside the framework – a sense, it should be said, that makes itself felt in the very earliest of Shakespeare's comedies, and is certainly present in *A Midsummer Night's Dream*, but deepens and operates increasingly as a counterbalancing force in the later comedies.

One important effect of this, structurally, is that the comedies develop multiple rather than single endings. These are in part a consequence of Shakespeare's liking for interwoven strands of plot and sub-plot, so that in *A Midsummer Night's Dream*, for example, the ending is prolonged over the whole of Act V as the unfinished business of the Athenian workmen's *Pyramus and Thisby* is staged, and in

Much Ado About Nothing the conventional marriage of Hero and Claudio is complemented by the much less conventional one of Beatrice and Benedick. In *As You Like It* and *Twelfth Night* the presence of the odd men out, Jaques and Malvolio, further complicates this process, and a stronger impression (though not, perhaps, so very much stronger than in *Much Ado About Nothing*) that the artifice of romance is in need of modification produces endings in which discordant notes offset the still prevailing concord. The result is a variation on the traditional happy ending which mingles both light and shade, conformity and nonconformity, and, ultimately, a blurring of the division between comedy and tragedy. Paradoxically, however, this is a process which seems to strengthen and enrich Shakespearean comedy. It becomes more flexible and supple, more imbued with the mingled rather than generically simplified qualities of life itself, and thus better able to withstand the buffeting and soaking of 'the wind and the rain'.

General Conclusions to Part 1

1. Shakespearean comedy is a mingling of romance and more realistic comic material. It delights in contrasts and surprising juxtapositions, and it relishes sudden descents from the sublime to the ridiculous. But if it frequently debunks, it rarely debases, the romantically high-flown. It is fully aware how a flawed humanity fails to live up to its ideals, but it also recognises the permanent appeal such ideals possess; and it likewise recognises, and offers rich poetic material that satisfies, the enduring appetite for exotic and colourful worlds that exist essentially in the imagination.

2. A keenly critical intelligence is at work in all of these plays, and there are marked elements of satire in them. But criticism is balanced with sympathy. Most characters have their 'case', even the pathetically inadequate Sir Andrew Aguecheek; and a modest, seemingly prosaic Corin is not to be put down even by the coruscating wit of a Touchstone. Reason, good sense, tolerance and the easy-going life of 'cakes and ale' are the comic standards by which attitudes and characters are judged; but minority figures such as Jaques and Malvolio, though clearly defined and placed as odd men out, are seen to have viable standards of their own.

3. Fools and their folly afford much of the material and entertainment of comedy; but not all fools are as foolish as they look. The dupes are balanced by the shrewd, clever fools, often professionals like Touchstone and Feste, whose supposed folly is a stalking-horse under which they shoot their wit.

4. The oldest definition of comedy is a narrative or play which has a

happy ending. Although Shakespeare's comedies conform with this, and their endings are adroit resolutions which bring concord out of discord, their closures are not rigid. Their prior complications involve tension and suspense, difficult situations and sometimes painful processes of self-discovery, which not infrequently border on the tragic; and not all characters are gathered into the fold of comic happiness at the end. If the play comes out of its clouds into the final sunshine, in the background there remains awareness of the wind and the rain.

5. Among the many memorable characters that these comedies exhibit perhaps the most memorable are their heroines – especially Beatrice, Rosalind and Viola. The preoccupation of the plays with love and courtship (itself the eternal subject of romance) partly explains this; the women's search for marriage partners is the central theme of all the comedies. But what makes the heroines so memorable is their all-round awareness of the complexities of love and their rejection of the unexamined formulae of traditional romance. What matters, too, is their manlike capacity to choose and contrive and act, though placed in a nominally subordinate position vis-à-vis their menfolk. The women are the foci of the comedies; it is their predicaments, and the intelligence and emotional variety with which they respond to them, which the comedies explore, and in so doing work towards a happiness qualified by realistic awareness and mature reservations.

PART 2

THE CONTEXT AND THE CRITICS

12

The Other Comedies and the Poems

Most critics would probably agree that one learns more about any given Shakespeare play by considering its relation to the rest of his work than from critical commentary as such. The whole of Shakespeare forms a uniquely interrelated organism in which themes recur, sometimes as echoes or anticipations of later ones, sometimes as attempts at treating subjects which have been dealt with before, but are now seen in a different light, or given new contexts; and characters also change and develop in ways that suggest a widening and maturing understanding of human nature. And – of special interest, and especially revealing as the plays and poems are studied in their relations to each other – Shakespeare's language and dramatic technique can be seen as interacting parts of one, unified artistic effort to give words an increasingly imaginative and dramatic expressiveness.

The plays with which *A Midsummer Night's Dream* (1595–96), *Much Ado About Nothing* (1598–99), *As You Like It* (1599–1600) and *Twelfth Night* (1599–1600) have the most immediate connection are the other comedies: *The Comedy of Errors* (1593–94), *The Taming of the Shrew* (1593–94), *The Two Gentlemen of Verona* (1594–95), *Love's Labour's Lost* (1594–95), *The Merchant of Venice* (1596–97) and *The Merry Wives of Windsor* (1598–99). (Not too much attention should be paid to these dates. The evidence is not always precise, and scholars vary in their interpretation; but the first four, along with *A Midsummer Night's Dream*, are certainly 'early'.) These are all (with certain qualifications applying to *The Comedy of Errors, The Taming of the Shrew* and *The Merry Wives of Windsor*) romantic love comedies concerned with wooing and winning, but which also contain within them secondary plots, or secondary groups of characters, of an anti-romantic nature. The non-dramatic poems, *Venus and Adonis* and *The Rape of Lucrece*, also belong to the years 1592–93 and 1593–94, respectively, thus making them contemporary with the 'early' comedies; and Shakespeare's Sonnets, as the usually accepted dates 1592–98 suggest (backed up by their greater stylistic variety), cover a wider period embracing both earlier and later plays. Of these the Sonnets have the closest relationship to the comedies, including, as they do, both idealistic and satirical treatments of love.

The courtship theme common to all the plays discussed in Part 1 is equally the preoccupation of the other comedies, and the complaint made by Lysander and Hermia at the beginning of *A Midsummer Night's Dream* that 'The course of true love never did run smooth' could form the epigraph for many of them. In *The Two Gentlemen of Verona*, for example, the crosses which impede the ultimate happiness of Valentine, Proteus, Julia and Silvia anticipate those of the four lovers in *A Midsummer Night's Dream*, and, in particular, the situation which results in the two men becoming rivals for Silvia, to the chagrin of Julia, initially the beloved of Proteus, is a clear forerunner of the rivalry of Demetrius and Lysander for the love of Helena, to the discomfiture of Hermia. Shakespeare's handling of similar complications in the two plays makes an interesting study in itself, and shows how much more skilful he has become even in the short time that separates them. The use of disguise in *The Two Gentlemen of Verona* (Julia dresses herself as the page-boy, 'Sebastian', so that she can remain near Proteus) also anticipates its use by Rosalind in *As You Like It*, and by Viola in *Twelfth Night*; and the psychological stress as Viola/Cesario has to witness the passion of the man she loves for another woman is a much more mature, and effective, handling of the tension created in Julia/Sebastian by Proteus's infidelity. It is also interesting to compare the lyricism of *The Two Gentlemen of Verona* with that of the later comedies: poetic decoration of the courtship theme is important in all of the plays, but it is revealing to see how much more skilfully Shakespeare integrates the poetry and the drama in the later work, especially *Twelfth Night*.

However, these plays are concerned not only with the crosses endured by true lovers, but also with the follies and absurdities of love. Several of Shakespeare's lovers have recourse to sonnets when they fall in love. If these are not, like Jaques's 'woeful ballads', made to their 'mistress' eyebrows', the ones written by the lovers in *Love's Labour's Lost* are brilliant parodies of the extravagant language used by many contemporary sonneteers; and the scene (IV.iii) in which they all find each other out as secret writers of love poetry to their respective mistresses (having sworn a mutual pact to have nothing to do with love) anticipates the comic exposure of the love between Beatrice and Benedick, which is capped by the discovery that they have each written a sonnet to the other. (In *As You Like It*, also, Orlando writes verses to Rosalind which Touchstone subjects to gross parody.) And this is symptomatic of a much more profound and far-reaching relationship in which Berowne of *Love's Labour's Lost*, who scoffs at love, but then falls head over heels himself, acts as forerunner of Benedick in *Much Ado About Nothing*. The whirling, high-spirited verse in which Berowne mocks himself for falling under the sway of 'This wimpled, whining, purblind, wayward boy, / This senior-junior, giant-dwarf, Dan Cupid' (*Love's Labour's Lost*, III.i.169–70), and the long, elaborate speech, full of fantastically witty extravagances, in which he defends love as spokesman on behalf of all the perjured lovers (IV.iii.286–361), makes a fascinating comparison with the equally vivacious, but more curtly trenchant prose in which Benedick laughs at love, and then cheerfully succumbs to it. Mockery of love's absurdities and affectation, while still preserving depth of feeling and commitment to true love, becomes a hallmark of mature Shakespearean comedy: Touchstone and Feste play important roles in this process, but it is most fully exemplified, as we have seen, in Rosalind and Viola.

The mingled light and dark elements in what still remain the comic happy endings of the mature comedies are likewise interestingly anticipated by aspects of the earlier plays. Towards the end of

Love's Labour's Lost, for example, 'the scene begins to cloud'
(V.ii.710) with the news that the Princess of France's father has died;
and the perjured male lovers, the King of Navarre, Berowne,
Longaville and Dumain, instead of being paired off with their
female counterparts, are put on trial for twelve months. Berowne, in
particular, is condemned by Rosaline to visit the sick, and with 'all
the fierce endeavour of [his] wit, / To enforce the pained impotent
to smile' (V.ii.841–2). As Berowne comments: 'Our wooing doth
not end like an old play: / Jack hath not Jill' (862–3). In *A
Midsummer Night's Dream* Puck's reassurance, as he at last squeezes
the love-juice in the right lover's eyes, that 'Jack shall have Jill'
(III.ii.461) sounds like a corrective to this – as the more extensive,
and more charitable, treatment of the amateur peformance of
Pyramus and Thisby similarly balances the performance in *Love's
Labour's Lost* of the pageant of the Nine Worthies. But the songs
which end *Love's Labour's Lost*, offsetting pastoral spring with a more
realistic winter, hint at 'the icy fang / And churlish chiding of the
winter's wind' in *As You Like It* and the melancholy 'wind and rain'
of Feste's song at the end of *Twelfth Night*.

In *The Comedy of Errors* confusion is caused by the mistakings of
two pairs of identical twins – Antipholus of Ephesus and Antipholus
of Syracuse, and their respective servants, Dromio of Ephesus and
Dromio of Syracuse – with uproariously comic consequences which
anticipate the 'errors' resulting from the resemblance of Viola and
Sebastian to each other in *Twelfth Night*. More generally, they also
provide a lead-in to the more subtle explorations of the nature of
illusion and reality in *A Midsummer Night's Dream* and *Much Ado
About Nothing*, and, yet again, in *Twelfth Night*. In addition, the
framework within which this comedy of mistaken identities is held –
the story of Aegeon, a shipwrecked merchant from Syracuse who is
condemned to death because of the enmity between his country and
Ephesus – suggests a pattern of tragedy, succeeded by comedy, succeeded by resolution of both the comic confusions and the intitially
tragic situation, which is prophetic of much that is to come in
Shakespeare's later work. The seemingly harsh sentence imposed on
Hermia at the beginning of *A Midsummer Night's Dream* gives some
echo of this, and one senses it again in the shipwrecking of Viola

and Sebastian at the beginning of *Twelfth Night*, and more particularly in the plight of Sebastian's sea-captain friend, Antonio. In *As You Like It* the framework provided by the story of Duke Senior's usurpation by Frederick, and the latter's conversion on his way to complete the destruction of his brother, is a significant part of the potentiality for tragedy which makes itself felt elsewhere in the texture of the play; and in *Much Ado About Nothing* the tragi-comic pattern is still more fully developed through the counterpointing of the Hero/Claudio and Beatrice/Benedick stories, and the benign deception constituted by the 'death' and 'revival' of the traduced Hero. And the pattern by no means ends here. It leads on to the tragicomic structures of *Measure for Measure* and *All's Well That Ends Well*, and ultimately to the fully-fledged treatment of death and renewal in the last plays (*Pericles, Cymbeline, The Winter's Tale* and *The Tempest*). In these plays the happy ending of comedy emerges from upheavals which are more profound and destructive than anything in the comedies at present under discussion; but to become aware of the former is to have a keener appreciation of what are at least potentially tragic implications in the comedies of the 1590s.

Consideration of these darker elements also gives further dimension to those 'odd men out' – Jaques in *As You Like It* and Malvolio in *Twelfth Night* – who were the subject of analysis in Chapter 9. The other character of particular interest in this kind is Shylock of *The Merchant of Venice*. Here Shakespeare touches on religious and racial issues involving differences of culture and values which reveal him both as a man of his time, reflecting the prejudices of his day (with regard, for example, to Jewishness and the practice of usury), and someone with the imaginative sympathy to stand outside those prejudices. It is an interesting question whether the same can be said of *The Taming of the Shrew*. Is Katherina an 'odd woman out' who represents self-destructive insubordination in a society which assumes that women find their natural fulfilment in marital submission? Or is she ahead of her time in making an aggressive bid for the independence of women? Is Petruchio's 'taming' of her a cunning form of bullying, or is it a way of shocking her into better self-knowledge? To many readers, and audiences, the happy ending to which she is moved in this comedy seems more like psychological defeat, in sharp contrast to the fulfilment that seems not only promised to, but is effectively the achievement of, Beatrice in *Much Ado About Nothing*, Rosalind in *As You Like It* and – a heroine with whom it is very interesting to compare these two – Portia in *The Merchant of Venice*. (Perhaps Viola of *Twelfth Night* also, though she seems less in control of events than either Rosalind or Portia.) And yet these heroines, intelligent, independent and energetic as they are, seem to use their powers to bring about the conventional, and conformist, happy ending – i.e. to arrive at a position which is not radically different from that which Katherina eventually reaches. Is Katherina, then, really a precursor of these 'manlike women', rather than an 'odd woman out'? Or are these 'manlike women' more refined versions of the 'odd woman out' to be seen in her less sophisticated and developed form in Katherina? The comparison between Katherina and Beatrice would be especially well worth pursuing, as the militant streak in both is strongly developed.

The more closely one looks at the four plays chosen for analysis, and at their relationship with the rest of Shakespeare's comic output, the more such questions suggest themselves – and the more one realises that Shakespeare is not working towards specific answers which (in the fashion of Bernard Shaw, for example) he expects his readers, or audiences, to endorse. The development is more towards greater flexibility and imaginative inclusiveness than towards particular ideas or doctrine. Questions are asked rather than answers supplied; and, as the example of *Love's Labour's Lost* suggests, experiment with departure from established norms ('Jack hath not Jill') does not necessarily lead to more and more radical departures from those norms. The later comedies remain comedies, with traditionally happy endings, but also with modifications of the kinds and degrees of happiness which suggest a ferment going on within the established patterns to make them more responsive to a growing sense, not only of the richness and variety of experience, but also to differences of value and outlook which the traditional range and the traditional form may not accommodate. The mould is there, but also an implicit recognition that not everything can be fitted into it.

13

Histories, Tragedies and Last Plays

Most of Shakespeare's history plays overlap with the dates of the comedies: the *Henry VI* trilogy is very early work (*Part I*, 1589-90; *Part II*, 1590–91; *Part III*, 1590–91), *Richard III* is usually dated 1592–93, *Richard II* 1595–96, *King John* 1596–97, *Henry IV, Parts I* and *II* 1597–98, and *Henry V* 1598–99. (*Henry VIII*, written in collaboration with John Fletcher, 1612, comes at the end of Shakespeare's career.)

Some of the satirically debunking spirit of Berowne and Benedick is seen in the speeches of Philip the Bastard in *King John*, particularly his sarcastic treatment of 'commodity' [= political expediency] at II.i.561-98. And, vicious as his character is, the outrageous conduct and scoffing language of the hunchback Richard III has something in common with their comic zest. Although he admits that he is 'not shap'd for sportive tricks, / Nor made to court an amorous looking-glass' (*Richard III*, I.i.14–15), he woos and wins Lady Anne in the very same scene as she mourns for the husband and father-in-law whom he has killed. Having so improbably turned the tables on her, he exults in his own wit: 'Was ever woman in this humour woo'd? / Was ever woman in this humour won?' (I.ii.227–8).

However, for comic wooing comparable to that which is found in the mature comedies one needs to turn to *Henry V*. This is a play dedicated to Henry V as a hero-monarch, committed to the glorification of his exploits at the Battle of Agincourt, and yet also one in

which the increasing sense of disillusionment with war and political
intrigue which characterises the preceding histories is strongly felt as
a counterbalancing theme. Henry's marriage to Princess Katherine is
dynastic – a political arrangement meant to seal Henry's claim to the
throne of France as well as England, and also the peace which is
being negotiated between the two countries. Romantic wooing,
therefore, of the kind found in the love poetry of the period is inappropriate, and in any case difficult to reconcile with the image of
Henry as the bluff warrior. It is here that the developments which
take place in the comedies, leading to the anti-Petrarchan debunkery
of Benedick and the mocking realism of Rosalind, in her role as
Ganymede standing in for Orlando's 'Rosalind', prove useful to
Shakespeare the historian. Stylistically, too, the deflationary zest and
colloquial ease that goes into the prose of the mature comedies is a
more suitable medium for a soldier's courtship than, for example,
the elegant sentimentalism of Orsino in *Twelfth Night*. Thus the
wooing scene in V.ii of *Henry V* becomes an extension of the mode
in the comedies which simultaneously flouts romantic attitudes and
language and expresses a love that is more firmly based in reality.
This is the posture adopted by Henry in his (nevertheless quite
lengthy) speech (lines 133–67) urging Katherine to take him as a
plain, but honest man, unused to, and unwilling to practise, the
over-sophisticated arts of the fashionable courtier:

> Marry, if you would put me to verses or to dance for your sake, Kate,
> why you undid me ... before God, Kate, I cannot look greenly, nor
> gasp out my eloquence, nor I have no cunning in protestation; only
> downright oaths, which I never use till urg'd, nor never break for
> urging ... I speak to thee plain soldier.

The fact remains, however, that this is political wooing. Sentiment
in the histories is subjected to some very probing analyses – and
never more so than by the great comic figure of the histories, Sir
John Falstaff, who makes the two Parts of *Henry IV* seem still more
an extension of the comedies. He, too, is reminiscent of Benedick;
but also of the anti-romantic Touchstone and Feste. For example,
the neatly patterned prose of Benedick mocking Claudio's surrender

to love and professing his own immunity (*Much Ado About Nothing*, II.iii.8–32) is more than matched (and with more devastatingly critical effect) by Falstaff's catechism of 'honour' (*Henry IV, Part I*, V.i.127–40), and Feste's verbal skill in 'proving' Olivia the fool (*Twelfth Night*, I.v) by his ingenious twisting of the word 'counterfeit' (*Henry IV, Part I*, V.iv.111–28). The other figure in the comedies with whom he has obvious affinity is Sir Toby Belch. They are both witty parasites and drunkards, and inveterate opponents of the puritanical; though Falstaff's disreputable behaviour covers a degree of cowardice which is alien to Sir Toby, and is more seriously at odds with the political order which ultimately has to prevail in the histories. Hence the more devastating rejection of Falstaff by Hal when the scapegrace Prince – whom Falstaff thinks he has in his pocket – becomes the reformed King Henry V.

Falstaff also appears – as a lover – in the comedy, *The Merry Wives of Windsor*, where, however, he seems more a comic dupe than the popular anti-hero that he clearly was for Shakespeare's contemporary audiences, and continues to be for most audiences today. His appeal is fundamentally anarchic (which is why the coming of his rejection, in *Henry IV, Part II*, V.iv.48–73, is inevitable). He shares his devastating capacity to expose cant and empty rhetoric with the clever Fools of the comedies, but, more radically than they, he appeals to the instinct deep in all of us to deride authority and cast off restraint. He represents a combination of energy and dissoluteness which is hedonistically attractive (akin to the 'cakes and ale' principle of Sir Toby), but also potentially destructive. As such it is irreconcilable with the brand of warrior-king patriotism celebrated in *Henry V* – where the memory of Falstaff is reduced to a brilliantly affective (but *reported*) death-scene (II.iii.9–26), and only the seedy figures of Pistol, Bardolph and Nym remain from the subversive comic scenes of *Henry IV, Parts I and II*.

That destructive potential is given its head in the tragedies, but allied with a rampant individualism, a ruthless self-seeking, and, at its worst, a satanic pleasure in evil for its own sake, which go far beyond anything envisaged in either the comedies or the histories. Yet a sense of continuity remains. On the one hand, such villains of the comedies as Don John in *Much Ado About Nothing* and the usurping Duke

Frederick (as well as Orlando's malicious brother, Oliver) in *As You Like It* can be seen as preliminary sketches, to be more fully developed, and given more serious roles, for the villains of the tragedies – Claudius in *Hamlet* (1600–01), Edmund in *King Lear* (1605–06), and Iago in *Othello* (1602–03). (What the comedies do not foreshadow, however, is the evil in such women as Goneril and Regan, in *King Lear*, and Lady Macbeth [*Macbeth* 1605–06]; nor the internal conflict, winding down to a desperate abandonment of good, depicted in Macbeth himself.) On the other hand, the critical role played by such characters as Beatrice, Benedick, Rosalind and the clever Fools of the comedies appears again, mordantly transformed, in the sardonic humour of Hamlet and the wit of the nameless Fool in *King Lear*. (In a decadent, corrupted form it is also still traceable, if barely, in the scurrilous wit of Thersites in *Troilus and Cressida* [1601–02] and the cynicism of Apemantus in *Timon of Athens* [1604–05].) The strongest link is between Feste and Lear's Fool: the song Feste sings at the end of *Twelfth Night* is echoed in a stanza sung by the Fool in *King Lear*, III.ii.74–7, and the two characters may have been played by the same actor, Robert Armin. The Fool's function, like Feste's also, is to educate his betters; as Feste corrects the sentimental excesses of Orsino and Olivia, Lear's Fool attempts to bring home to his master the folly of what he has done in disowning Cordelia and giving everything to Goneril and Regan. The same dramatic metaphor of a wise Fool in the pay of a foolish employer, and the possibilities of ironic meaning this throws up, is exploited in both plays; and, still more profoundly, the sense one gets in *Twelfth Night* of a comedy which verges at times on the tragic is complemented in *King Lear* by tragedy, of the most searing kind, mingled with painful jesting and absurd language and behaviour, which creates an atmosphere of the grotesque. By the standards of classical tragedy – and, more particularly, the severely purist form of such tragedy exemplified in the work of the seventeenth-century French dramatist, Racine, which rigidly excludes anything frivolous or ludicrous – *King Lear* is laughably indecorous. It is a confusion of genres, neither comedy, nor tragedy. But it is a confusion which works, employing the intelligent barbs of comedy to intensify the predicament of its tragic hero, and blending light and shade to create a powerful emotional chiaroscuro.

The relationship of the comedies to what are often known as the 'problem plays', *All's Well That Ends Well* (1602–03), *Measure for Measure* (1603–04) and *Troilus and Cressida* (treated above as a tragedy), has already been touched on. The first two could, indeed, be classified as comedies – they work towards a happy ending, and *Measure for Measure* has low-life scenes which excite laughter, even if some audiences would find them coarse and unsavoury compared with those in *A Midsummer Night's Dream* and *Much Ado About Nothing*. They are 'problematic' because they raise issues, like Angelo's attempt to bargain with Isabella for her virginity in return for sparing her brother's life, which become so incompatible with the values of romantic comedy that the retention of the traditional framework seems impossibly strained. In particular, the 'bed-trick', whereby a legitimate wife (or betrothed) is substituted for an illicit partner, seems a legalistic device which shirks all the serious moral issues. These are plays which seem to have more in common with the tragedies that mainly preoccupied Shakespeare at this stage in his career. Yet Helena, the heroine of *All's Well That Ends Well*, is both reminiscent of the strong, directing woman found in several of the previous comedies and an interesting link between them and the 'last plays', where comedy is plucked out of tragedy, and – in *The Winter's Tale* at least – a strong woman, Paulina, is again instrumental in bringing this about.

The 'last plays' are sometimes, and perhaps more appropriately, called the 'romances'. They show a renewed interest in the romance stories and themes which Shakespeare had used in his earlier work, with an even stronger drive towards the comic happy ending. But these are endings achieved only after disruptions and disturbance so intense that they often seem like the aftermath of tragedy. Their structural similarity to *The Comedy of Errors* and the Hero/Claudio plot of *Much Ado About Nothing* has already been noted; but in some respects their links to *As You Like It*, though less apparent, are more significant.

The first three Acts of *The Winter's Tale* are a deeper and more extended treatment of the treachery that robs Duke Senior, Rosalind and Orlando respectively of their righful inheritances (though the emphasis in *The Winter's Tale* is on the sexual relationship between

Leontes and his Queen, Hermione – with unmistakable resem-
blances to the jealousy which foments the tragedy in *Othello*). And
the move in Act IV to the idealised countryside of Bohemia brings
with it a powerful renewal of the pastoral themes, and characters,
which dominate *As You Like It* from Act II onwards. In both plays
the move is from court to country, with important interplay between
courtly and pastoral values. *The Winter's Tale* has its courtly sophisti-
cate, Autolycus, who prances self-consciously before the rustics as
Touchstone shows off his superior refinement before Corin and
William (though a comparison of Touchstone and Autolycus would
show even more important differences as well); and the sense of the
countryside as a refreshing counterbalance to the corruption of the
court world is also significant in both plays. The repentance of Duke
Frederick and the reconciliation of Oliver with Orlando may seem
perfunctory compared with the deep contrition undergone by
Leontes, but both lead to happy restoration and the approved comic
ending.

The one marked difference, however, is the opting-out of Jaques.
No one is left out in *The Winter's Tale* – even Paulina is paired off
with Camillo. It is to *The Tempest* that one must look for a thematic
equivalent to the Shylock/Jaques/Malvolio 'odd-man-out' figure.
Here again harmony is brought out of disorder, with the young love
of Miranda and Ferdinand sealing it and promising its continuity
into the future, as had been the case with the love of Perdita and
Florizel in *The Winter's Tale*. But at the courtly end of the spectrum
the disaffected Antonio is never properly brought into the circle of
renewal, and, more strikingly still, at the rough, unpolished natural
end of the spectrum (quite unlike the pastoralism of either the
Forest of Arden or the sheep-shearing festival of Bohemia), Caliban,
though he says he will 'be wise hereafter, / And seek for grace'
(V.i.294–5), represents a crude, primitive vitality that cannot be
accomodated to the courts of Milan and Naples.

Other differences are to be found in *Pericles* and *Cymbeline*,
including, for example, the peripatetic structure and deliberately
archaic narrative mode cultivated in *Pericles*, and, in *Cymbeline*, the
combination of fairy-tale witchcraft with Italianate sophistication,
plus the attempt to bridge British and Roman culture which brings

the dissident Cymbeline back into the fold of empire. These are plays in which Shakespeare is manifestly going back to things which interested his earlier self; but, just as the comedies reveal him repeating without ever merely copying himself, so the 'last plays' show old themes being given new twists and new emphases. (And, stylistically, there is still more difference, Shakespeare's verse having passed through the great dramatic crucible of the tragedies which burnt and purged away almost all the leisurely decorativeness of his earlier work, to emerge in these plays as a completely flexible and immensely variable instrument.) The organic relationship between the total *oeuvre* is proved by the interconnections which can never be exhaustively analysed, but equally, the organic force is constantly growing new shoots.

14

Theories of Comedy and Criticism of Shakespeare's Comedies

Theories of Comedy

Theories of comedy do not figure so largely in the history of literary criticism as theories of tragedy. Aristotle, for example, has little to say about it in his *Poetics*; and in the Middle Ages comedy, as in Dante's *Divine Comedy*, which moves from hell via purgatory to paradise, suggested a structure culminating in happiness and bliss. The self-consciously learned writers of the Renaissance, following classical precedent, emphasised the realistic, low-life nature and the didactic, corrective function of comedy, as in the work of Ben Jonson, which purports to expose vice and folly to healthy ridicule; but the tradition to which Shakespeare's comedies belong has its roots in popular festivals, and receives its theoretical justification, as opposed to theatrical practice, only in more recent times.

For the student, D. J. Palmer's *Comedy: Developments in Criticism* (in the Macmillan Casebook series, 1984) provides a useful introduction to theories of comedy, and a series of extracts from major critics (with particular emphasis on twentieth-century ones). Parts One and Two ('The Classical and Medieval Tradition' and 'From the Renaissance to Bergson') contain brief extracts – among others, from Plato, Aristotle, Cicero, Sir Philip Sidney, Jonson, Fielding, Goldsmith, Lamb and Meredith – the trend in the English eighteenth and nineteenth centuries being, as Palmer suggests, towards a 'growing distaste for scornful or aggressive laughter' (*Comedy: Developments in Criticism*, p. 14). But the most substantial thinking about comedy is to be found in the French philosopher, Henri Bergson's *Le Rire* (1899). Bergson refines the corrective theory away from its ponderously didactic emphasis, which often seems inconsistent with the joyful, liberating effect of actual comedy, to relate it to his own concern with that quality of flexibility and resilience which he sees as necessary to the living, adaptable human being. Laughter, he maintains, is directed at behaviour which has lost touch with this essential life force and has become virtual automatism. This is a theory which may usefully be applied to a character like Malvolio; and, considered not only as a theory explaining the laughter directed *at* comic dupes, but as one which explains the positive attractiveness of comic figures whom one laughs *with*, it also casts light on characters such as Benedick, Beatrice and Rosalind (and perhaps Bottom as well) who excel in nimbleness and adaptability.

Part Three contains more substantial extracts, and is divided into two sections: 'The Traditions of Comedy' and 'Conceptions of Comic Form' – corresponding to Palmer's sense that modern criticism tends to be occupied either with the origins and traditions of comedy, or with more theoretical questions. An extract from F. M. Cornford's *The Origin of Attic Comedy* (1914) delves into the primitive rituals which lie behind the more popular forms of comedy, and includes such themes as the contests between spring/summer and winter, and youth and age, as well as fertility rites concerned with death and resurrection. (Obvious connections exist here with the Shakespearean comedy discussed above. For example, the songs at the end of *Love's Labour's Lost* have spring and winter as their subjects; the dialogue between Silvius and Corin in *As You Like It*, II.iv echoes youth v. age; and the oppositions of winter/spring and death/resurrection are potently orchestrated in the plot and language of *The Winter's Tale*.)

However, it is Northrop Frye who turns these 'origins' into a fully-fledged structure which he sees as providing the distinctive pattern of Shakespearean comedy. Palmer's source is 'The Argument

of Comedy', which Frye published as an essay in 1948, but it is also
the informing principle behind such works by him as *An Anatomy of
Criticism* (1957) and *A Natural Perspective: The Development of
Shakespearean Comedy and Romance* (1965). Frye speaks of 'the
drama of the green world', the theme of which is 'the triumph of life
over the waste land, the death and revival of the year impersonated
by figures still human, and once divine as well' (reprinted in
Comedy: Developments in Criticism, p. 80). He emphasises the co-
presence of both tragedy and comedy in Shakespearean comedy, but
with the fundamental proviso that the tragedy is contained within,
and ultimately cancelled out by, the comedy. The plays deal with situations and characters who hinder and obstruct this process – hence,
for example, the sterile animosity of Egeus to the union of Hermia
and Lysander in *A Midsummer Night's Dream,* the usurpation of
Duke Senior's dukedom by Duke Frederick and the denial of
Orlando's inheritance by his brother, Oliver, in *As You Like It*, and
the killjoy opposition of Malvolio to Sir Toby's 'cakes and ale' in
Twelfth Night. But translation of the action into the 'green world' of
the wood outside Athens, or the Forest of Arden, or the land of
Illyria – magical settings remote from the London-based realism of
Jonsonian comedy, and essentially empowered with the 'divine'
resources of archaic tradition and folklore – enables the play to tap
into deep, creative forces which thaw out the wintry obstructions of
tragedy and assure the ultimate triumph of life.

The other major critic included in section 1 of Part Three is
Mikhail Bakhtin. Bakhtin also relies heavily on folklore and popular
tradition, but his interest is in the anti-authoritarian nature of this
tradition, and especially the licence which is granted in carnival time
to subvert orthodoxy and the establishment. Laughter becomes the
cocking of a snook at authority which offers the ordinary populace a
kind of alternative, second world. As Bakhtin puts it, in medieval
times the parodic rituals of carnival 'offered a completely different,
non-official, extra-ecclesiastical and extra-political aspect of the
world, of man and of human relations; they built a second world
and a second life outside officialdom' (reprinted in *Comedy:
Developments in Criticism*, p. 95). And later he says that 'carnival is
the people's second life, organised on the basis of laughter. It is a

festive life' (ibid., p. 98). There is a link here, obviously enough, with Cornford and Frye, but for Bakhtin the significance of this is less historical than artistic. 'Carnivalisation' becomes a kind of literary counterpoint in which officialdom's formal voice is offset by one or more unofficial voices which, both in style and attitude, challenge the received wisdom. It is characteristically irreverent, ribald, unbuttoned, slangy-colloquial and open-ended; it makes for a variety of meanings rather than one, officially endorsed, 'monologic' meaning. And, since laughter is its most potent instrument, it finds a natural home in comedy. Moreover, given the multiple plots and the multiple, often dialectically opposed, positions dramatised in Shakespeare's comedies, 'carnivalisation', it could be argued, is a concept particularly appropriate to his work. It even fits nicely with his throwaway titles – *Much Ado About Nothing, As You Like It* and *Twelfth Night* (the latter, especially, alluding to the carnival atmosphere of the Christmas period, and suggesting by its alternative, *What You Will*, an almost Rabelaisian relaxation of formal control).

Palmer's 'Conceptions of Comic Form' embraces extracts from R. S. Crane, Susanne Langer, Friedrich Durrenmatt, Eric Bentley and Elder Olson. Susanne Langer tackles the elusive theme of laughter in real life v. laughter in dramatic comedy. As she says, 'we tend to laugh at things in the theater that we might not find funny in actuality' (reprinted in *Comedy: Developments in Criticism*, p. 128), and it is the essence of her argument (which still, however, remains somewhat elusive) that comic situations in drama are made *un*like those in real life by devices such as stereotyping, exaggeration and excessive use of coincidence. The comedy, she would suggest, is not holding the mirror up to nature, nor – as in the classical approach – reinforcing the accepted values of society, but imitating the 'comic rhythm' which is an expression of the inherent liveliness of life itself. Hence it is essentially amoral. It does not have an end in view, an ulterior motive. Its business is constructing an artefact which intensifies an audience's sense of well-being through the exercise of humour. In real life things are only funny if we happen to be in the mood for them: 'It is different in the theater: the play possesses us and breaks our mood' (ibid., p. 127).

Durrenmatt and Bentley, however, see comedy as a much more

disturbing experience. Durrenmatt, acutely conscious of the grotesquely violent elements in the modern world, concludes, not that tragedy is its appropriate form, but that 'Comedy alone is suitable for us'; and he makes the seemingly odd comment that 'many of Shakespeare's tragedies are already really comedies out of which the tragic arises' (reprinted in *Comedy: Developments in Criticism*, p. 132). And, far from endorsing Langer's 'comic rhythm', he sees comedy as a kind of 'mouse-trap in which the public is easily caught' – a series of devices (or 'conceits') working on the brittle lack of community which (in his absurdist view) is what life has become for us.

For Bentley, too, there is something aggressive about comedy, and he maintains that at its greatest (in Machiavelli, Jonson, Shakespeare, or Molière), 'we find the dark undercurrent at its fastest and most powerful' (reprinted in *Comedy: Developments in Criticism*, p. 136). In his view, although conventionally comedy is considered 'a gay and lighthearted form of art', it is, like tragedy, 'a way of trying to cope with despair, mental suffering, guilt and anxiety' (ibid., p. 140). Tragedy does this by a process of confrontation, but comedy's method is 'indirect, ironical' (ibid., p. 141); there is a dynamic contrast 'between a frivolous manner and a grim meaning' (ibid., p. 148). Nevertheless, Shakespearean comedy reveals a 'contrary tendency' in which 'for grim statements in a gay style are substituted benign statements in a style not without solemnity' (ibid., p. 148). The inconsistency of this concession (he also makes it with regard to Mozart opera – especially *The Marriage of Figaro*) seems a disconcerting reversal of his argument, but underlying it is his sense that the romantic elements in such plays as *As You Like It* and *Twelfth Night* walk perilously over a matchboard floor beneath which pain and suffering are constantly to be detected. Bentley generalises, while at the same time being averse to generalisation. Instead of applying theory to comedy he prefers to look at particular examples of comedies, and in doing so he finds what is conventionally regarded as 'comic' repeatedly contradicted by qualities allied to the tragic. (And the corollary would seem to be true: that tragedies, particularly Shakespearean ones, constantly border on the comic.) A properly inclusive notion of comedy must therefore risk seeming a contradiction of itself. Dogma must not be allowed to distort the seeing of what is actually there; and this includes his own insistence on the underlying presence of despair in comedy.

Three Critics of Shakespeare's Comedies

There are many commentators on Shakespearean comedy, and many books devoted to individual comedies, as well as the excellent introductions to editions of the plays in such series as the Arden and the Oxford Shakespeares. There is only space here to concentrate on a limited number of these. But the three chosen for consideration (albeit briefly – and it cannot be emphasised too strongly that what is written here is no substitute for the books themselves, which should be read and studied in their entirety) represent, not only changes of fashion in critical approach, but also different aspects of the comedies which are to some extent complementary to each other. None has a monopoly of truth, but each has something worthwhile to contribute to a subject which in its richness and complexity transcends them all. The three are taken in chronological order of publication, without, however, any implication that latest necessarily means best.

The first book is H. B. Charlton's *Shakespearian Comedy* (London: Methuen 1938). Charlton starts from the assumption that Shakespeare was giving his Elizabethan audience what they wanted, i.e. tales of romance, and romantic courtship in particular. 'Romantic comedy is pre-eminently the comedy of love,' he says. 'It is its specific occupation with wooing which distinguishes it most markedly from classical or Roman comedy' (p. 21). But there were difficulties in the way of translating this into effective dramatic comedy which Shakespeare found himself up against in the early attempt, *The Two Gentlemen of Verona*, and which led to a 'recoil' in the 'rollickingly anti-romantic' *The Taming of the Shrew*.

The first successful staging of romance was *A Midsummer Night's Dream*. This shows adroit skill in bringing together plot material of three different kinds; but its real achievement is in moulding them 'into one by a controlling point of view, by an idea, not a philtre' (p. 103). This idea is that love is a vital, but adolescent, romantic fury which needs to modulate into the more settled maturity of marriage, under the guiding good sense of a Theseus. The latter's speech at the beginning of Act V becomes the core statement of the play's values: 'With Theseus, the philosophy of comedy is finding its voice, and his "cool reason" is its prevailing spirit' (p. 122). Other critics give a more central importance to Oberon and Titania, but for Charlton these characters are 'the undomesticated irresponsible beings of fairyland'. The flaws in their marriage are allied to their non-human status and are implicitly judged by a more humane standard. On the other hand, he recognises the overwhelming appeal of Bottom, who provides essential ballast to the more romantic aspects of the play. Bottom represents 'substance in the seemingly insubstantial cloud-world of *A Midsummer Night's Dream*' (p. 119).

Chapters are devoted to Shylock, Falstaff and the 'problem plays' (which Charlton calls the 'dark comedies', and somewhat confusingly treats as if they were preparatory, rather than subsequent, to the mature comedies). But the drive is towards Shakespeare's supreme comic achievement in *Much Ado About Nothing, As You Like It* and *Twelfth Night*, dealt with in the final chapter, entitled 'The Consummation'. Here Shakespeare 'most fully satisfies the curiously Elizabethan aesthetic demand for a drama which would gratify both the romantic and the comic instincts of its audience' (p. 266).

Charlton says that classical comedy is 'conservative' – by which he means that it uses laughter to return aberrants to the established norms of a settled society; but Shakespearean comedy, he argues, is of a more exploratory kind:

> It speculates imaginatively on modes, not of preserving a good already reached, but of enlarging and extending the possibilities of this and other kinds of good. Its heroes (or heroines, to give them the dues of their sex) are voyagers in pursuit of a happiness not yet attained, a brave new world wherein man's life may be fuller, his sensations more exquisite and his joys more widespread, more lasting, and so more humane ... . Hence Shakespearian comedy is not finally satiric; it is poetic. It is not conservative; it is creative. The way of it is that of the imagination rather than that of pure reason. It is an artist's vision, not a critic's exposition. (p. 278)

The realisation of this creative ideal is to be found most particularly in the heroines of the mature comedies, Beatrice, Rosalind and Viola. But the great virtue of these women (whom Charlton treats *as* women, disregarding the fact that in Shakespeare's theatre they were played by boys) is that, warm and glowing as they are, they behave neither as visionaries nor didactic prophets. They are creatures of this world, eminently well balanced, excelling in instinct and intuition, but anchored in realism and good sense – qualities which Charlton (in a manner that might not commend him to more recent feminists) attributes to their 'essential femininity' (p. 286). Generosity and shrewdness of wit are harmonised in them, making them the movers and shapers of the mature comedies; and they also act as criteria by which other characters, such as Jaques and Malvolio, are judged and found wanting. They represent 'Shakespeare's enthronement of woman as queen of comedy' (p. 285).

In effect, what we have here is a projection of the nineteenth/twentieth-century liberal humanism to which Charlton himself subscribes. (See, for example, his statement that 'the foundation of all lasting pleasure is the gift of intuitive sympathy, and the habit of forbearance and of tolerance', p. 293.) It is this which informs his interpretation of the heroines; and it is this which governs his sense that Shakespeare's career as a comic dramatist consists of a dialogue between realism and romance, culminating in a successful accommodation between the two. It is an attractive and eloquently written thesis, in which much of lasting value is achieved, but at the expense of those darker undercurrents detected by Durrenmatt and Bentley. And it lacks the more precise linguistic analysis to be found in subsequent criticism. Its strength is in the general case it makes for regarding the comedies as vehicles for a humane and reasonable optimism.

C. L. Barber's *Shakespeare's Festive Comedy* (Princeton: Princeton University Press, 1972) is partly explained by its subtitle: *A Study of Dramatic Form and its Relation to Social Custom*. Further explanation is offered in the introductory chapter, where Barber states: 'To get at the form and meaning of the plays ... I have been led into an exploration of the way the social form of Elizabethan holidays contributed to the dramatic form of festive comedy' (p. 4). There is some debt to the work by F. M. Cornford and Northrop Frye already touched on in the above consideration of D. J. Palmer's Casebook on *Comedy*: there is a similar concern with folk elements, popular tradition and the celebration of vitality. But 'holiday' also means for Barber a certain kind of interaction between freedom and restraint, the finding of a balance between the two which adds up to a way of life that is truly civilised. Its features include May games, the election of Lords of Misrule and the praise of folly. Much of this is low-life counterpoise to officialdom (akin in some respects to the 'carnival' spirit of Bakhtin), but reflected also on the aristocratic level in, for example, the pageants created for the entertainment of Queen Elizabeth. It is a perhaps idealised image of a unified culture at ease with itself; and the ease deriving from having its roots in the good old times of 'cakes and ale'. But it is balanced, too, in having its mockery of killjoys (who appear in Shakespeare's comedies as such figures as Shylock and Malvolio) offset by an equally sceptical treatment of 'highflown idealism' seen as 'a not unnatural attempt to be more than natural' (p. 9).

With regard to *A Midsummer Night's Dream*, this approach results in much greater emphasis on the importance of the fairies than in H. B. Charlton's work. The play becomes a night of Maying presided over by Oberon and Titania, who are seen as 'a pair of country gods, half-English and half-Ovid', whose function is comparable to that of the classical deities who play a part in the reception of Elizabeth on her visit to Elvetham in 1591 – the likeness coming particularly close in Oberon's lines at II.i.155–64. The status of the fairies, however, is also ambiguous: actual belief in them is countered by the recurrent theme of 'the folly of fancy', and in Puck Shakespeare creates an intermediate figure who plays the mocking festive games in a spirit of uniquely self-conscious gamesmanship. Barber's attention to the play's imagery also differentiates him from Charlton. He analyses a series of 'metamorphic metaphors' which, like the status of the fairies, suggest an elusive fluidity of being: 'The teeming metamorphoses which we encounter are placed ... in a medium and in a moment where the perceived structure of the outer world breaks down, where the body and its environment interpenetrate in unaccustomed ways, so that the seeming separateness and stability of identity is lost' (p. 135). Artificiality – in no derogatory sense – is the keynote of it all. Even Bottom and his Athenian workmates contribute to this effect. Their naive taking of things too literally throws into relief the imaginative scepticism on which the play is predicated: 'They exhibit just the all-or-nothing attitude towards fancy which would be fatal to the play as a whole' (p. 149).

In common with Charlton, Barber finds the culmination of Shakespeare's comic vision in the mature comedies, discussed in his final chapters on *As You Like It* and *Twelfth Night* respectively. 'The Forest of Arden, like the Wood outside Athens, is a region defined by an attitude of liberty from ordinary limitations, a festive place where the folly of romance can have its day' (p. 223). Though it is a region of freedom and fulfilment, it also contains antidotes to itself in the satirical and sceptical attitudes dramatised via Touchstone and Rosalind. Touchstone's, for example, is a 'one-sided realism', reducing love to desire in his affair with Audrey, but in so doing forestalling 'the cynicism with which the audience might greet a play where his sort of realism had been ignored' (p. 232). Rosalind, on the other hand, combines mockery with passion, participation with detachment. The result is a comedy as finely balanced as Metaphysical poetry, expressing in dramatic (rather than lyrical) terms that 'alliance of levity and seriousness' which T. S. Eliot praised in the poetry of Marvell (p. 236).

The final chapter on *Twelfth Night* focuses on the festive carousing of Sir Toby and company, but with awareness of the way it illustrates both right and wrong styles of festivity. (Sir Andrew, in consequence, gets comparatively harsh treatment, and Sir Toby a little too much indulgence.) And the sense of style – especially as it is refined and extended for the Elizabethans by their interest in the more aristocratic conception of 'courtesy' – pervades the rest of the play through the importance attached to customs, manners and patterns of speech. Malvolio's part in all this is to display a self-centred style that suggests careerism cut off from the more liberal/conservative standards (in no political sense, of course) implicit in the rest of the play. The supreme irony for him is that his duping leads him into ridiculous parodies of festive behaviour such as his wearing of yellow stockings and deliberate beaming of preposterous smiles. Barber has little sympathy with Charles Lamb's portrayal of Malvolio as a figure of pathos (see the Casebook on *Twelfth Night*): 'To play the dark-house scene for pathos, instead of making fun out of the pathos, or at any rate out of most of the pathos, is to ignore the dry comic light which shows up Malvolio's virtuousness as a self-limiting automatism' (p. 256). What matters is the living variety and balanced holiday atmosphere of the festive tradition; and Malvolio, if not strictly a Puritan (Barber cites Maria's 'The devil a Puritan that he is, or anything constantly but a time-pleaser', *Twelfth Night*, II.iii.137–8), could be said to have got his revenge in the Civil War of the 1640s. In a very subtle and intelligent mode Barber's study is a commendation of the 'good old days', and the way Shakespeare embodied the best of that concept in his comedies.

The third book is Ruth Nevo's *Comic Transformations in Shakespeare* (London: Methuen, 1980), which again traces Shakespeare's development from the early comedies up to and including *Twelfth Night*. The opening chapter (somewhat arid, and to that extent giving a misleading impression of what the book is like as a whole) argues that 'Shakespeare's early comedies are a gallimaufray of experiments' (p. 1), varying and redistributing the constituent parts of an overall structure derived from the 'New Comedy' associated with the Roman dramatist Terence, which directs the personae of comedy through hazards and complications to final harmony and resolution. But this process is not one of identification with 'a favourite character': 'We participate rather in a dynamic process, acting out imaginatively, and restructuring, impulses as often as not dialectically opposed' (p. 11). Moroever, a strong element of detachment and irony is required to forestall identification, and this is provided by the all-important figure of the Fool. Refining on Bakhtin's insight, Nevo particularly emphasises the deflationary wit of the Fool as it is developed, for example, in the 'multi-impersonator' Falstaff; but also recognising that 'Polity cannot survive this demon of jest' (p. 16), she turns her ultimate attention to the more practical combination of romantic and anti-romantic as it is worked out in the post-Falstaffian comedies of *Much Ado About Nothing*, *As You Like It* and *Twelfth Night*.

There are interesting chapters on *The Comedy of Errors* and *The Taming of the Shrew*, in which Nevo argues that farce has a more integral place in the dynamics of Shakespearean comedy than is usually allowed, and, with regard to the *Shrew*, that the battle of the sexes amounts to more than the taming of Katherina by crude bullying. In both plays there is evidence of what is to become the primary theme of the later work, encapsulated in the sentence: 'The more [protagonists] lose themselves in a spiralling whirligig of misapprehensions, the more their latent selves emerge, or are acted out' (p. 26).

Viewed in this perspective, *A Midsummer Night's Dream* is 'a highly intellectual, highly speculative comedy' (p. 96). Egeus's objection to Lysander as wooer of Hermia is an obstacle to be overcome, but not the main one. More important is the conflict between Lysander and Demetrius for the same woman, and Helena's unrequited love. These involve the 'errant faculty' of the 'mind', as implied in Helena's lament that 'Love looks not with the eyes but with the mind'. In accordance with the principle that 'The strategy of comedy is to maximalise error before matters will mend' (p. 105), relations are complicated, not in a merely mechanical way by Puck's misplaced love-juice, but by the immature rivalries of the lovers allied with 'that fluidity and instability of imagination' which causes them 'to represent reality in images generated by the desires of the mind' (p. 104). The dream-world of their experiences in the wood near Athens becomes a kind of 'alembic' which they pass through to a truer perception of reality. Similarly with Oberon and Titania: the sibling-like rivalry that afflicts the lovers is reflected in Oberon's jealousy of the relationship between Titania and her Indian queen, and the conflict over the boy which results from it. The pity Oberon begins to feel for Titania's doting on the ass-headed Bottom belongs to a 'recognition scene' in which he sees his consort 'perhaps for the first time ... with detachment and tenderness' (p. 109). (Bottom , it is argued, shows a like immaturity of 'mind', in wanting, for example, to play all the parts in *Pyramus and Thisby*, but it would seem that he is impervious to the alchemy of the 'alembic'.)

If Nevo's argument is a little strained in its application to *A Midsummer Night's Dream* (though interestingly so), it is vindicated in the chapter on *Much Ado About Nothing* (one of the best in the book). Here, as Nevo points out, the usual relationship between plot and sub-plot is, if not inverted, at least challenged. Although at first it looks as if the unusual portrayal of the battle of the sexes in the 'war' between Beatrice and Benedick is intended to set off the normality of the courtship of Hero by Claudio, later 'we perceive that it is the conventionality, and subsequent frailty, of the Hero/Claudio relationship that provides a flattering reflector for the freewheeling, impulsive, individualist demands of Beatrice and Benedick' (p. 163). The originality of this conjunction is also reflected in the way the pattern of doubling, frequently found in Shakespeare's comedies (and in the comic parts of the histories), is used. Beatrice and Benedick become the unconventional anti-romantics, seemingly detached from love, who, via the entanglements of the action, find real love, while for Hero and Claudio 'the courtly love conventions camouflage a courtship of convenience, the substance of which will be tested and found wanting' (p. 164). The play takes us into misapprehensions and misperceptions, along the lines of *A Midsummer Night's Dream*, in the comic mixture of recognitions, half-recognitions and non-recognitions of the masked ball in II.i (particularly well analysed by Nevo); and further forms of masking and false appearances are dramatised in the eavesdropping scenes designed to draw Beatrice and Benedick together, the deceiving charade of Borachio's 'wooing' of 'Hero', and the 'burlesque eavesdropping' of the Watch. And out of these spiralling and maximalised errors comes the deepening self-realisation that, at least for Beatrice and Benedick, produces the climactic revelation and reversal of Beatrice's command to Benedick to 'Kill Claudio'. (As an interesting variant on the play's doubling, Nevo also suggests that this is a reversion to 'the oldest of chivalric tests – to kill the monster and rescue the lady, thus proving [the hero's] valour and his love', p. 174.) This is no mere piece of melodrama, but a challenge which brings the swivelling relationship of this pair of lovers to a crisis, and climaxes the underground process by which attraction and repulsion have hitherto acted as foils to each other. Nevo's treatment of the Hero–Claudio relationship cleverly dovetails with this, but is less inwardly felt and convincingly argued, betraying an imbalance which is perhaps inherent in the execution of the play's design. But the overall sense of that design, and its vigorous realisation in the love of Beatrice and Benedick, is admirably achieved.

The thesis works less well with *As You Like It* (which Nevo comes near to admitting is structurally a departure from the Terentian tradition), but is again strongly reinforced in *Twelfth Night*, where the accelerating complications (after an initial spell of more leisurely verbalising) of Acts III and IV and the virtual impasse of Act V are finally resolved by the appearance of Viola and Sebastian for the first time side by side. Once again, these, it is argued, are not an end in themselves, but the means by which the 'instability or volatility' in Orsino, Olivia and Viola's 'perception of themselves' is clarified and resolved; and Nevo's analysis of the shades and ambiguities in the sexual postures wilfully or unwillingly adopted by, or thrust upon, the three main protagonists, together with the processes by which they are moved towards clarifying change, is excellent.

Finally, in a short chapter on 'Comic Remedies' Nevo raises an interesting and fundamental question about the very nature of the complication/resolution theory of comedy on which her overall argument has been based. Which prevail, the anarchic, satirical and saturnalian aspects of comedy (those which Nietzsche would designate 'Dionysian'), or the orderly, constructive and reintegrative aspects (in Nietzschean terms, the 'Apollonian')? How radical, she asks, is the comic muse?

> Does comedy divert us, entertaining us the while with the absurd follies and errors, the ribald misdemeanours or riotous exploits of its characters, so that, when our vicarious participation ends we may return, liberated and enlightened, to a balanced and rational and orderly existence? Or does it subvert, rather than divert, undercutting the structure of norms and *mores*, of the accepted, the comprehensible, turning upside-down the assumptions and values, the accustomed responses and distinctions upon which our rational personalities are constructed, and leaving us with a world as unformed as Orsino's ocean itself in which nought enters 'of what validity and piitch soe'er, / But falls into abatement and low price'? And if it is subversive, is it nevertheless ultimately socially therapeutic? (p. 217)

Nevo's own answer, with regard to Shakespeare's comedies, inclines towards the ultimately 'therapeutic'. She develops an extension of the idea of 'catharsis' (that purgation of the emotions which has a central position in Aristotle's theory of the beneficial effect of tragedy), applying it to the effect the comedies achieve by plunging their protagonists into laughable, but disturbing complications, and changing them for the better in the process so that they are 'purged' and restored to a world both emotionally richer and more mature. These comedies, she insists, 'do not deny the dark side'; on the contrary, 'they occupy always a danger zone of potential radical harm to the individual'. But they take what must be seen finally as 'a tolerant and genial view of the vital spontaneities, the imperious instincts, the recalcitrant emotions and the chaotic appetites and desires' (p. 224).

This is a fitting conclusion to the view of the comedies elaborated in Nevo's book. But it does not altogether settle the question that Nevo herself raises. Evidence for the two opposite principles, the Apollonian and the Dionysian, the integrative and the fissiparous, is in ample supply throughout Shakespeare's development as a comic writer. And though the structure used in most of the comedies does point towards restoration and reintegration, this does not clinch the argument in favour of order. The structure is constantly under pressures that make it bend and buckle, producing happy endings that are nevertheless qualified and compromised by much that is less than happy, and sometimes verging on the tragic. To focus on the beneficial change undergone by protagonists is likewise to risk getting the 'odd men out' and the 'fools' (of both categories) somewhat out of focus, and to underestimate the extent to which Shakespeare's imagination is often deeply engaged by characters who are resistant to change, or stand at a bizarre and challenging angle to the accepted heroes and heroines. (Nor is this to ignore the point that an essential element in the most vital of these heroes, and especially heroines, is itself unconventional and anti-heroic.) Shakespeare is also, as a man of the theatre, very much seized by what works on the stage; and what works may (fruitfully) disrupt the patterns and structures perceived by the critic. (Hence, for example, the nominally disproportionate attention given to the *Pyramus and Thisby* play within the play of *A Midsummer Night's Dream,* and the potentially unbalancing memorableness of the gulling of Malvolio in *Twelfth Night.*) Often the plays seem to be almost bursting at the seams, as Shakespeare crams in more and more that seizes his imagination and excites his sense of dramatic possibility; and though his architectonic skills are stimulated to find ever more appropriate ways of containing this abundance of material, the instinct to reach out and respond, as well as the awareness of dark undercurrents which forever question the optimism on which comedy is predicated, seems more powerful than the will to subdue. It is this openness of the imagination which is the distinguishing mark of Shakespearean comedy, and the thing that makes it at once so lastingly entertaining and so endlessly capable of disturbing.

Further Reading

There is no substitute for reading the plays themselves. As already suggested in Chapter 12, the best help to understanding any one of the comedies singled out for study in this book is to read the rest of Shakespeare's comedies, and after them his other plays – histories, tragedies, 'problem plays', last plays – and his non-dramatic poems. And to help in the study of particular plays it is advisable to use well-annotated editions such as those in the Arden, Cambridge, Everyman, Macmillan, Oxford and Penguin Shakespeares. Many of these also have excellent introductions covering textual problems and surveying the history of critical development and stage production, as well as giving the editor's own considered opinions on the play in question. The following are particularly recommended: *A Midsummer Night's Dream*. ed. Peter Holland (Oxford: Oxford University Press, 1994); *Much Ado About Nothing*, ed. A. R. Humphreys (London: Methuen, 1981); *Much Ado About Nothing*, ed. Sheldon P. Zitner (Oxford: Oxford University Press, 1993); *As You Like It*, ed. John F. Andrews (London: J. M. Dent, 1997); *As You Like It*, ed. Alan Brissenden (Oxford: Oxford University Press, 1993); *Twelfth Night*, ed. Roger Warren and Stanley Wells (Oxford: Oxford University Press, 1994).

In addition, there are numerous critical commentaries and collections of essays on individual plays, of which the following may be mentioned: *Shakespeare: A Midsummer Night's Dream*, ed. Antony Price (Basingstoke and London: Macmillan, 1983); Peter Hollindale: *Shakespeare: A Midsummer Night's Dream* (Harmondsworth: Penguin, 1992); David P. Young: *Something of Great Constancy: The Art of A Midsummer Night's Dream* (New Haven: Yale University Press, 1966); *Shakespeare: Much Ado About Nothing and As You Like It*, ed. John Russell Brown (Basingstoke and London: Macmillan, 1979); Peter Reynolds: *Shakespeare; As You Like It* (Harmondsworth: Penguin, 1988); *Shakespeare: Twelfth Night*, ed. D. J. Palmer (Basingstoke and London: Macmillan, 1972); R. P.

Draper: *Twelfth Night by William Shakespeare* (Basingstoke and London: Macmillan, 1988).

Among more general studies, besides those already discussed in Chapter 14, Moelwyn Merchant's *Comedy* (London: Methuen, 1972) provides a stimulating short introduction to the varieties of comic form, and G. J. Watson's *Drama: An Introduction* (Basingstoke and London: Macmillan, 1983) covers drama more widely, but has a useful chapter on 'Comedy and Satire', with special reference to *A Midsummer Night's Dream*. Studies devoted more specifically to Shakespeare's comedies include: John Russell Brown, *Shakespeare and His Comedies* (London: Methuen, 1957, revised edn 1968); Alexander Leggatt, *Shakespeare's Comedy of Love* (London: Methuen, 1980); and Patrick Swinden, *An Introduction to Shakespeare's Comedies* (Basingstoke and London: Macmillan, 1973).

Anne Righter's *Shakespeare and the Idea of the Play* (London: Chatto and Windus, 1962) is a seminal study of the consciousness of theatre and audience in Shakespeare's work; Pauline Kiernan's *Shakespeare's Theory of Drama* (Cambridge: Cambridge University Press, 1996) stresses the importance of the dramatic in the non-dramatic as well as dramatic work; and Carol Rutter's *Clamorous Voices: Shakespeare's Women Today* (London: The Women's Press, 1988) brings together comments by actors such as Juliet Stevenson and Fiona Shaw on their experience of playing women's parts in Shakespeare, including those in *As You Like It*.

For background material useful volumes to consult are F. E. Halliday's *A Shakespeare Companion, 1564-1964* (Harmondsworth: Penguin, 1964) and *The Cambridge Companion to Shakespeare Studies*, ed. Stanley Wells (Cambridge: Cambridge University Press, 1986). A variety of scholars contribute to the latter book, including Inga-Stina Ewbank on 'Shakespeare and the arts of language', Peter Thomson on 'Playhouses and players in the time of Shakespeare', David Daniell on 'Shakespeare and the traditions of comedy', Lawrence Danson on twentieth-century criticism of the comedies, and Terence Hawkes on 'Shakespeare and new critical approaches'.

Index